GW00362373

KING FAHD and
SAUDI ARABIA'S
GREAT EVOLUTION

ROUZEGAR E NOW LTD.
NEW SOUTH WALES HOUSE
15 ADAM STREET, THE STRAND
LONDON WC2N 6AH

DONATED BY
MR. JAAFAR RAED
C.A.I.S. LTD.
5 STREATHAM STREET
LONDON WC1A 1JB

KING FAHD and SAUDI ARABIA'S GREAT EVOLUTION

Dr. Nasser Ibrahim Rashid

Chairman, Rashid Engineering
Riyadh, Kingdom of Saudi Arabia (K.S.A.)

Dr. Esber Ibrahim Shaheen

President, International Institute
of Technology, Inc., Joplin, Mo.
United States of America (U.S.A.)

International Institute of Technology, Inc.
IITI Building, 830 Wall St.
Joplin, Missouri 64801 U.S.A.

Copyright © **1987 by Dr. Nasser Ibrahim Rashid and Dr. Esber Ibrahim Shaheen.** All rights reserved. No portion of this book may be reproduced or transmitted in any form or by any means, electronic or mechanical including photocopying and recording, without permission in writing from the authors.

Library of Congress Cataloging-in-Publication Data

Rashid, Nasser Ibrahim.
  King Fahd and Saudi Arabia's great evolution.

  Bibliography: pp. 316–332
  Includes index.
  1. Saudi Arabia–History. 2. Fahd ibn 'Abd al-'Azīz, King of Saudi Arabia, 1920–   . I. Shaheen, Esber I. II. Title.
DS244.63.R37   1987   953′.8   86–27869
ISBN 0–940485–00–1

Printed in the United States of America

DONATED BY
MR. JAAFAR RAED
C.A.I.S. LTD.
5 STREATHAM STREET
LONDON WC1A 1JB

Table of Contents

Preface	vii
Acknowledgments	xi
Chapter 1	
The Era of Abdulaziz Ibn Saud, Founder of the Kingdom of Saudi Arabia	1
Chapter 2	
King Fahd Bin Abdulaziz and Education in the Kingdom	57
Chapter 3	
Fahd, The National, Regional, and International Man of Moderation	135
Chapter 4	
Saudi Arabia Redefines Progress	161
Chapter 5	
Defense	241
Chapter 6	
A Look Into the Future	261
Appendices	267
References	316

Preface

The spectacular achievement realized by the Kingdom of Saudi Arabia in its quest for modernization and industrialization is fascinating and mind-boggling. Miraculous progress that has taken place in slightly over a decade is, indeed, unparalleled in the history of mankind. This reality is in sharp contrast with the shallow imagery that occupies the western mind about Arabia. The mere mention of the name brings images of a barren desert expanse and nomadic bedouins astride rocking camels. This is nothing but a mirage! The tip of the iceberg! This is a blessed land. The birthplace of the Prophet! The Mecca for nearly one billion Moslems around the globe who cherish it and face it five times every day.

This great land is a vast mass of desert floating on a sea of oil, with proven oil reserves of 169 billion barrels that will last over a century. The massive infusion of capital from this God-given resource brought the most modern technology to the Kingdom and truly made the desert bloom! All this was accomplished in line with Saudi traditions, always protecting society from thunderous jolts and runaway inflation. Despite the voices of doubt and reservation about the development plans, optimum results prevailed. The leadership knew this great burst in income was for a short duration, so they optimized it and now they continue to sail the ship with proper stablization and steady movement. Their development process touched the far corners of the Kingdom, from the big cities to the smallest hamlets and villages.

This book aims at documenting these miraculous achievements for students of history and for men and women who seek knowledge, fairness and justice everywhere. The Saudi experience in modernization and progress became a model for other countries around the globe.

Security, justice, dedication, foresight and compassion are basic ingredients in the foundation for progress. Without these, the environment would not be conducive in triggering the ingenuity of man toward excellence. Thus, the need for a background presentation on the history of Arabia is imperative.

The First Chapter is on the "*Era of Abdulaziz Ibn Saud, Founder of the Kingdom of Saudi Arabia.*" Here, a historical perspective will take you, the reader, through the long history of the development of Arabian beginnings, divisions and consolidation through bitter conflicts. The development and improvement of a little known culture will amaze you. The captivating story of *Abdulaziz* and his descendents will astound you. Beginning with this giant of a man, they have forged a modern nation that brought compassion for its people and became a great moderating force among the world's family of nations. The reader will find spine-tingling accounts of King Ibn Saud's life-threatening rise to the throne. A vivid description gives an account of the long and arduous struggle for unifying the Kingdom under the banner of justice and the rule of law. The story of black gold unfolds with its vital role in keeping the wheels of progress turning in Saudi Arabia and other nations around the world. Then come the mesmerizing and thrilling stories about the qualities of Abdulaziz as a leader with unique courage and determination and as a man of compassion and justice for his fellowman. Abdulaziz forged a nation from a sea of lawlessness and anarchy. He truly is the founder of the Kingdom of Saudi Arabia.

While Abdulaziz was the father of the nation, *King Fahd* on the footsteps of his father and predecessors, became the pioneer and founder of the modern Kingdom of Saudi Arabia. The Second Chapter on "*King Fahd Bin Abdulaziz and Education in the Kingdom,*" gives the true picture about the moving force behind the legendary progress, the father of modernization and learning in the Kingdom of Saudi Arabia. Background description on Fahd's youth, his qualities as a father, educator and world leader along with his humanitarianism, populist character and compassion, are portrayed in many facets of his life. The Majlis is depicted with pictures reflecting that people from all walks and levels of life are free to meet their leaders in an atmosphere of justice, respect and compassion.

King Fahd's first love was and remains education. In the last fifteen years the Kingdom made tremendous progress in the field of education, which was one of the basic foundations for modernizing the Kingdom. Education in the country grew by leaps and bounds on every front. In a matter of a few years, seven universities were operating in the Kingdom. The chapter illustrates in detail and with attractive diagrams and pictures the story of education in the Kingdom. This parade of progress continues to be vividly portrayed in other chapters.

The Third Chapter on "*Fahd, the National, Regional, and International Man of Moderation*" gives insights into the wisdom and moderate, peaceful policies of King Fahd. The core for guidance is the *Shari'a* and preservation of old traditions. The populist attitude of King Fahd brings him closer to the hearts of the people, where mutual love, admiration and compassion are genuine. Fahd, on regional, moslem and international matters, carries his weight of leadership in a policy based on wisdom, peace, and justice. Law and order are a cornerstone of the Saudi policy. They are based on the Shari'a and the tenets of Islam.

The Fourth Chapter on *"Saudi Arabia Redefines Progress"* is a vivid pictorial description of what has been achieved in slightly over a decade. Imagine the magnitude and vast impact of this progress, keeping in mind that only a few years ago introducing the telephone and telegraph required the ingenuity of Abdulaziz to convince the populace that, certainly, this machine is not "an instrument of the devil."

The *five-year plans* were devised and designed to lay the proper foundation for the gigantic modernization and industrialization that has taken place. A massive boom touched all walks of life from communications and transport to industrial development, human welfare and social justice. Various funds are presented here because of the central role they played in the development plans. What a great and dynamic change from just a few years ago! One witnesses progress everywhere! This procession of great achievements is self-evident and mirrored in the beautiful gardens and slick marble buildings that dot the desert landscape. King Fahd continues his mission of progress and modernization.

The Fifth Chapter on "Defense" testifies to a mission of peace that demands strength in a turbulent world. The bedrock foundation of national safety and security are described here. The pillars of Saudi defense are the National Guard, the Ministry of Defense with its Army, Navy, Air Force, Air Defense and Internal Security & Coast Guard through the Ministry of the Interior.

Saudi Arabia carries a basic and genuine policy of peace and friendship toward other nations of the world. The strengthening of its defenses is at the heart of carrying out such a policy. The Saudis are strongly against the interference in the internal affairs of other nations and they, certainly, practice what they preach. Their military deterrence is truly a force for peace in the region.

The last Chapter, *"A Look Into the Future,"* gives insight, thought and predictions into what awaits Saudi Arabia. The private sector and joint-ventures will play a good role in the years ahead. Employment of Saudis will be on the rise. As Saudization takes hold, the number of expatriates will decrease substantially. Saudi women will realize more progress as they reach new milestones in education. Security, law and order will continue to be at the heart of Saudi internal policy. King Fahd and his dedicated men in the Saudi leadership will continue their wise and moderate policy toward peace and achievement. Their oil policy in the past, present and future will remain moderate and stable.

Finally, the *Appendices* contain a great wealth of information. They, certainly, complement this parade of progress. The reader will find an interesting *"Profile: the Saudi Today."* A *"Brief History of the Arabs"* gives information on the Arabs as a whole. Black gold, with its great impact on global energy needs, brought strategic importance to the Arab land. Although the Arab world accounts for a good share of world news, it still is least understood among other nations. This topic will shed some light on the Arabs as a whole.

Interesting *charts*, such as a simplified diagram for the government of Saudi Arabia and a list of the major battles of unification, along with the names of those accompanying Abdulaziz in his recapture of Riyadh are also included in these Appendices. Lists and descriptions of the brothers and children of Ibn Saud are presented, along with other information. An interesting and useful *glossary* of Arabic words is included. Also, the Appendices contain a very detailed and updated list of *references* that should prove to be of much use and interest to the reader.

Dr. Nasser Ibrahim Rashid
Riyadh, K.S.A.
Dr. Esber Ibrahim Shaheen
Joplin, Mo., U.S.A.
January, 1987

Acknowledgments

The authors extend their deep gratitude to the many people who helped in this project. Special thanks are given to H. E. Mr. Ali Al-Shaer, Minister of Information in the Kingdom of Saudi Arabia, for making available to us authenticated documentation that helped us extensively in our research. Thanks are due H. E. Mr. Hisham Nazer, former Minister of Planning (1975–1986) and now Minister of Petroleum and Mineral Resources, for his help in making available to us material relating to the various Five-Year Plans for development. The Ministry of Education and the Ministry of Higher Education also were supportive in our search for statistics and information on the educational progress in the Kingdom. Aramco was helpful in permitting us to use a few maps.

Our deep thanks and gratitude go to the select few who were dedicated, loyal, compassionate and very encouraging. Sincere thanks are expressed to others who are too numerous to name here.

Chapter 1

The Era of Abdulaziz Ibn Saud, Founder of the Kingdom of Saudi Arabia

The Late King Ibn Saud, affectionately known to his countrymen as Abdulaziz.

A giant of a man, with legendary courage, wisdom, passionate love for security and justice, deep compassion and devotion for his countrymen. This, combined with great charm, good luck and good looks too make him the founder of a nation forged from a sea of lawlessness and anarchy. He truly is the father of the Kingdom of Saudi Arabia.

Introduction

The mention of Arabia brings to the mind of most people in the West a shallow imagery of great expanses of barren desert, nomadic Bedouins astride rocking camels, men in flowing robes and women whose faces are shielded from view with veils. To these superficial views in very recent years also has come a mental picture of oil-rich sheikhs with vast wealth.

All of these are but the surface; the tip of the iceberg. Here and in the chapters ahead, you will learn about Arabia–mother–land of the Arabs, heartbeat of the Arab world. You will learn much more about a fascinating story that will unfold in the pages to come.

This will take you, the reader, through the long history (extending to 7000 B.C.) of the development of Arabian beginnings, divisions and consolidations through bitter conflict. The development and improvement of a little-known culture will astound you.

Most poignant of all perhaps will be the alluring and condensed captivating story of the father of today's progressive Kingdom of Saudi Arabia, the unchallenged star in the firmament of all present day Arabian nations. It is the story of intrepid King Abdulaziz (Ibn Saud) and his descendents and how, beginning with Abdulaziz, they have forged a modern nation that brought compassion for its people and a moderating force among the world's family of nations.

The reader will find spine-tingling accounts of King Ibn Saud's life-threatening rise to the throne, accounts that make fiction's plots of danger and intrigue pale by comparison.

This also is the story of Black Gold–how it was found, how immense this God-given treasure is and how vital it is to keeping the wheels of progress turning–in Saudi Arabia and other nations around the globe.

Here, too, the reader will find little-known accounts of the King's top level secret meetings and communications with United States President Franklin D. Roosevelt, regarding a problem that is commanding the headlines of today.

Come with us now for a journey to the Arabia of old, and the Saudi Arabia of today.

Historical Perspective

Since the beginning of time, around 7,000 B.C., people in the Eastern part of Arabia developed trading ties with the Ubaid culture in the north. Early civilizations flourished between the regions extending from Egypt to Mesopotamia. Arabia, the beating heart of this region, was called: "the Cradle of Civilization."

People of the Arabian Peninsula mingled with old civilizations of the time and left a permanent and everlasting impression.

The Southern portion of Arabia was known to the Romans as "Arabia Felix," which means "Happy Arabia." It was prospering and considered the major source for frankincense and myrrh. These were extensively used in perfumes for many Temples and in the cremation ceremonies of the Romans for the royal and noble people.

This region also was a focal point for the trade in silk, ivory, spices for flavoring as well as preserving food, and other goods on their way to the Mediterranean countries. Trade through the Indian ocean was brought by ship to Arabia. Ships unloaded at Aden. From there, transportation was mainly by land to markets in the Western Mediterranian, Egypt and Mesopotamia.

Southern Arabia was the only part of the Peninsula that was agriculturally self-sufficient. The people imported some luxury items, but never foodstuffs. This was possible because of their ingenuity in irrigation. They designed systems to catch runoff waters from the infrequent rains that occasionally flooded the wadies. The dams were used to direct this water into channels.

By the year 613 A.D. the Holy Qoran (also written as Koran) was revealed to the Prophet Mohammed in Mecca. The birth of Islam and the lightening speed with which it spread, brought about great Arab conquests. The Arabian Peninsula became the heartbeat for the Arab world as well as all Moslems everywhere.

Antiquities at Madain Saleh–Arabia reaches back into the beginnings of time.

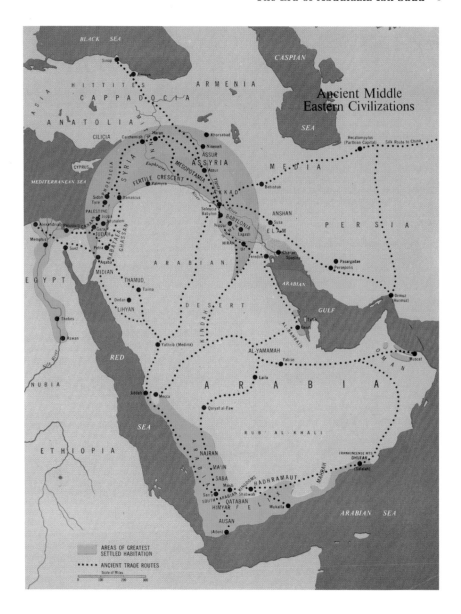

Ancient Middle
Eastern Civilizations

The Arab Empire reached its climax during the reign of Horoun Al-Rashid. However, the fall of this Empire led to a dark period in Arab history. This was when it suffered under a cloud of Ottoman rule of oppression, that lasted until the early part of the Twentieth Century.

With the fall of the Arab Empire, Moslems lost the drive and enthusiasm for practicing the faith of their ancestors. Erroneous practices and behavior veered away from the religious simplicity originally preached by the Prophet Mohammed. Many animistic practices were resumed in the Interior part of Arabia and were integrated into the rituals of Islam.

While Islam was still strong in the Hijaz, it became weak and diluted in other parts of Arabia. Certain settlements of Najd were practicing and teaching Islam. Also at Uyaynah, which was not far from the main Saudi settlement of *Diriya*, people were practicing Islam.

The Saudi ancestors came from the Qatif region and settled in the historical community of Diriya in the middle of Wadi Hanifa in the northwest corner of Riyadh. Saud Ibn Mohammed Ibn Moqrin became the ruler of Diriya from 1720 until his death in 1725. Then, *Mohammed Ibn Saud* became the ruler. His rule lasted nearly forty years, extending from 1726 until his death in 1765. During this period the title of Imam was adopted for Al-Saud (see chart for a simplified version of the Al-Saud Family).

SIMPLIFIED VERSION OF THE
AL-SAUD FAMILY

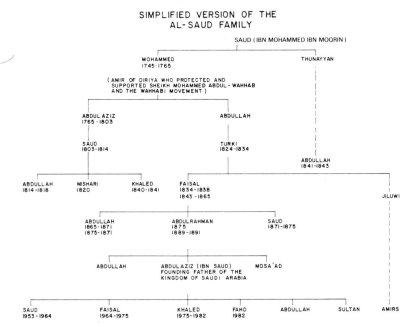

Fusion of Wahhabism with Saudi Leadership

The rule of Mohammed Ibn Saud coincided with the rise of a religious movement whose leader was *Sheikh Mohammed Ibn Abdul Wahhab*. He was born in 1703 in Uyaynah and was from the Banou Sinan tribe. His family was deep-rooted in Islamic law and they sent him to several Islamic cities to advance his religious studies and expertise.

Sheikh Abdul Wahhab enthusiastically advocated the return to the simple message of the Qoran and the great teachings of the Prophet Mohammed. Wahhabism gave moral basis for unifying the Arabian Peninsula under the House of Al-Saud. The words Wahhabi and Wahhabism were applied to the followers of this religious leader.

Initially, the preachings of Wahhabism were not well received at home and, in 1744, Abdul Wahhab was forced to leave his hometown. He was welcomed by Mohammed Ibn Saud, the ruler of a neighboring town called *Diriya*. They became strong allies in a mission of true Jihad seeking purity in Islam and Unity of the nation.

The founding of Saudi Arabia was a culmination of the coupling and fusion of the Wahhabi movement and Saudi family leadership, which remained a dedicated champion of the Wahhabi movement. This relationship flourished and was cemented through intermarriages. Leading among these was the marriage of Mohammed Ibn Saud to the daughter of Sheikh Abdul Wahhab.

Wahhabism gained in dynamism and momentum and through eloquent preaching, many people became zealous believers. Even the people who had driven Abdul Wahhab from his home were converted to his puritan ways. By the time the Amir died in 1765, most of Najd was a Wahhabi domain.

The alliance of Wahhabism, with his successor Abdulaziz who ruled from 1765 to 1803, was renewed and finally the city of Riyadh was taken over in 1773. Although there were many enemies, the fervor and dynamism of the Wahhabi movement, coupled with the courage and political stamina of the Saudi leadership, propelled the Saudi State to spread with speed and vigor.

Abdul Wahhab died in 1792. By then, Wahhabism reached as far south as the *Rab'a al-Khali* (*Empty Quarter*). While the south and east accepted the movement, the Hassa area, especially the oasis of Qatif and Houfouf, were defeated in battle. Karbala, a Shiite Holy City in present-day Iraq, was taken over in 1802.

By now the Saudi State had extended its domain to cover most of the Arabian Peninsula, including Oman, Hijaz, and some portions of Yemen. The Holy cities of Mecca and Medina were under Saudi control

(Mecca was taken in 1801 and Medina in 1805). Both cities were cleansed of any religious infractions. By 1811 some plans were made for Baghdad.

Shari'a, the sacred Islamic law, was practiced and safeguarded by the Qadis in many towns and communities. Tribal feuds were solved by Wahhabi authority.

Expansion of the movement became worrisome to the Ottoman Empire in Constantinople. The Pasha of Baghdad appealed to the Ottoman authorities for help in crushing it. His requests were initially ignored since the influence of the movement was underestimated. However, the loss of the Holy cities, which meant a loss in prestige and income, made the Ottoman government more decisive in undermining its progress. The viceroy in Cairo, Mohammed Ali, was asked to stop this movement and to crush it.

The first expedition was led by the viceroy's son in 1816. Modern weaponry was of no practical use against the special tactics of the desert tribesmen. Although Mecca and Medina had fallen, the stiff resistance displayed by the people of Arabia forced Mohammed Ali himself to come and lead the military campaign. Reinforcements came under Ibrahim Pasha, another son of Mohammed Ali.

The defenders were strong and formidable but were finally shaken with the death of their leader Saud in 1814. However, by 1814–1818, his successor Abdullah retreated to Diriya.

The Egyptian leader reached Najd in 1818. He bombarded and ravaged Diriya until it was turned to ruins. The town fell in that year after an arduous struggle and siege. Abdullah, the Saudi chief, was taken to Constantinople and beheaded.

Despite this debacle and defeat, the Saudi House regained political power over central Arabia, and the Wahhabi movement gained new momentum. Abdullah's uncle Turki organized his troops and vowed to oust the Egyptians from Najd. He established his rule in Riyadh because Diriya had been destroyed. He moved on to reconquer Najd and the Eastern Province. The Egyptian garrison was harassed and attacked until it was forced to transfer to Hijaz.

Turki warned against political oppression of the people. He reminded the governors that true Islamic spirit was at the heart of the movement and any political oppression would not be tolerated. As a result of internal tension and squabbling that ravaged the movement, Turki was assassinated in 1834. The assassination was carried out by a rival from within the family.

The son of Turki, named Faisal, took up the reigns of the government and ruled for the years 1834–38 and 1843–65. Although Faisal suffered some early defeats from the Egyptians, he later re-established Saudi rule in Najd and the Eastern Region of Arabia. His strong supporters in these military feats were led by Abdullah Ibn Rashid of Jabal Shammar in the Northern Region of Arabia.

Mohammed Ali decided to bring Arabia into his own sphere of influence around 1834 and supported a rival claimant to Saudi leadership: Khaled Ibn Saud (1839–41), a cousin to Faisal who had been imprisoned in Egypt since Abdullah's capture some twenty years earlier. Faisal was a token prisoner for the Egyptian forces, who then occupied Najd & Hijaz and directed the functions carried out by Khaled. However, they overextended themselves in a number of areas. The British rebuffed them in Yemen. Also, securing the Arabian interior was not an easy task. All this caused Mohammed Ali to withdraw in 1840.

By 1843 Faisal escaped from Egypt and regained his position of leadership. Like his father Turki, he did his best to bring law and order to the land. His effective rule was based on creating order in the family and among the tribes.

Faisal died in 1865 and the rivalry between his sons brought on a civil war that lasted for many years. All the stability and cohesion built during Faisal's era were in shambles and ruins due to this civil war that erupted between his sons: Abdullah (1865–71, 1875–89) and Saud (1871–75). This provided a window of opportunity for the Turks to occupy the Eastern region in 1871.

When the rule of Saud, the son of Faisal, was established, anarchy was dominant in the region. People suffered from famine and even the weak tribes became difficult to control. After Saud's death in 1875, Abdul Rahman (1875, 1889–91), the younger brother of Saud and Abdullah announced his succession. Abdullah regained power after one year and then ruled until he died in 1889, when Abdul Rahman became the ruler again.

Disputes between sons and brothers caused serious damage and distractions that led to challenges from the growing power of the Rashids, who had been placed into power by Al-Saud in the Hail area, governing the Northern Province of Arabia named Jabal Shammar.

By the time Faisal's youngest son, Abdul Rahman, was finally forced out of Riyadh, much of Najd was under the control of Mohammed Ibn Rashid. In 1891 the house of Rashid appointed a governor and established a garrison in Riyadh. Leaving the city of his ancestors, Abdul Rahman and his family were exiled in Kuwait.

A bright young man of the family was an eleven-year-old son named *Abdulaziz*, who, in the years to come, would become the father and founder of the Kingdom of Saudi Arabia. The Rashid successor was a son of minor administrative talent. He governed harshly and succeeded in alienating the tribes under his rule, thus paving the way for the eventual recapture of the region by its true and just rulers. This was achieved through the sheer courage, superb genius and daring of Abdulaziz.

Capture of Riyadh

When Al-Saud were forced to leave Riyadh in 1891, among their midst was a brilliant young man whose date with destiny was in the making. Abdulaziz was born at the Amir's Palace in Riyadh on December 2, 1880.[1] His mother was Sarah Al-Sudeiri. She had a proud heart and a strong physique; she was a great lady with a good organizational mind whose father fought Ibrahim Pasha. She died in Riyadh in 1910. Thus, Abdulaziz was the direct descendent of Mohammed Ibn Saud, and the daughter of Mohammed Abdul Wahhab. Among his ancestors were Pious men and many Kings across many generations of coura-geous fighters. Great ancestory was credited to his name. Beyond that, destiny did not grant him any material wealth or any established rule.

"Among all the members of the family there was only one who had any inkling of what was happening in this passionate heart: a younger sister of his father. I do not know much about her; I only know that whenever he dwells on the days of his youth, the King always mentions her with great reverence.

She loved me, I think, even more than her own children. When we were alone, she would take me on her lap and tell me of the great things which I was to do when I grow up: "Thou must revive the glory of the House of Ibn Saud," she would tell me again and again, and her words were like a caress. "But I want thee to know, O Azayyiz," (Affectionate diminutive of Abdulaziz), she would say, "that even the glory of the House of Ibn Saud must not be the end of thy endeavors. Thou must strive for the glory of Islam. Thy people sorely need a leader who will guide them on to the path of the Holy Prophet—and

---

[1] There is a discrepancy as to the birth date of Abdulaziz; Zarkali says he was born in the year 1876; others say he was born on February 1881 (according to the Birth of a Kingdom); but the best date is 1880, according to Rihani and also according to the confirmation of King Abdulaziz himself.

thou shalt be that leader." These words have always remained alive in my heart."[2]

When he was barely eight years of age he was taught to use the sword and the rifle along with jumping on a horse while moving. He was taught to cope with difficulties and especially the severe conditions normally encountered in the desert. He was taught patience and was trained to exercise self-control.

He was told that a true bedouin should know how to economize on a small piece of date, a drink of water and should be fresh and ready for action with even three hours of sleep. With discipline and similar principles, his ancestors were able to build an empire.

Abdulaziz grew to be tall and handsome. But his towering figure gave him headaches when he was in Kuwait. Other boys in the castle would make him a target of their jokes. He was seldom in a state of rest, always bustling with energy and enthusiasm. His preferred exercises were wrestling and walking for a long time. He was strong and endowed with exemplary courage.

Safety and security were nonexistent. Destruction from the Turks and the civil war were both rampant. The two older brothers of Abdul Rahman were engaged in a struggle that brought destruction and civil war.

Abdulaziz's father was a religious man who wanted to avoid this struggle and vicious circle of destruction. Despite this, he was forced to defend himself many times. With all these dangers and the imminent threat from the north, Abdulaziz's youthful upbringing was to be influenced by all this and more; so in 1890 when Ibn Rashid conquered the city of Riyadh, the two fighting brothers of Abdul Rahman were slain and Abdul Rahman was permitted to live in a corner of the castle.

A man named Salem was appointed to rule Riyadh. Once there was a meeting between Salem and Abdul Rahman. Salem devised a plot requesting that all the family of Abdul Rahman be present, having in mind a sinister plan to slay them all at one time. However, Abdul Rahman took his sword along with his men as a precaution. Before Salem could execute his murderous plan, he himself was slaughtered. The young man present at the time was Abdulaziz who learned a lesson about intrigue and bravery. He was sitting in the lap of a big man who protected him from becoming a victim in this bloodbath.

Abdulaziz was to say later in life: "I learned here that I should be the first to hit when I am exposed to danger."

---

[2] Related by M. Asad in the Road to Mecca.

Preferring not to fall as a prisoner or become a victim, Abdul Rahman gathered about twenty of his supporters and his family along with some food supplies and left from Riyadh in the darkness of night. The party moved on southward looking for shelter in the desert. After a short time, they divided into two groups: one made of his wife and some servants went to Bahrain, while the other group remained with the father and headed south.

After a number of days, numerous difficulties and harshness were encountered in the desert. The father was in despair and told his companions: "it seems that our end is here and near. Let us pray together the prayer of the dead."

But young Abdulaziz answered: "No! We will not die here."

His father asked, "What makes you have such faith?"

Abdulaziz replied: "When I become a man, I will rule the Arabian island," (Jazeerat Al-Arab).

However, being in the Rab'a al-Khali does not give great hope for a bright future!

The tribe which inhabited the Empty Quarter was known as Al-Murrah. They were famous for their toughness and adaptation to the harsh desert environment. Young Abdulaziz strengthened these traits and learned about survival in the desert. For a brief period, the family was in Bahrain and then Qatar. Finally, permission came for the Saudi family to have their refuge in Kuwait, where they would be in the hospitality of Al-Sabbah for nearly ten years.

When Abdulaziz reached twenty years of age, it became clear that he was gifted with qualities of greatness which destiny rested upon his shoulders. It was evident then that great achievements would come to him and the House of Saud. He was also gifted with an extraordinary personality that was well matched with his great character. He was over six feet tall, a giant of a man, truly blessed with the natural look of a great King.

The British traveler Gertrude Bell[1] met Abdulaziz when he visited the British base in Basra, Iraq. Here are her impressions from a secret report:

"Ibn Saud is now barely forty, though he looks some years older. He is a man of splendid physique, standing well over six feet, and carrying himself with the air of one accustomed to command.

Though he is more massively built than the typical nomad sheikh, he has the characteristics of the well-bred Arab, the strongly marked

---

[1] Cox was a British civil servant in Basra. Gertrude Bell was on his staff. She was assigned as a guide, showing military hardware, around 1916.

aquiline profile, full-fleshed nostrils, prominent lips and long, narrow chin, accentuated by a pointed beard. His hands are fine, with slender fingers, a trait almost universal among the tribes of pure Arab blood, and, in spite of his great height and breadth of shoulder, he conveys the impression, common enough in the desert, of an indefinable lassitude, not individual but racial, the secular weariness of an ancient and self-contained people, which has made heavy drafts on its vital forces, and borrowed little from beyond its own forbidding frontiers. His deliberate movements, his slow, sweet smile, and the contemplative glance of his heavy-lidded eyes, though they add to his dignity and charm, do not accord with the western conception of a vigorous personality.

Nevertheless, reports credit him with powers of physical endurance rare even in hard-bitten Arabia. Among men bred in the camel-saddle, he is said to have few rivals as a tireless rider. As a leader of irregular forces he is of proved daring, and he combines with his qualities as a soldier that grasp of statecraft which is yet more highly prized by the tribesmen. To be 'a statesman' is, perhaps, their final word of commendation."

Abdulaziz had a great heart. When his wife died in 1919 he made no secret of the sorrow which befell him or the fact that he mourned her passing for a long time. He treasured small articles which he kept as souvenirs of a beautiful love. He confided that his wife was the most charming, very wise, and the sweetest woman in Najd. For a long time, he could hardly fight his tears when he thought of her.

While in Kuwait, his character was developing and his resolve was hardening. Not having all the luxuries of life added more to his resiliency, which gave him more strength and patience. In due time, all these virtues helped him tremendously in grasping the opportune moment to reclaim the kingdom and domain of his forefathers. During this period he meditated. He planned his future and what awaited him in history. He came to the definite conclusion of reclaiming the land of his ancestors through the capture of Riyadh and then by reclaiming the rest of the land through courageous and determined holy war. He was convinced that reclaiming the land of his forefathers would only be won through an arduous struggle and absolute dedication to a unifying objective.

Abdulaziz learned the tortuous path of practical politics in Kuwait. By 1896, the Kuwaiti ruler Mubarak allowed Abdulaziz to sit in some of the meetings and to listen to the discussions with such governments as the British, Russians, Germans and Turks.

Mohammed Ibn Rashid died January 10, 1897, and his successor

Abdulaziz in a moment of serenity

was having designs on Kuwait. Abdulaziz took this opportunity, convincing Mubarak that he should go with a force to Riyadh and thus force Ibn Rashid to fight on two fronts. The battle, in Al-Sarif in the Kasim, between Mubarak Al-Sabbah and Ibn Rashid ended in favor of the latter (on 3–7–1901), and Ibn Sabbah returned to Kuwait.

While Abdulaziz reached Riyadh, he knew he would be hard put to stand the strength of Ibn Rashid without the burden of another front, so his father called him back to Kuwait and he returned–but only for a short time.

He was preparing again for a second adventure into Riyadh. He was very anxious to carry on this holy mission and his eagerness led him to confront his father with two choices: "Either he will order one of his servants to cut his head so he will be leaving this life for good or go right now to the house of the Sheikh of Kuwait and not return without a promise to ease the departure of Abdulaziz to carry on his fight in the heart of Najd." It wasn't very difficult for Mubarak to agree!

Abdulaziz left for Riyadh with forty men from the Al-Saud family and their supporters, along with twenty more followers. He led his weary and tired men to the northern fringes of the Empty Quarter, where he spent several months hoping to recruit more support from the local tribes. Support was not forthcoming and he grew impatient in his wait, especially since life was difficult for his men under the harsh conditions of this barren expanse of sand dunes. Being true and dedicated to Wahhabism, he fasted with his men during Ramadan, although he did not have to fast while traveling.

On the last day of Rajab 1319 A.H. (12/10/1901), he received a message from his father and Sheikh Mubarak. Ibn Rashid appealed to the Turks, who exerted pressure and threats. The message urged Abdulaziz to return to Kuwait because the consequences of carrying his plans would be devastating.

On that date Abdulaziz met with his men in the oasis of Yabrin. He read his father's letter advising their immediate return. He told them: "You are free to choose whatever you desire for yourselves. As for me, I will not expose myself to be the subject of ridicule in the streets of Kuwait. Whoever needs to relax, be with his parents, sleep and fill his stomach, turn to my left. . ."

Not all forty, but the sixty of them went to his right! They were deeply moved! They removed their swords giving the oath to accompany him to the end.

Then, Abdulaziz looked to the man sent by his father and told him, "Give our greetings to the Imam! Inform him about what you

AL-RUWALAH
Turaif
'ANAZAH
AL-'AMARAT
Badanah
BANI SAKHR
Wadi al-Sirhan
AL-SHARARAT
Sakaka
al-Jauf
AL-MUNTAFIQ
BANI 'ATIYAH
Tabuk
'ANAZAH
AL-SULABAH
Rafha
AL-DHAFIR
AL-RASHAYIDAH
SHAMMAR
Hafar al-Batin
Wadi al-Batin
Qaisumah
Ras al-Mish'ab
Taima
Hayil
al-Hinnah
AL-'UJMAN
BANI KHALID
Nariya
Abu Hadriya
Jubail
AL-'ULA
SHAMMAR
MUTAIR
Qatif
Ras Tanura
Dammam
Dhahran
al-Khobar
al-Muwailih
al-Wajh
HARB
Wadi al-Rumah
Bursaidah
'Unaizah
Ma'aqala
Abqaiq
al-'Uqair
HUTAIM
Khaiber
Yanbu' al-Nakhl
Medina
Yanbu' al-Bahr
'UTAIBAH
UTAIBAH
Marah
al-Dawadimi
al-Qa'iyah
'Afif
al-Dir'iyah
Riyadh
al-Sulaimaniyah
al-Dilam
Haradh
Wadi al-Sahba
'Urai'irah
'Ain Dar
Hofuf
al-Hani
Salwah
Doha
Sharja
Abu Dhabi
AL-SHUHUH
BANI KA'B
NU'AIM
Muscat
Mahd al-Dhahab
al-Hariq
Yabrin
AL-MANASIR
BANI YAS
AL-DURU'
AL-DAWASIR
HARB
al-Muwaih
AL-SUHUL
Laila
QAHTAN
AL-'AWAMIR
AL-MANAHIL
AL-'IFAR
AL-JANABAH
Jiddah
Fatimah
'Ushairah
al-Khurmah
Mecca
Tayif
Turabah
SUBAI'
SUBAI'
AL-DAWASIR
Wadi al-Dawasir
al-Lidam
AL-WAHIBAH
ZAHRAN
HUDHAIL
GHAMID
RUB' AL-KHALI
AL-HARASIS
AL-JANABAH
al-Qunfudhah
QAHTAN
SHAHRAN
AL-RASHID & BAIT YAMANI
BAIT KATHIR
MAHRAH
AL-BATAHIRAH
'ASIR
YAM
Najran
AL-'AWAMIR
AL-MANAHIL
AL-MAHRAH
KATHIRI &
RASHIDI
GROUPS
AL-QARA
Murbat
Jaizan
AL-AMALISAH
WAYILAH
AL-SAI'AR
DAHM
'ABIDAH
BAL-'UBAID
(AL-KARAB,
ETC)
Wadi Hadhramaut
San'a
Hodeida
AL-HUMUM
Saihat
AL-DAYYIN
AL-'AWALIQ
Mukalla
Mocha
YAFI'
Ahwar
Aden

Scale of Miles
0   100   200   300   400

Tribal Map of the
Arabian Peninsula

have seen! Ask him to pray for us and tell him: God willing our rendez-vous will be in Riyadh."

On the twentieth of Ramadan, Abdulaziz moved with his party of sixty men; his destination—Riyadh.

He celebrated Ramadan in the area called Abou Jifan on the road to Hassa. On the third of Shawwal, the following month, he continued his trip to the outskirts of Riyadh. They were moving at night and by day they were hiding behind rocks and sand dunes. They were finally within an hour and a half walking distance from Riyadh.

They hid between the trees until the fall of dusk. That night Abdul-aziz told his companions that he was determined to enter the city and conquer it. Whoever wanted to go with him was welcome, and whoever was reluctant should stay. He moved on, with seven of his men. He told the rest around nine o'clock at night, that "by dawn if you do not receive a word, you should run for your lives, because we would have all been killed; and if God grants us success, whoever wants to join us, God be with him."

Abdulaziz moved with the company of his seven men toward the heart of Riyadh with the purpose of taking the Castle of Musmak, which is the fortress where the appointed governor of Riyadh, Ajlan, resided. However, the city had a defense wall surrounding it. Abdulaziz and his men cut a palm tree and used it as a ladder to climb the surrounding wall.

Some houses were near the outside wall of the Castle. One of these was inhabited by Jouwaisir, a cattle merchant, known to Abdulaziz. He knocked on the door and a woman answered: "Who is it?"

Abdulaziz answered: "I am sent by Amir Ajlan to buy him two cows from Jouwaisir."

The woman said, "You should be ashamed of yourself . . . Does anyone knock on a woman's door at this time of night unless he had bad intentions? Go away."

Abdulaziz said, "You be quiet! In the morning I shall tell the Amir and he will rip Jouwaisir apart."

When Jouwaisir heard the threat, he opened the door and Abdulaziz was able to enter into the house and get information about Ajlan. Abdulaziz held the man and threatened him not to make a move or he would be killed instantly. While the women were gagged and quieted in a cellar, the cattle dealer fled. Abdulaziz and his men had to enter another house to be able to reach the house where Ajlan's wife lived. In the second house they found a man and his wife. They tied them up with their bed clothing, gagged the wife and threatened them with death if they made any sound.

Abdulaziz waited for a short time to see if the fleeing cattleman alerted the city. Luckily, he did not.

Abdulaziz by now sent word to his brother Mohammed, who was stationed in the palm groves to bring the thirty-three men for support.

Ajlan's wife had a two-story house, so they had to step on each other's shoulders to reach the roof of the second story. After reaching this house they forced the roof door open, crept quietly, and seized the servants one by one. Finally they reached Ajlan's bedroom. Ibn Saud had his rifle and another man followed him with a candle.

They found two persons in bed, but Ajlan was not there. Two sisters were in bed. One of them was Ajlan's wife. While they jumped, screaming, he told them, "Enough! I am Abdulaziz." They were threatened with death if they did not cooperate and remain quiet.

It was learned from them that Ajlan left the fortress after the morning prayer and normally returned to this house. The wife, her sister, and the servants were all locked up. The rest of Abdulaziz's men were brought in from the house next door. All forty men settled down around two o'clock in the morning. They drank Ajlan's coffee, ate some dates and prayed, while wondering and thinking about the next step.

The decision was to wait until morning when the big gate of the fortress would open and Ajlan would come out. Four men were to stay in the house to cover the group with their rifles. After sleeping about an hour or less, dawn was approaching. Abdulaziz got up and prayed. The plan was to surprise Ajlan as he entered the house.

With the sunrise of January 15, 1902, Ajlan was coming out of the main gate of the fortress and he had about twenty men with him.

When Abdulaziz's eye focused on his enemy, the sight was too much for restraint! Abdulaziz had a gun with one bullet in it. He could not wait any longer. He charged out of the door and moved on to surprise and attack Ajlan. When Ajlan's bodyguards saw Abdulaziz they ran for the fortress gate, but it was already shut. So they moved through a small postern-gate two feet high, designed so that a man could enter head first, thus exposing himself to the sword if he was undesired.

Ajlan was left alone to face the onslaught of Abdulaziz. He drew his sword to strike Abdulaziz, who covered his face with his arm and fired his rifle point-blank and heard the sword fall to the ground.

Ajlan, injured, plunged into the postern. Abdulaziz caught his legs and tried his best to keep him from going in. Ajlan's man inside pulled his arms. He then kicked Abdulaziz in the stomach with a strong kick, that nearly fainted him. Abdullah Ibn Jiluwi, a cousin of Abdulaziz, threw a spear at Ajlan but missed! The spear went through the gate

Postern Gate at Fort Musmak—Here, and for a fleeting moment, the history of Arabia hung in the balance.

Fort Musmak, captured by Abdulaziz and his forty men, signaled the beginning of an arduous struggle for unifying Arabia.

of the fort. The steel point is still imbedded in the wood until this day.

In the confusion, the defenders did not slam the postern gate shut. Abdullah Bin Jiluwi threw himself into the hole and wiggled his way through. The defenders were too confused to kill him as he was going with his head first. Other followers of Abdulaziz moved in, and threw the main gate open.

Abdulaziz's men were outnumbered at least two to one. But they moved through the courtyard and towers of the fortress in a bloodthirsty fight that ended in slaughtering many of the defenders. Ibn Jiluwi finally shot Ajlan and killed him with one bullet.

The following is an account by Abdulaziz, who reminisced in later years: "He made at me with his sword, but its edge was not good. I covered my face and shot at him with my gun. I heard the crash of the sword upon the ground and knew that the shot had hit Ajlan, but had not killed him.

He started to go through the postern gate, but I caught hold of his legs. The men inside caught hold of his arms while I still held his legs. His company were shooting their firearms at us and throwing stones upon us. Ajlan gave me a powerful kick in the side so that I was about to faint. I let go of his legs and he got inside. I wished to enter, but my men would not let me.

Then Abdullah Ibn Jiluwi entered with the bullets falling about him. After him ten others entered. We flung the gate wide open, and our company ran up to reinforce us. We were forty and there before us were eighty. We killed half of them. Then four fell from the wall and were crushed. The rest were trapped in a tower; we granted safe-conduct to them and they descended. As for Ajlan, Ibn Jiluwi slew him."

Ajlan's guards were surprised and demoralized with the loss of their leader. They lost the will to fight. Abdulaziz went to the center of the area and declared, "There is no sense in further resistance." He promised to save their lives if they give up the fight. The battle was over!

At this moment of victory one of his men went to the highest point in the fort and declared, "The rule is for God! and then to Abdulaziz Ibn Abdul Rahman Al-Saud. You are in his safety and guaranteed security."

The capture of Riyadh paved the way for a holy struggle that eventually led to the founding of a great nation, a spiritual center for all Moslems of the world, and a great economic power whose impact is felt throughout the globe, making it the epic center for justice, safety, wisdom and an abundant source of energy. This closely-knit union is the most cohesive one ever known in history. One would hardly realize, remember or recognize the recent past of lawlessness, disintegration and division.

The Struggle to Unify the Country Under the Banner of Justice and The Rule of Law

The capture of Riyadh on January 15, 1902 gave the nucleus for the founding of Saudi Arabia. The struggle for this unification would prove to be long and arduous. At this time Abdulaziz Ibn Mit'ab Ibn Rashid was preoccupied by warfare against Kuwait. Thus, he delayed his response until late in the fall. His campground was at Hafr Al-Batin. He did not give the situation in Riyadh the weight and importance it proved to deserve. He waited to act until it was too late.

Abdulaziz rebuilt the defenses of Riyadh and the city was fortified and prepared to withstand adverse conditions of attack or blockade. His father came back from Kuwait and was placed in charge of the city, while he moved on to unify the nation. Their relationship was exemplary in every way.

For years Abdulaziz dwelled in tents, moving from place to place, often as a fugitive, and frequently with a price on his head. Sometimes eating, but more often going hungry. He moved across the desert, sometimes hunting, sometimes hunted. Soft and comfortable beds knew him not! A hole dug in the sand for his hip, and he had to be content with a brief rest for his bruised and aching body.

Abdulaziz did not come by a single square foot of Arabian territory without fighting for it. Every war he fought, he made it a religious war, a war for a principle. His idea finally took the form of welding the destructive and endlessly warring Bedouins of Central Arabia into a cohesive unit. He assured them peace and security the like of which they had never seen before.

With his charisma, great charm and dynamism, Abdulaziz won the hearts and help of people from southern Najd. By the time Ibn Rashid decided to move on south, he did not attack Riyadh directly, but made a move on Al-Kharj. However, Abdulaziz was waiting for him in an ambush and when his army advanced, a fierce battle raged on. Ibn Rashid retreated to Hail. Winning this battle was a great moral victory, uplifting the spirit of Abdulaziz and his men. His rule was established in the city of Riyadh southward on to Rab'a al-Khali.

Being very proud of these achievements, his father acknowledged

Riyadh during the early days of Abdulaziz.

his son's heroism and effective leadership. He abdicated the title of Amir, and bestowed upon him the authority over the Emirate. The father retained the title of Imam.

Toward the end of May, 1904, Ibn Rashid organized an army strongly supported by Turkish troops and their heavy armaments. The Turks were concerned about the expansion of Abdulaziz; because he was a friend to Mubarak, the ruler of Kuwait who, in turn, was a friend of the British. Moving from the town of Buraidah in al-Qasim, Abdulaziz led his force to meet the advancing forces of his enemy. In the heat of the battle the Turks and Ibn Rashid were defeated. Many of them fled for their lives! However, the controversies continued and hostilities led to another showdown which took place near Buraidah in April, 1906, during which Ibn Rashid was killed while trying to rally his troops (His successor was Mit'ab Ibn Abdulaziz Ibn Rashid). This was practically the beginning of the end for the contest between Abdulaziz Al-Saud and the Rashids. It took four years and three months after the capture of Riyadh.

The struggle for unifying the land was steady, coupled with dedication, determination, wisdom, and sheer courage. By now, the successors of his opponent were in disarray and confined to the northern portion of Najd, while the central and south of Najd were under the solid control of Abdulaziz.

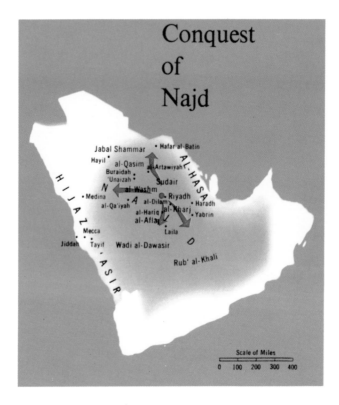

Problems cropped up frequently. Whenever one was settled, another or many more popped up. By 1908, Sherif Hussain was appointed by the Turks as the Amir of Hijaz. A brother of Abdulaziz, named Sa'ad, was captured by him. He held the brother as a hostage until Abdulaziz was pressured to acknowledge the Ottoman Suzerainty along with recognizing the hegemony over Kasim. However, as soon as his brother was released, this Ottoman control was deleted.

The Ikhwan

Since allegiances and loyalties changed from time to time, Abdulaziz devised a genius plan to settle the nomad tribes. By doing so, he reasoned, a great service would be rendered to the people and a stronger union would result. Once the bedouins were settled, some differences which developed between warring factions would be minimized or eliminated.

While bedouins were living as nomads, moving from one point to another in the desert simply by folding their tents and moving on with their herds, allegiances swayed easily from one side to the other. Especially since the harsh life of the desert made them suspicious in general. However, when settled in a certain way of life, this would become impractical. Their former way of living with shifting loyalties brought with it only reprisals and severe consequences through the loss of personal belongings, homes and agricultural settlements.

Since possessions are very dear to the heart of man and especially the bedouin, settlements should help in stabilization, allegiance, and improving the socioeconomic standard of the people. Abdulaziz devised the *Hijra* Plan for settling the bedouins. This became the focal point of his long-range planning.

Hijra meant an agricultural oasis settlement. Here, the bedouin settled to a peaceful and fruitful life. Mud houses replaced tents. The bedouin was better able to protect himself from the seering heat in the summer and from severe cold in the winter. The inhabitants of the Hijra were taught basic methods of agriculture and were given seeds.

Basic Islamic teachings were stressed. Religious teachers were sent to teach the tribesman and preach the new approach. This effort met with tremendous success. Learned religious leaders were delegated to lead the Hijra settlements. The settled bedouins were known as *Ikhwan*, which means brethren.

Artawia, the first farming settlement of the Ikhwan, was established in 1912. Many other agricultural settlements were established all over the realm of the Arabian Peninsula. Their number totaling 122 during the life of King Abdulaziz.

Wahhabism was practiced and a powerful force was ready and available to carry its Holy mission of unifying the nation. By 1912, this force of Ikhwan reached eleven thousand. By 1916 all the bedouin tribes were ordered to become part of the Ikhawn and also to pay Zakat as all Moslems should. The Sheikhs of the tribes were required to attend the Islamic law school at the Mosque in Riyadh. Many of them were encouraged to become a part of Abdulaziz's Court, further strengthening their allegiance, which was badly needed in carrying major campaigns of unification. The organized Ikhwan with their great zeal and enthusiasm became a very powerful force under the leadership of Abdulaziz.

With the religious fervor of the Ikhwan, the genius and great courage of Abdulaziz, the wars of unification became truly Holy Wars that would with time overcome the enemies and their selfish desires in keeping the country divided and torn in a state of anarchy and lawlessness.

The beliefs were strong in austerity, purity of Islamic concepts

Cavalry is an old tradition of the Arabs. Abdulaziz made good use of camels and Arabian horses in his long struggle for unifying Arabia.

and the founding of an Islamic society that practices decency and justice. However, some of their concepts were primitive and their zeal sometimes bordered on fanatic extremism.

Abdulaziz, with his genius and vast experience was able to cope with the situation and make successful use of their enthusiasm and religious zeal.

With this tremendous force at his disposal, in 1913 Abdulaziz felt powerful and daring enough with the Ikhwan at his side, to strike the Turks at the Hasa Province on the Arabian Gulf that was once under the realm of Najd but was occupied by the Turks for some fifty years.

This was not the first time Abdulaziz was warring against the Turks, he encountered Turkish troops and armament during his war with Ibn Rashid. But this was a very daring attack, since Hasa was directly administered by the Turks, who were considered a great power of the era. However, Abdulaziz needed the Hasa region and its ports under his domain, so he would not be left cut off from the rest of the world and unable to obtain desperately needed armaments and food for life.

The risks were great, but his needs were greater. Thus, his decision was to carry on the campaign. So on the eve of World War I, April, 1913, the Turks were eliminated from the Hasa region, and the territory extending from Kuwait to Qatar was under Saudi leadership.

With Hasa wrested from the Ottomans and with the newly extended territory, Abdulaziz came in close contact with the British. While Abdulaziz did not take an active part in World War I, at the end of the war he found himself in open dispute with Sherif Hussain. He did not attack him during the war since a common desire was to dislodge the Turks from the Arabian Peninsula. The British armed and supported Sherif Hussain, who concluded a secret agreement with them.

Although the British were aware of the emerging power of Abdulaziz, they aligned themselves with Sherif Hussain, but nevertheless they tried to enlist Abdulaziz against the Turks. After a number of negotiations, a treaty was signed between him and the British in 1916 where the British recognized Abdulaziz as the Amir of Najd and Hasa. They gave him a subsidy to encourage his efforts against the Rashids and the Turks and also to discourage an all-out war against Hussain. Bolstered by the Ikhwan forces, Saudi control was extended to the outskirts of Hail in 1917. While a consolidation of his control was taking place, he refrained from attacking Hijaz.

The western edge of the Wahhabi territory was attacked by Hussain in 1919 and the uneasy truce ended in war. The destruction of Hussain's army opened the way to Mecca. Abdulaziz contented himself with small territorial expansion. Other territories were acquired and by 1920 he added the inland districts of Asir. In 1921, he conquered the Rashid headquarters of Hail, thus ending a long dispute and competition. After three months of blockade, the city of Hail gave up the rebellious fight. This long rivalry between the two Houses was finally put to rest. The domain was extended north and west of Hail. This consolidation of territory took place in 1923.

Abdulaziz, the supreme commander and natural-born leader.

Abdulaziz was always generous in victory. After the fall of Hail, he prevented the troops from any looting. The hungry people were fed from his army's supplies. Surviving members of the Rashids were taken to the capital city of Riyadh. They lived at his expense as his personal guests.

Some captains of the Rashid army were taken into Abdulaziz's army. Two captains at the gates of Hail who refused to be bribed during the siege of the city were promoted rather quickly relative to the one who accepted the bribe. The man who held the fortress at the final stand, became the honored father-in-law of Abdulaziz, who also married the widow of Saud Ibn Rashid. He adopted her children and made peace with her relatives. Thus, the powerful institution of marriage helped to foster the peace and cement a relationship of loyalty and understanding.

Hussain of Mecca provoked another conflict with Abdulaziz in March, 1924, through his proclamation making himself the Caliph of Islam after the Ottoman Caliphate was abolished in republican Turkey. The passionate desire of Abdulaziz and the Ikhwan to capture Hijaz was formidable, especially since they were not allowed to make the pilgrimage while the Holy Shrines were under the control of Sherif Hussain.

Warfare began in September with the fall of Taif. Trying to halt the Wahhabis between Taif and Mecca was in vain. Hussain was defeated and escaped to Jeddah, where he was forced to abdicate in favor of his son Ali. Siege operations followed, until Medina capitulated on the fifth of December, 1925. On the nineteenth of December, Ali abdicated, and four days later Abdulaziz entered the city of Jeddah.

By 1926, Asir which was previously independent, was added to the conquered territories by a treaty. Finally, in 1927, Abdulaziz was crowned King of Hijaz, Najd and its dependencies. In 1927 a British treaty was signed in Jeddah, recognizing the territories conquered by Abdulaziz extending from the Arabian Gulf to the Red Sea.

After the great conquest of Hijaz, the Ikhwan leaders, who were very helpful and instrumental in this undertaking, grew more zealous and attacked an Iraqi border fort. The attack was carried against the clear orders of Abdulaziz. This challenge to his authority was a serious breach, but he used his wisdom in every way possible to avoid a conflict with the Ikhwan.

However, they grew more overbearing and refused to curb their raids across Iraq and the Jordanian frontiers. The raids were in direct conflict with an agreement that was concluded with the British at Uqair in 1922. The insubordination and rebellion could not be tolerated.

The Ikhwan were distrustful of the urban life which was different from what they had known before. They had suspicions and lack of trust for the readiness that Abdulaziz had shown in accepting facets that contributed to the progress of his people.

When the siege of Jeddah ended in 1925, some of the Ikhwan were against the use of the telephone because such modernization exemplified to them an intrusion upon the puritanical way of life they wanted to practice and preach. To gain their approval, he had them listen to some verses from the Qoran that were read over the telephone. By this he convinced them that the devil had fled "from this instrument which was suspicious and undesirable to them."

With time however, the Ikhwan grew more restless and rebellious. Their extremism was interfering with the safety of the state and was destined to disrupt plans for progress and development. Automobiles, telephones, telegraph and radios were considered "inventions of the devil." By January, 1927, a conference was held with the Ikhwan leaders and Ulema in Riyadh. The topic was a discussion of all matters causing disagreement and conflict. The Ulema issued a Fatwa or religious opinion that declined to make a decision on these instruments of modern life.

With the attacks on Iraq, a clear disobedience to his distinct orders, Abdulaziz had to face this challenge decisively. However, the British, who installed one of Sherif Hussain's sons as King of Iraq and another as King of Transjordan, were leary of the growing strength of Ibn Saud. They were discreetly fomenting trouble along the border with Iraq, and their intrigue was aiming at weakening his authority.

In September 1927 Ibn Saud telegraphed from Mecca to Baghdad:[1] "I hear that my border tribes are in a state of great excitement because of the illegal fortifications that are being built. The situation is dangerous, since the tribes threaten to attack on their own initiative." As usual, he waited long for an answer. It was three months this time. By then the crisis was over.

"By the end of October, Sheikh Faisal Ad-Dawish had advanced to the head of his Mouteir Bedouins, destroyed the B'ysey'a fortifications, and killed the soldiers and workers, without harming the Iraq tribes who lived in the neighborhood. British flying squadrons appeared, surveyed the situation, and, contrary to their usual custom, returned without throwing a single bomb.

At this point Ad-Dawish marched forth into Iraq territory and dispatched a few raiding parties. This continued for ten days, and though the invaders could easily have been bombed by English airplanes no measures were taken against them. On other occasions such as the

---

[1] Weiss, "Trouble In Arabia," The Living Age, 1928.

end of January, 1928, a British air squadron flew over the Najd boundary and dropped a number of bombs, thereby giving the Bedouin tribes an excuse for a revenge on Iraq. As these lines are being written the news comes to Riyadh that the northern Bedouin tribes are already in motion and have sent small detachments across the Iraq frontier.

When the truth was recognized, Ibn Saud had already gone far. He had become the ruler of the greater part of Arabia, a mighty bloc between the Suez Canal and India. Great Britain is now trying to hamper the development of this bloc. She is well aware that the native population of Iraq hates the Sherif Faisal and loves Ibn Saud, recognizing him as the only really free ruler in the Arab-speaking world. Furthermore, some of the Iraq Bedouin tribes also support him. The British, however, are trying to lull these sympathies, and are fomenting rivalries between the various tribes, rearing a barrier between Najd and Iraq. This is the source of the trouble in Arabia."

Faisal Ad-Dawish of the Moutair tribe, whose leadership was decisive in the battle for Hail, aligned himself with other Chieftains of the Ikhwan. Among these was Sultan Bin Bujad, who was the Sheikh of the powerful Utaiba tribe. They quickly forgot the great achievements of Abdulaziz and how much they owed him for their existence and organization.

In the fall of 1928, Abdulaziz called a congress of the chieftains and Ulema to Riyadh to solve these differences. Tribal leaders came with the exception of Sultan Bin Bujad and Ad-Dawish, who were behaving as outlaws. They were strong in opposition, and they were derogatory and rebellious against Abdulaziz. They declared him a "heretic" because he made treaties with the infidels and brought to the land instruments of the devil such as the telephone, telegraph, airplane and the automobile.

The Ulema at this conference declared that these instruments are permissible by law and indeed most desirable from a religious point of view. They increased the strength and knowledge of Moslems. Also, by authority of the Prophet of Islam, treaties with non-Moslem nations were very desirable, especially if they bring peace and freedom to the Moslem world.

The patience of the king was wearing thin. Finally, after a number of skirmishes between rebels and loyal tribes, the decisive battle of Artawia was fought in the spring of 1929. Abdulaziz crushed the rebellion after eighteen months of intermittent warfare that led to the open revolt in 1928.

Bin Bujad surrendered and was taken to Riyadh. Ad-Dawish was wounded severely and was thought to be dying. Abdulaziz, gracious as ever, sent his personal doctor to care for him.

Abdulaziz defeated all the rebel leaders and finally dismantled the power of the rebellious settlements of the Ikhwan. Northeastern security was established. Then Abdulaziz became the undisputed leader of `Arabia.

On September 22, 1932, the united land became the Kingdom of Saudi Arabia. Abdulaziz was proclaimed the King. With his courageous struggle to unify the country, and his great achievements, he became a world leader. Many foreign powers now focused their eyes on his new Kingdom.

No sooner than Abdulaziz thought all his conquests were over, trouble erupted in the Southern Province. Imam Yahya of Yemen captured Najran. He was helping and encouraging liberal tribes to carry on mischief and revolt.

The two sons of Abdulaziz, Saud and Faisal, led an expedition into the mountains and captured the port of Hodeida in Yemen. The dispute was settled and a peace treaty was signed in May, 1934, at Taif. As usual, the terms of King Abdulaziz were very moderate. Simply, they were minor adjustments to the Southern border and the payment of 100,000 sterlings in gold to compensate the government for the expenses of the campaign.

Now that his headaches were over and the scars of war had healed, Abdulaziz focused his attention on resources and development. His luck and ingenuity would strike again! Not only the water wells, he sought . . . but also a desert underbelly of "black gold."

Oil Discovery

The well-being of the people and development of the country made it imperative that resources of the Kingdom be diversified and productive. Up to this time most of the income for running the country came from raising animals and some small subsistence farming from the fertile areas, with a little income from pilgrimage.

The worldwide depression of the 1930's affected the economy through the decrease in the number of pilgrims visiting Mecca. King Abdulaziz was able to develop proper relations with the western nations so the economy and political development of Saudi Arabia would take place on a solid footing. However, the French and the British were determined to limit the Arab desire for independence.

On the other hand the United States of America declared its support for self-determination. Abdulaziz worked very carefully in establishing better relations with America while cultivating a relationship to avoid any irritation or antagonism toward Britain, the major power of the time.

He was very eager to make basic contributions toward education and health services so they would be made available to all his people. He intended to modernize primitive transportation and communication systems.

The King also wanted to extensively increase the number of automobiles, airplanes and telegraph. His dire need and desperation for new financial resources prompted him to grant the first oil exploration rights to a British firm in 1923. The concession was not used and the contract was not renewed in 1933.

Prior to that period, Americans who visited Arabia in the 1920's and early 1930's made a very positive impression on King Abdulaziz. Thus, he later chose an American company to prospect and do the oil exploration.

Potential resources of the Kingdom were discussed with King Abdulaziz in Jeddah in 1931 by an American mining engineer whose name was, Karl Twitchell. A special emphasis was placed on the untapped water resources of Hijaz. The Saudi Arabian Mining Syndicate, ltd. was established in 1934 to mine the Mahd Al-Dhahab. This gold mine was about fifty miles south of Medina.

Abdulaziz made the decision to open new discussions for petroleum exploration in the Kingdom. This proved to be one of his most important decisions. In 1933, exploration rights were granted to the Standard Oil Company of California (SOCAL). By September 23, 1933, two American geologists were joined by Karl S. Twitchell. They were Art P. Miller and S. B. (Krug) Henry. A month later they were joined by J. W. (Soak) Hoover, who came with the necessary equipment from the United States of America. The equipment supplied by the government that was brought from Jeddah also was used. Each party was accompanied by an escort and guide. The explorers encountered no difficulties with the Bedouin, especially since King Abdulaziz established peace and security throughout the land.

By the summer of 1934 and after search, exploration and scouting, a decision was made to test the Dammam Dome. This structure is similar to the one in Bahrain only twenty-five miles away. Other personnel joined the group, thus establishing the nucleus for exploration operations in the Kingdom.

With their increase in number, so did their personal needs and requirements for everyday living. Thus, the supply line was established between Saudi Arabia and the United States of America. Drilling equipment was erected on Dammam Number 1 on the west slope of Jabal Dhahran. At the same time the construction of the first Dammam camp was moving simultaneously.

Signing of oil exploration
agreement on May 29, 1933
between the Saudi finance minister
Abdulaziz al-Suleiman and Lloyd
Hamilton of Standard Oil
Company of California U.S.A.–a
bright future awaited the Kingdom
of Saudi Arabia.

King Abdulaziz inaugurating oil discovery in Dammam No. 7 in March
1938–a discovery that changed the history of Saudi Arabia.

Tests from the Dammam Dome were not very encouraging, but
the hope and determination were alive for continuing drilling and
exploration. Drilling was continued to a depth exceeding thirty-two
hundred feet. A total of eight additional wells were drilled, but again
results were not very encouraging.

By the spring of 1937 and upon completion of the Dhahran residential camp, American wives and children joined their men in the field.
By July, 1937, there were 53 American employees exploring for oil in
the Kingdom of Saudi Arabia.

The drilling of well Number 7 which started in 1936 was halted.
It was resumed in the fall of 1937. This proved to be a great decision

Beneath a barren desert, the good luck of Abdulaziz strikes again–this time–Black Gold (oil).

and the turning point in the history of Saudi Arabia and the Company's good fortunes.

When this well was drilled to a depth of 4,727 feet, large quantities of oil were gushing out and a new history was beginning to unfold for the Kingdom and the World. This well was completed in March, 1938, many years after the drilling of Dammam Number 1.

After five years of arduous effort, oil exploration yielded fruit and petroleum in large quantities was discovered in 1938. *The Arabian American Oil Company (ARAMCO)* was formed.

Because of World War II the development of the oil fields was rather slow and revenues from oil did not exceed four million dollars. However, as oil became in demand for modern warfare, Aramco started large-scale production in 1944. By 1948 the revenue from oil was around eighty-five million dollars. This was continually increasing every year and the dream of King Abdulaziz for economic development, welfare, and progress of his country was being realized steadily, step by step.

His great love and devotion for the nation and the people all along with his deep religious beliefs were the driving force in the initiation of many programs and services which led, some years later, to the development of major projects and great achievements.

With this great gift from God, oil revenues were increasing. They exceeded other revenues and King Abdulaziz was able to use these funds for initiating the building of roads, telecommunications, schools, health and welfare, industrial developments and other needed infrastructure befitting a nation of the Twentieth Century.

The proven oil reserves in Saudi Arabia now stand at over twenty-five percent of the world's crude oil reserves, giving the country the distinct capability of being the largest exporting oil producer in the world.

King Abdulaziz (Ibn Saud): The Leader and the Man

The struggle for unifying the Kingdom of Saudi Arabia was long and difficult. It became only a reality under the leadership of a genius, a determined lucky man whose personality and character were disarming, overpowering and most impressive indeed. No one would visit King Abdulaziz without being impressed and charmed. "One American, high in the world of oil and accustomed to think of himself as unimpressionable, compared him in old age to an ancient god." He was a man of justice and compassion, but capable of tough response and notable anger. The strength of his mind and personality combined with his superior qualities of youth helped in uniting his warring and divided people under the banner of Islam.

He founded the Kingdom of Saudi Arabia and guided it into a mighty economic power that must be reckoned with throughout the world, a nation which became the essence of justice and safety. Many nations of the world could draw useful lessons set by King Abdulaziz. He dedicated his life for the unity and independence of his country and for the welfare of his people. Prior to his emergence on the scene of the Arabian Peninsula, the land was rampant with lawlessness and internecine rivalries. People were not even able to go to the Holy Moslem Shrines in peace and tranquillity.

Abdulaziz considered the discovery of oil as a gift from God that was given to the heart of the Arab land, the birthplace of Islam. The strong conviction that God was on his side and that Wahhabi purification of the Moslem world was a must, both contributed to his tremendous inner drive that led him to victory upon victory.

In a land where Ghazu was a way of life, pilgrims who came to fulfill their religious duty at the Holy Moslem Shrines were endangering their safety by taking such pilgrimage where thieves, robbers and wolves were commonplace at the time.

From this land with its great span of diverse interests and desires, a giant of a leader, King Abdulaziz, asserted his unquestioned authority and the practice and respect for law and order, bringing equality and justice to all, and protecting the innocent from all aggressors. "And thus, King Abdulaziz established in the Arabian Peninsula a rule of justice, peace, and security that were total, and the like of which was not known even in the days of the Rashideen Caliphs at the height of the Arab Empire. So as if one person dropped a sack on his way, the sack would remain in place, no one will touch it until the government authorities come to move it."

His son, the late King Faisal, once said about him, "In our upbringing he balanced tolerance with discipline and he did not distinguish between us and the children of the people. He did not have two scales for justice, where he will use a scale for his children and another for the children of the people. All are equal in his eyes, and all are his children. Once, I remember that one of my younger brothers fought with the youth of another person. His Majesty punished him and sent him to detention. He did not forgive him because he is the son of the King."

According to Amin Rihani: King Abdulaziz was the greatest reformer of the Arabs. Even during the height of the Arab Empire, no

King Abdulaziz, the undisputed leader of Saudi Arabia.

leader was able to fully unite Arabia or care for the Bedouins except for using them as warriors (wood for wars), nor did even Saleh Eddine, as it appears, try to improve Bedouin conditions by eliminating their deep-rooted enmities.

It took one thousand and three hundred years until a second age has been written for them through the emergence of Abdulaziz Ibn Saud, who united them, united their objectives, found and strengthened an Arabic Kingdom "of the people, by the people, for the people."

His tastes were very simple. His way of life was frugal. He was true to his friends. He cherished warm affections for them. Some of these were from other lands. Among them: Philby, Rihani, Percy Cox and General Clayton. No! He did not have distaste and suspicion for people from other countries with different religions. He had most pleasant memories for his loyal friends.

In peace, his manners were mild, commanding a fine sense of humor. The love for his countrymen and men's companionship were deep and sincere.

The warrior King would rise an hour before dawn. He would read the Qoran, then pray when the Mouezzin called for prayer.

In the evening, he would hold a General Council. Someone would normally read for an hour and a half, covering various topics on religion, literature and politics. He was always interested in the news.

To his countrymen, he is simply and affectionately: Abdulaziz, the man they could approach at all times, claiming a right or voicing a grievance. His hospitality brings to his table the mighty and powerful along with the most humble Bedouin of the desert.

During World War II King Abdulaziz exercised his great wealth of wisdom and leadership. Although he favored the Allies, he kept the relative neutrality of Saudi Arabia during the war, avoiding the torment that would befall his land. However, as the war progressed and the balance of power was readjusting, the interest of his Kingdom was reassessed. He moved from his neutral position and declared war on Germany on the first of March, 1945. Prior to this time, some correspondence of great historic value was taking place between him and the American President Franklin D. Roosevelt.

King Ibn Saud and President Roosevelt

King Abdulaziz was a champion of justice not only in his land but throughout the world. Among all leaders and nations of the world, history will note that he defended the Palestinian cause with great dedication, compassion and enthusiasm. He used his convincing power and every means at his disposal to defend the rights of innocent people and especially those in Palestine.

Two great men were destined to become friends and share philosophies of common interest. King Abdulaziz had just concluded his successful struggle for uniting his country; which, by 1932, became the Kingdom of Saudi Arabia. Franklin D. Roosevelt became President of the United States of America in March, 1933. Both were dedicated men in the service of their respective countries. Both sacrificed remarkably in contributing their share for peace and justice in a turbulent world ravaged by war and division. While the Kingdom chose to be neutral at the beginning of World War II, so did the United States of America for some time, until it was pushed against the wall by the Japanese. Both men were of similiar age. They espoused philosophies that had many viewpoints in common. They were farmers in the depth of their heart and they both had some physical injuries. The President was forced to use a wheelchair; the King was able to move with difficulty; he was not able to climb the stairs because of wounds in his legs.

The first political moves of the United States in the Middle East took place during the Versailles Conference for Peace, held in 1919 after World War I, coming on the heels of President Wilson's declaration on human rights and freedom. These rights, along with self-determination, were declared in Congress on January 8, 1918.

Abdulaziz was lending a good ear to these developments and to the awakening of a new giant coming on the horizon. British power and influence on Arab affairs was waning.

American ingenuity coupled with the massive oil potential of the Kingdom, along with the sharp minds of two great leaders, all these created an atmosphere of rapport between two charismatic personalities.

As the Palestine problem was getting more acute by 1936, King Abdulaziz extended his hand of cooperation to the Arab countries. He concentrated his efforts on Britain, under which Palestine was a protectorate. His efforts were also geared toward the United States, which was emerging as a world leader. On the 29th of November, 1938, a letter was sent to President Roosevelt in which the King alerted the President to the fact that it would be impossible to establish peace in Palestine without preserving Arab rights and without guaranteeing that Palestine would not be given to a foreign group of people whose principles, objectives, and morals are very different from those of the Arabs.

In his answer, President Roosevelt, on January 9, 1939, expressed that the position of the United States on Palestine was expressed in a formal announcement, the essence of which was that any changes relating to the British protection on Palestine must receive the approval of the United States. At that time, the announcement expressed that a project for establishing a home for the Jews in Palestine received large sums of gold and American capital, which played a major role.

In a dinner reception held September 30, 1943, in honor of the late Kings Faisal and Khaled in Washington D.C., President Roosevelt expressed his good wishes toward the Kingdom and assured his visitors that the United States of America is a nation that seeks to exploit no other nation no matter what her status may be. He also mentioned the great resources of the Kingdom. He said, "I think we all know that the King is a very great man. I read this evening a magazine and all of it was written about the King. There was a short passage at the end which I admired very much. Everything in it coincided with my personal philosophy."

On the 30th of April, 1943, King Abdulaziz sent a letter to President Roosevelt, again urging him to take the just course for Palestine. He expressed his deep concern along with that of Moslems and Arabs of the world, since Zionist maneuvers were plotting to create a home for the Jews in Palestine. The people of Palestine would be driven out of their homes!

He concluded by saying, "We do not wish to erase the Jews and we do not demand that. We demand that the Arabs not be deleted from Palestine and be replaced by Jews. If every nation of the Allies shared in the responsibility a tenth of what Palestine had endured so far, the Jewish question would be solved. All we ask in this present position is the help of your honor to stop the flow of immigration and to stop it completely."

In his answer of July 15, 1943, Roosevelt repeated his assurances that the United States would not make any decision to change the basic status of Palestine, without complete consultation with both the Arabs and the Jews.

With the country's fabulous wealth just lying beneath the surface, American oil interests were developing momentum. This prompted President Roosevelt to declare in 1943 that defending Saudi Arabia was of vital interest to the United States of America. This way, the Kingdom became eligible for a lend-lease assistance program. However, this assistance was to be delivered through the British, since they still were the power in the region. This courting and coziness were looked upon disapprovingly and suspiciously by the British.

President Roosevelt invited King Abdulaziz to visit him aboard an American destroyer in the Suez Canal upon his return from the

"President Roosevelt listens intently to King Ibn Saud"–A charming encounter on February 10, 1945 aboard an American warship anchored in Great Bitter Lake in the Suez Canal, near Cairo. The visit took place as the President was heading homeward after the Yalta Conference.

Yalta Conference. Preparation for this meeting was conducted with the utmost of secrecy, especially because of the prevalent dangers at that stage of the war. When the King left at 4:30 P.M. aboard the destroyer Murphy, rumors were rampant in Jeddah.

People were left bewildered and astonished. Malicious rumors had the King leaving the country, running from his people like Sherif Hussain. Others said he had been kidnapped by the Americans. Of course none of that was true. Ibn Saud was carrying a mission of peace, honor and justice. After two nights and one day, the destroyer anchored at the point of destination in the Suez Canal. The meeting was a historic one! Positive impressions from both sides led to better and warmer relations.

At ten o'clock in the morning, February 10, 1945, the American destroyer Murphy was next to the American ship Quincy, which brought the President to Yalta. The atmosphere was very cordial. The meetings were very informative. A conference for one and a half hours and the dinner was ready! The President took one elevator, while the King took another, to meet in the dining room. While in his elevator, President Roosevelt pushed the emergency red button and stopped the elevator between the decks of the ship and smoked two cigarettes. Although the President was a chain smoker, he did not smoke in the presence of the King at all, out of respect for him and his Wahhabi beliefs! They continued their political discussion from nearly eleven-thirty in the morning until three-thirty in the afternoon. The honorable Colonel William A. Eddy, who was chief of the American delegation in Jeddah, Saudi Arabia from 1944 to 1946, said, "King Ibn Saud and President Roosevelt had great understanding."

The King came seeking friendship and it was realized. He did not mention at any time the subject of economic or financial aid. He traveled to meet the President, searching for friendship not money, despite the fact that in 1945 he was governing a land that was not able to produce the necessary amount of food. The war and the poor treasury had prevented him from importing other necessities of life.

President Roosevelt mentioned that the end of the War would be near and Germany would be defeated. He said there still was a dangerous problem. He would like to have the King's advice on it! How to save the rest of the Jews in Mid-Europe and how to find a home for them?

The answer of King Ibn Saud was tough but brief and to the point, "Give them and their children the best land and best homes of the Germans who victimized them." President Roosevelt countered by saying that the Jews have a tremendous desire to reside in Palestine and that he depended on Arab generosity and the help of the King in solving the Zionist problem.

The King answered, "Let us make the tyrant enemy himself pay the price. This is the method which was followed by the Arabs in their wars. The criminal must pay the price and not the innocent observer."

This conference led to the founding of a genuine friendship between two great men. The King also defended the independence of Syria and Lebanon, which were under French protection. The President of the United States personally assured the King that he would not carry on any actions that would be contrary to the Arabs. He promised that the government of the United States would not cause any basic political change in Palestine, without complete consultation beforehand with the Jews and the Arabs.

Afterward the King met with Winston Churchill, Prime Minister of Great Britain. When Churchill learned about the meeting between Roosevelt and Ibn Saud, he was "thoroughly nettled. He "burned the wires to all his diplomats" desiring to meet with Ibn Saud and others who met Roosevelt.

Sir Winston Churchill meets with His Majesty King Ibn Saud (February, 1945) – on the heels of a meeting with President Roosevelt. Years later, he wrote of the King: "My admiration for him was deep . . ."

Upon returning to the United States, President Roosevelt declared that he learned about Palestine and the Middle East in five minutes of conversation with Ibn Saud, more than he learned from the exchange of several letters. A secret memo sent by Colonel William Eddy stated that the King said to a number of foreign representatives meeting in Jeddah in February, 1945, "America and Britain must choose between Arab land where peace and tranquillity dominate or a Jewish land drowned in blood". This memo was released on the eighteenth of May, 1969 by the Secretary of State's office.

Following the meeting on the tenth of February, 1945, King Ibn Saud had other correspondence with the President defending the Palestinian cause with impressive and convincing documentation. On the fifth of April, 1945 he received an answer from President Roosevelt reaffirming his previously stated position.

In a letter dated February 16, 1945, which was sent to William Eddy, the President said, "It was for me a most interesting and stimulating experience and I want you to know how fully aware I am of the important part which you played, not only in the arrangement but also, in the conversation itself in making our meeting such an outstanding success."

Destiny had other plans for the fate of Palestine! President Roosevelt died two months after this successful meeting and the promises on Palestine were nullified by the rise to power of Harry S. Truman as the next President of the United States.

Zionist influence was massive. Despite strong appeals for justice and respect for mutual interest and human rights, the road was paved for establishing Israel in Palestine. Truman, under formidable Zionist pressures, summoned his ambassadors from the Arab World to Washington. He brazenly declared, "I'm sorry, gentlemen, but I have to answer to hundreds of thousands of people who are anxious for the success of Zionism. I do not have hundreds of thousands of Arabs among my constituents." Of course, communist Russia was equally eager to recognize the state of Israel.

After 1945, Saudi Arabia did not participate in any belligerent acts in the war. However, through a declaration of war against Germany, the Kingdom of Saudi Arabia became eligible to participate in the United Nations. It was represented by the late King Faisal, who attended the meeting in San Francisco. King Ibn Saud also was a strong force behind the founding of the Arab League in 1945.

It is very fitting to conclude this section with what King Abdulaziz said about the story of his life, "I liberated this Kingdom from foreign domination. I am a master in it and she is a master herself. So here I united five countries: Najd, Hijaz, Assir, Hail, and the Hasa; for everyone of these there were rulers and princes, so I built from it all this nation. I opened in front of the people the doors of life; I prepared for them the ways for progress and I caught with them the bandwagon of civilization. We achieved in tens of years what was not imagined by anyone that we could reach in hundreds of years." How true!

On the morning of November 9, 1953, King Ibn Saud, the great statesman, desert warrior, father and founder of the Kingdom of Saudi Arabia, was dead. His spirit and holy mission are both alive and well! They go on.

Interesting to Know

King Abdulaziz was a giant of a man in his achievements and strong leadership, enhanced by a majestic physique and warm personality. It would be very interesting to portray some of his thoughts, traits, pronouncements and his great passion for justice and love for his countrymen. We thought you would be pleased and maybe fascinated to know more about this wonderful human being.

Unique in Character and Personality

• In his youth Abdulaziz was very smart and very active; as was witnessed by his friends when he was with his father in Kuwait. He was the "leader of the group" while playing. He very much enjoyed listening to the history of his grandfather, Imam Faisal, as it was told to him by some old Sheikhs.

He learned how to read and write and memorized many soras from the Qoran. He read it entirely with the help of learned men.

• When he was in Bahrain, the ruler asked him, "Abdulaziz! Is Qatar better or Bahrain?" He answered spontaneously, "Riyadh is better than both of them." Then, the ruler said, "This kid will be somebody someday!"

• His determination and perserverance were unique. Once he set his eyes on a goal he did the impossible to achieve it.

• He practiced and believed that in this life, the basic foundation for fine character is the truth and good virtue. Every life that is not based on this fact does not have any value at all, because the truth rewards man in both this world and after death.

• The strength of his mind and the depth of his thoughts were fascinating. He was gifted with a sharp memory. His marvelous depth of mind accurately assessed other minds and situations. This was crowned with an agile and wise personality that was portrayed in his towering figure that exuded his manhood and left a deep and everlasting impression on all who sat with him. His greatness, charm and magnetism fascinated and captured whomever met him. The strength of his determination was supreme and enabled him to overwhelm the minds of other people. Many a time, chieftains of tribes came in to his court with arrogance and animosity. His personality overwhelmed them. He won them over with his magnetism, convincing power and charm.

All this was crowned with his interesting conversations and fine oratory. The exercise of self-discipline made him a master at saying the right thing at the right time, at the right place, in the right form. His stories and scintillating talks were sprinkled with intelligent proverbs and touches of wisdom, all narrated in a mesmerizing style that captures the audience, wanting him to go on and on . . .

• When an Arab leader sought refuge at his court in 1941, at a time when Britain was a major power in the region, he said, "Britain is capable of taking anyone of the children of Abdulaziz, but she will not be able to take a man who sought refuge with Abdulaziz, as long as we are alive!".

• "I am not one of those men who will throw their words without judgement, I am a practical man, if I say I do; it is a shame on me, on my religion and honor to say something that I will not follow through, because this is one thing I am not used to, and I do not like to become used to, ever! And if what's between me and God is well and good, let whatever is between me and man be ruin".

• "Every man should say whatever his conscience dictates, with complete frankness, and one should not veer away from right because of the blame of anyone. Everyone should declare what he believes to be helpful, because the domain for discussion, compromise and analysis will lead to the good and best results. Man should try and God will grant success."

• He had guts and his courage was exemplary. He was a warrior of the first caliber and his resistance to pain was unique. Once he suffered from a serious wound in his stomach for six months before he received the proper treatment from his personal doctor. He was hit with two bullets that lodged in the skin of his stomach. When his doctor was getting the anesthetic ready for the operation, Abdulaziz asked, "What are you doing?" The doctor explained what he was going to do. The King exploded laughing and ordered him to put the anesthetic aside. King Abdulaziz took a knife in his hand and cut the skin above the bullets, then ordered the doctor to continue his job. His courage was always coupled with wisdom and good planning.

• In a speech to the graduates from the Scientific Saudi School in Mecca, the King said, "Countrymen! You are the first fruit from what we planted in this school. So, realize the value of what you have learned from this education. You should know that education without work is like a tree without fruit. Education can help a person, it can also work against him. The one who learns is not like the one who does not learn. Little blessed education is better than much that has not been blessed, and the blessing is in work."

• The British Arabist and writer, Philby wrote, "The King once mentioned that his personal court is similar to the British Parliament and said, 'Don't you see that we are discussing matters with complete freedom and democracy and we always have an opposition represented by Philby?' "

• Said he, "In my opinion, people are of three kinds: One of them is of the truth; this one I equate him with myself and I will sacrifice myself for him. The second is the man of good and bad; this one I pray God will elevate his good above his bad, and God save us from his bad. The third is from the bad; God save us from him! I ask God that he will guide him and help him avoid the evil of himself and that God will lead him to the right path."

• Ibn Saud enjoyed the company of his children and had an excellent reputation as a father. In every kingdom, until the recent past, royal marriages were a means of uniting peoples or achieving national aims, but in monogamous countries their use was limited. Ibn Saud, however, was able to marry into every important tribe in his domain, and so bind them all to himself by family ties.

King Abdulaziz practiced a royal habit of wisdom in training the princes on the functions of government. Whenever a child reached an age of significance, he was given a job befitting his experience. Then he was promoted to other jobs of higher responsibility, depending upon his eligibility and experience. He loved his children very dearly. He was a disciplinarian in their upbringing. He demanded from them to be always ready to receive his orders at a moment's notice and without prior warning.

• Once he made the Hajj with his father, who was very old. They toured around the Ka'aba, as the tradition requires. By the third tour, the father was tired, too weak to continue. Instantly, Abdulaziz carried his father and continued the ritual. He could have ordered his entourage to carry him. But not Abdulaziz, who honored and respected his father!

• King Abdulaziz loved and respected his father, even when he became the Sovereign leader of a nation unified and created by his great courage and leadership. His behavior toward his father was with great respect and humility, to the point that he would never set foot in a room of the castle if his father was in a room below. He would say, "How can I allow myself to walk over my father's head?"

In his father's presence he would stand up until he was invited to sit down. A close associate recalls that one day in Riyadh, probably December 19, 1927, he was visiting the King's father on a courtesy call. They were sitting on the ground on cushions, Arabian style. An attendant announced that the King was coming and Ibn Saud was standing by the doorway. Certainly, the associate wanted to rise and greet him, but the father clutched his wrist and told him to sit down. "You are my guest," he said.

This was certainly an embarassment and words could not express its depth, for the associate to be seated while the King was greeting his father from a distance, standing at the doorway while waiting for permission to enter the room. However, the King winked at the associate to put him at ease, while the father continued his story without interruption. After a few minutes the father told Abdulaziz, "Step closer, oh, my boy, and sit down!"

Sometime later, when he received word about the death of his father, he was deeply grieved and jumped with a terrible roar, "My father is dead! My father is dead!" he cried. For two days after his father's death he refused to see anyone. He refused to eat or drink, spending days and nights in prayer. Similar stories go on and on . . .

Justice and Safety

After conquering Hijaz, crimes were rampant. The last years of Sherif Hussein's rule were years of criminal acts including theft, kidnapping, murder and other crimes. Outlaws were numerous. Innocents were robbed, especially the pilgrims who were moving unprotected. It was repugnant for the King to see these acts taking place in the Holy Shrines of Islam. He was determined to apply the rule of Shari'a to the fullest. Justice was swift and soon led to peace and tranquillity.

● His love for justice and security were supreme. He was religious, honorable, and straightforward. The Shari'a was swiftly and properly applied to bring the right to the people and to severely punish the criminals. One of his famous mottos: *Justice is the foundation for successful rule.*

● Once a Bedouin came to Abdulaziz and said he found a sack of flour on the way, at a spot that he pointed out. The King asked him, "And how did you know the fact that the sack had flour in it?" The Bedouin said, "I felt it with my toe!" Abdulaziz ordered him in prison and told him, "If you find a sack from thereon, do not touch it even with your toes!"

The safety and security are the envy of many people and nations around the world. An American writer once said; "If you had ten thousand dollars in a wooden box without a lock and you have it tied only with a rope, and you send it by car with a driver who is not armed that would travel a distance of one thousand miles in a given direction here in the United States of America, and if the purpose of the trip was not kept secret, how far do you think the driver and the money will go? But, in the Kingdom of Saudi Arabia, they will travel the entire distance in complete safety and without anyone disturbing them. This in brief is what King Abdulaziz of Saudi Arabia has done. He is counted as one of the greatest men of our time."

● He was always very interested in knowing the latest news about his Kingdom, going from major matters of policy to the smallest requests.

Once in his court in Mecca, an old man came with a request concerning his land. This was conveyed to the late King Faisal. A year went by, and the man came to the Royal Court and declared that his problem was not solved! The King ordered that the man should be let in immediately.

After talking to the man, he told him that his problem would be solved in two days. The King then asked Faisal, who said that the request was turned in to two of his employees, but it was not found. The King ordered a thorough search until the request was found. The two employees who neglected their duty were terminated and the old man received what he had requested. This was a good lesson for government employees who realized that delinquency in their duty, no matter how simple it may be, will not be hidden from the King.

• Once a woman came requesting the death penalty against the killer of her husband. The King asked her, "Where is the proof for what you are complaining about?" She answered, "This man was up in a date tree. He was picking some dates and my husband was sitting peacefully underneath. Suddenly the man falls from above and breaks my husband's neck, so I am now a widow and my children are orphans." The King said, "And did you see him fall purposely to kill him?" "I do not know," she replied, "but my husband died. I am after him alone, with no one to take care of me." "And, would you accept court compensation or are you still demanding the life of this man?" "The Shari'a of Allah gives me judgement against his life," she explained. Ibn Saud thought for a moment and said with a hidden smile: "I do not deny this right to you, but the method of his death is in my hand, so let us see what we can judge. The date tree is thirty yards tall. Let the man be tied on the trunk at the base of this tree, and you climb until you reach its top. Then you fall on him and kill him. This is your right, so go and receive it!" He was quiet for a while, then said, kindly, "Or, will you prefer a judgement of compensation!" The woman accepted indemnity without hesitation.

• Once Prince Abdullah Al-Faisal told the story about a killer who entered his home and asked his help. So he was in a dilemma and went to his grandfather, awakened him and said, "I have a problem and I came so you will help me in my sadness." "And what is your problem?" "The killer you have been hunting! I found him seeking help in my home! I brought him to you now, so you will order what you see fit!" Ibn Saud said, "If the Shari'a judges on any man, no matter how big he may be, I will not hesitate to execute the judgement. Go and call on the family of the victim. Give them money and ask them if they will drop their rights to punishment. If they drop their right, I will give him clemency from the public right. If they do not agree, all you have to do is give him the course of justice."

• Once a contractor came complaining to the King about one of his children. The man had property near the land of the Prince. During the man's absence, the Prince built a house. It appeared that the structure protruded into the neighbor's land. When the King heard the complaint, he asked the Prince to tell him what happened. The Prince said, unintentionally, the workers trespassed on his neighbor's land. The King then said, "The plaintiff has a choice of destroying the structure of the Prince so that he will reclaim his land or he will receive four times the price of the land, plus the proper monetary compensation from our son who trespassed on his land." The man accepted the price and the indemnity, and then prayed for the welfare of the King.

• Once a Bedouin complained that one of the King's children had hit him. The King called on his children to come to his court. He asked the plaintiff to point to the one who hit him. So the man obliged and pointed out the guilty. With a strange vibrance in his voice, His Majesty asked the child, "Did you hit him?" The son was quiet and did not answer. The just father realized that his son had committed the act. So he looked at the Bedouin and asked him, while his features showed anger and deep hurt, "With what did he hit you?" "With a stick!" the Bedouin replied. "Get up and hit him! Revenge from him. Get up!" the King said. Whispers of anxiety and anticipation filled the air. The man answered "I cannot!" "Get up, God enlighten you, get up, old man, and do not be afraid! Justice has equated between you and him, but you are greater than him because justice is on your side and he is younger than you are. He is the guilty one. Get up and hit him." "Excuse me! This is sufficient from you. Justice has erased the guilt of your son. What you have done is the best reward for me. I decline my right completely." At this stage, everyone thought the matter had been solved since the plaintiff dropped his complaint. After this symbolic compromise, which the plaintiff did not even dream of, all of a sudden Abdulaziz stood up, angry and screaming at his son with a strong voice, "You hurt him and you do not fear God. Do you think that your belonging to me gives you the right to transgress, or that you will escape punishment?" He then hit him, hit him hard, and he ordered that he be taken to the court and be imprisoned alone! This event led him to make the following pronouncement which was distributed throughout the land:

• "From Abdulaziz Ibn Saud to the people of the Arabian Island (Kingdom of Saudi Arabia): Everyone of our people who feels that injustice befell him, must come forward with complaint. Everyone that comes with a complaint should send it by telegraph or the free mail, at our expense. Every employee of the post or telegraph must receive the complaints from our subjects even if they were directed against my children, my relatives, and the people of my home. Let it be known to every employee who tries to dissuade our people from presenting a complaint no matter what it is, or try to influence the plaintiff, so that he will minimize the impact of its language, we will punish him severely. I do not want to hear in my life of a single one oppressed, and I do not want God to have me carry the burden of oppressing anyone and not helping an oppressed or extracting the right of an oppressed. This is made known, so God is my witness."

Wisdom and Tolerance

• He was patient and forgiving. Once a cousin in fury said that he was more courageous than Abdulaziz. When the King heard this, he was not disturbed. He smiled a big smile and said: "What my cousin said is correct. He is more courageous than I am, but I am luckier than he is." On another occasion he said, "If God will give my children the luck that he bestowed upon me, they will be able to rule the whole Arab World."

• With his legendary courage and warrior capacity came his compassion, tolerance and forgiveness. Instead of crushing his enemies after defeat in battle, he manifested genuine tolerance toward them. Once an enemy is conquered, he exercises his respect and tolerance. One of the best examples is his forgiveness for Ad-Dawish on a number of occasions.

At the end of the war between Abdulaziz and the Sherif of Hijaz, few of his supporters continued to oppose the King. He gave them all full clemency in 1935. Some of them had positions where they proved to be loyal in their work for the rest of their lives.

• After the founding of the Kingdom, the Royal Court included a large number of men from Shammar. In victory, he forgave his adversaries who became admirers of his greatness and professed loyalty and trust. They became his supporters. Many Rashids, and their children grew in Riyadh. They were loyal and true, respected and honored.

At the end of the struggle against Ibn Rashid, the King called the Rashid's emissary in Damascus, Syria, Reshaid Ibn Layla, who was the middleman between Ibn Rashid and the Turks. The emissary had received armaments and money to help Ibn Rashid against Ibn Saud.

Abdulaziz told him, "What should be your penalty? "Whatever you
desire, and I do not regret what I have done." Abdulaziz said, "You
were true and loyal in serving your friend and your friend is gone.
There continues to be in you the sense of loyalty, so go back to Damascus!
Now, you are my representative!" The man represented him in Syria.
He was true and loyal in his work to Abdulaziz until the last day of
his life.

Compassion, Hospitality and Generosity

● One day an old woman stood by the door of his castle and complained about an inheritance matter. She told His Majesty that she
had no one to defend her rights. The King called her and took the
papers from her hand. He promised her that he would personally represent her in defending her rights. As a matter of fact, he examined the
documents in her hand and sent the matter to the Court of Justice.
Everyday he would personally ask about the matter, until the court
made the judgement. He then informed the woman about it and ordered
its implementation.

● In one of the royal processions, a voice was heard, "Oh, Abdulaziz! Mazloum!" (oppressed). The King ordered his driver to stop.
He told the man to get closer and asked him for his need! "I need
medicine, I need clothing," the man said. The King ordered his men
to give him medicine, clothing and twenty sterling. The procession
of mercy moved on.

● An incident which occurred in 1928 comes to memory. Ibn Saud
was sitting at a window and a Bedouin came and stood before it. The
King asked him to move away.
The Bedouin asked, "Oh, Abdulaziz, how can you sit there and
see me starve?" The King answered; "How come you are starving?"
The Bedouin recited his story, explaining that he arrived to Mecca
about nine o'clock at night. When he came to the guest house, he
was told that he was too late for dinner! He then said; "I would be
happy with any food that you may have." A bureaucratic answer was
given saying that the proper hour for dinner had passed and that food
will not be served again. The man went away with an empty hand
and an empty stomach.
The generosity of Abdulaziz was injured. Upon hearing this story,
he ordered that the manager and the assistant at the guest house be
brought immediately before him so he could hear their side of the
story. When asked about their behavior in not practicing the treasured
generosity of Abdulaziz by not giving food to a hungry man, their

reply was a hideout behind regulations and bureaucracy, saying that the man came too late for dinner.

"If the cooked food was finished, asked Abdulaziz, why was the man not furnished with dates or other similar food?" The guest house manager and his assistant did not answer!

"Quivering with rage, for these servants had "blackened" his face in outraging the laws of hospitality, Ibn Saud ordered them a beating, the first installment of which he administered with his own cane." They were also suspended from their duties for a few days, then allowed to resume their job on the promise that in the future no one would be refused food, no matter what the hour may be when he asks for a meal . . .

• A writer said, "I saw with my own eyes a midget Arab entering the court of King Abdulaziz. He wanted to kiss him on the forehead. When he was unable to reach him because the King was so tall, he held the head of his Majesty and brought it closer saying, "How are you, Oh, Abdulaziz?"

• The Reader's Digest reported in 1943 that once King Abdulaziz Ibn Saud was on his way to Mecca for the pilgrimage, as he does every year, when one of the tires of his car blew out, so he sat on the sand until it was repaired. At the time a shepherd on his camel passed by and asked him if he had seen the King pass by. Abdulaziz said, "What do you need him for?" "I heard that he is on his way to Mecca, so I said maybe he will give me some money, and this way I myself will be able to go to the Hajj." The King opened his briefcase containing the gold sterlings that he keeps by him all the time, and he filled the man's hand with gold pieces. The shepherd was astonished! He looked at the golden pieces and said to the King, "Thank you, Oh, Abdulaziz! I was not able to recognize your face, but I knew you from your generosity."

Indeed, the King was very generous, not only to his subjects but to many of the needy abroad.

Was this giant of a man a Napoleon of the desert? Certainly more! He was not a tyrant. He was a man of great compassion and justice. He forged, almost singlehandedly, a viable nation from a sea of lawlessness and anarchy. What an impossible task! A dream come true! Great leaders would have marvelled at his feat. Garibaldi of Italy, Bismarck of Germany, and George Washington of America, would have been bewildered! Scholars and history students would certainly be amiss not reading the fascinating story of Abdulaziz.

After this great leader's death, his sons followed in his footsteps of dedication and love for their country and world peace.

On November 9, 1953, the successor to the throne was King *Saud* the son of Abdulaziz. In his twenties, he led many campaigns in the battles of unification. Attempts were made at building some roads, hospitals, schools and improvement of Hajj facilities, but the financial situation deteriorated with time, so did his health. Finally, he abdicated from the throne and *Faisal* was proclaimed King in 1964.

Faisal was born in Riyadh on April 9, 1906, less than four years after the capture of Riyadh. His birth coincided with the day Abdulaziz won a decisive battle in his struggle to unify the country. The battle was Rawdhat Mhanna.

Since youth, Faisal received traditional education and was interested in racing horses and camels. He learned the Qoran, and enjoyed poetry. However, his best education according to him came from his father "Abdulaziz who was the best teacher from whom Faisal learned his lessons and experience." At the age of thirteen he accompanied his father in battle. His talent in the battlefield impressed Abdulaziz very much. A born-commander, Faisal was a great asset in the long struggle for unification.

In 1919 he visited Britain, France and Belgium. His travels to Europe broadened his horizons. Upon returning to the Kingdom, his father, obviously pleased with his son's performance, smiled and said: "We were right to name you after your grandfather, Faisal Bin Turki." After the conquest of Hijaz, Faisal was appointed Viceroy with his headquarters in Mecca. This position was very important throughout the Moslem world, especially since the Holy cities were under Faisal's domain.

Abdulaziz recognized Faisal's talent and experience by appointing him the first Foreign Minister for the Kingdom in 1930. Matters of international nature fell under his realm. He always listened to the voice of wisdom and received proper guidance from his father. In 1945 he headed the delegation representing Saudi Arabia at the founding of the League of Nations in San Francisco, U.S.A.

The many visits of Faisal to Europe, Britain, France, Germany, Poland, the Soviet Union, Turkey, Iran, Italy, Iraq and Kuwait, among other nations took several months and lead to good results that strengthened relations with the Kingdom of Saudi Arabia. In 1953, upon the establishment of the Council of Ministers, Faisal was appointed Deputy Prime Minister. A few weeks later, Abdulaziz died and Faisal became the Crown Prince. His ascension to the throne on the 27th of Joumada thani 1384 A.H. (1964), paved the way for the basic steps in modernizing the Kingdom. Two years prior to that, Faisal declared the *ten principles* that became historically associated with his program in governing. Briefly, these principles are:

1. Rules are to be enacted according to the Holy Book and the Sunna of the Prophet.
2. Organizing local administration in various regions of the Kingdom in order to help in the administrative, political and social progress of the nation.
3. Establishing a Ministry of Justice, a Supreme Council for Jurists and an independent judiciary.
4. Proclaim a Council for "Fatwa" from the Ulema to look into Moslem matters and to give the proper Fatwas when needed.
5. Work to spread the mission of Islam, strengthen its foundation, and defend it by words and deeds.
6. Good morality to be practiced in line with the high Moslem objectives.
7. Improve living standards of the nation by offering free medical care, education and by subsidizing basic foods so that the citizen will be able to have them at reasonable prices. Establishing social insurance to give the proper care for the elderly and the workers.
8. Organizing economic and social progress.
9. Executing programs for building roads, dams, exploration for water, building manufacturing plants both for heavy and light industries, and establishing a general Petroleum and Minerals Organization (Petromin).
10. Completely abolishing slavery and granting freedom to all.

Faisal had done his best to practice these ten principles. On top of this, and for the first time in the Kingdom's history he opened new doors for Saudi women so that women will receive education along the same footing as their male counterpart, going from kindergarten to the university level. Faisal worked strongly toward laying the foundation for modernizing the Kingdom. He made great effort toward improving Arab unity and toward better relations with the Moslem world. His work for world peace was reflected in his genuine peaceful relations with all nations of the world.

His experience, sharp mind and dedication lead to laying the foundation for the first Five-year Development Plan. His keen intelligence, pious traits and wisdom steered the country into proper foreign policy and successful domestic policy as well.

However, King Faisal did not live long enough to see the fruits of his labor. He was assassinated on the 25th of March, 1975, by his nephew Faisal Ibn Musa'ad Ibn Abdulaziz.

His successor was King *Khaled* who was born in Riyadh in 1913. Since youth, Khaled enjoyed the desert life and treasured Arabian traditions. He felt at ease and at home in the desert. He was very much trusted by the various tribes of the Kingdom. He helped his father on a number of missions during the struggle for unification. Khaled became the Governor of Hijaz in 1932 and a Minister of the Interior in 1934. He was involved in agricultural work. His brother Faisal took him to the United States of America and also to a number of European countries. When Faisal became King, Khaled was made a Crown Prince; he then became the King in 1975. After the death of Faisal, a smooth transfer of power took place, and King Khaled appointed *Fahd* as the Crown Prince and First Deputy Prime Minister. He also made Prince *Abdullah* the Second Deputy Prime Minister and Head of the National Guard.

The second Development Plan ended during his time in May, 1980. This plan centered on diversification of the economic base so that the government will not be dependent only on petroleum for its income. In cooperation with his trusted men, Khaled held the historic Summit Conference of moslems which included thirty eight nations that were represented in Taif and Mecca in 1981. In this same year, he initiated the founding of the Six-nation *Gulf Cooperation Council* (GCC). During his time and in the span of a decade, the standard of living was substantially raised, at least threefold. The per capita income increased to nearly thirteen thousand dollars by 1980. Noticeable progress covered all sectors of the economy and all social, educational and human services.

King Khaled continued the mission of his predecessors in promoting peace and goodwill among the Arab and Moslem nations as well as the world community. During this time the Kingdom occupied its position of prominence in world affairs, on both the political as well as the economic fronts.

When King Khaled acceded to the Throne in 1975, his *righthand man was chosen to be Crown Prince Fahd.* The two made a very successful team. Extensive administrative duties for running the Kingdom were delegated to Crown Prince Fahd. The second Five-Year Plan was successfully finished with great accomplishments. The third Five-Year Plan was begun in 1980. The industrial and educational evolution was well underway when King Khaled died in June, 1982.

On June 13, 1982 Crown Prince *Fahd* Ibn Abdulaziz became the new King of Saudi Arabia. He is a man of great wisdom and decades of experience in top government positions. His policies and foresight, coupled with the contributions of his predecessors, brought to the Kingdom of Saudi Arabia great progress and development, the likes of which are unparalleled in the history of mankind.

While Abdulaziz was the father of the nation, Fahd, on the footsteps of his father and predecessors, became the pioneer and founder of the Modern Kingdom of Saudi Arabia.

Chapter 2

King Fahd Bin Abdulaziz
and
Education in the
Kingdom

Custodian of the two Holy Mosques, King Fahd Bin Abdulaziz.

His father's teachings of true leadership, wisdom and deep compassion for his fellowman, were the foundation of an illustrious personality, the amalgam of a great man, who truly became the dynamo behind a legendary progress, the father of modernization and learning in the Kingdom of Saudi Arabia . . . surely!

"Like father, like son".

The birth of King Fahd was a special good luck star in the galaxy of Abdulaziz. Riyadh was his birthplace, and the year was 1920. He was born around the time peace was made and strengthened with the Rashids. A messenger of peace and unity was born.

His birth brought a rapid succession of good luck in the decisive battles for unity. By this time Abdulaziz was consolidating his victories by conquering the territories north and west of Hail. The end of Sherif Hussain was near. Taif and Mecca fell in 1924. December 5, 1925, brought the capitulation of Medina. On the 23rd of December, 1925, Abdulaziz entered Jeddah. Total conquest of Hijaz was achieved and the expansion for unity was essentially complete.

The dawn of Fahd (meaning leopard in Arabic) to this world brought with it the final touches of success for a long and arduous struggle for unity.

Fahd was barely twelve years old when the Kingdom of Saudi Arabia was born on September 22, 1932.

This young man had a rendezvous with greatness. It was as if he was destined to fulfill the mission and dreams of Abdulaziz! He was a bright child who attended the Princes' School in Riyadh. Later he studied at the Institute of Science in Mecca. His traditional education was enriched with other studies and several trips abroad. Since childhood, his parents were genuinely impressed with his superior intelligence and curiosity for learning. They taught him Arab history and traditions. They impressed upon him the teachings and golden values of religion. He was quiet, thoughtful, attentive and alert.

Observing these rare traits in his son, fresh memories of yesteryears must have flashed through the fascinating mind of Abdulaziz! He, himself, was the bright young man attending the Court of his own father and learning the intricacies of political life! Soon to return, capture

Fahd as a young man (on the far right)

Riyadh and create a Kingdom against all odds! It was only natural for Abdulaziz to have Fahd in his private Court. Here, the young man endeavored to quench his thirst for knowledge. His father's teachings of true leadership, wisdom and deep compassion for his fellowman, were the foundation of an illustrious personality, the amalgam of a great man, who truly became the dynamo behind a legendary progress, the father of modernization and learning in the Kingdom of Saudi Arabia. Surely! "Like father, like son."

His father's Court or Majlis included top men from the Arab world, men of religion, men of knowledge, and loyal men of vision from other lands.

As a young man, Fahd listened attentively while grasping a vast wealth of knowledge. He saw firsthand how his genius father handled governmental affairs, and how he wisely and compassionately settled tribal differences and human problems.

Fahd lived up to the task and to the high expectations of his father, who delegated to him assignments of responsibility commensurate with his experience.

He was sent on official missions abroad. He represented his father in meeting tribal chiefs and solving their problems. Vast experience was acquired in handling tribal and bedouin problems.

Fahd was gifted in his own right. He was endowed, not only with a legendary man as his father, but also with a great mother whose name was Hussah Al-Sudairy. She gave birth to seven sons and four daughters. Fahd was the eldest.

She was a loving mother truly dedicated to the good upbringing of her children. Abdulaziz treasured her until the last day of his life. Her sons were trained to be fiercely loyal. She held weekly meetings with them, reviewing their progress and discussing achievements of the royal family.

She was the proud mother of King Fahd and his successful brothers and sisters. Prince Sultan is Second Deputy Prime Minister, Minister of Defense and Aviation and Inspector General. Abdul Rahman is Vice Minister of Defense. Prince Turki, formerly Vice Minister of Defense, is now in private business. Prince Naif is the Minister of Interior, a very sensitive position of great importance for internal security. He has direct responsibility for security police and the regular police forces, along with the Frontier Guard, the Coast Guard as well as Immigration and Naturalization. Internal affairs fall under his domain. All governors of the Kingdom, in the various regions, report to him. Prince Salman is the Governor of the historic capital city, Riyadh. He is the Chairman of the Higher Authority for the Development of Riyadh. His contributions in modernizing the capital are very impressive. Prince Salman

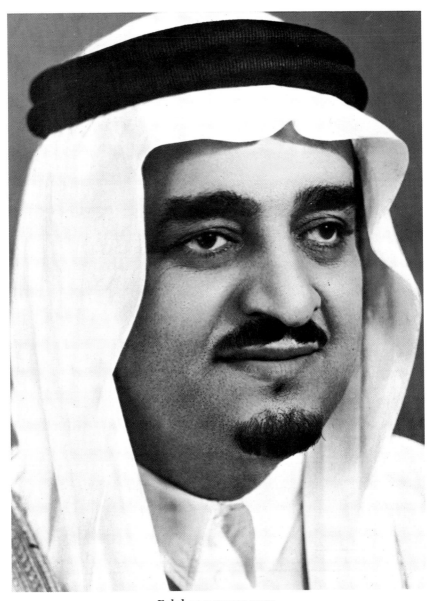

Fahd as a young man

is a valued advisor to King Fahd. He is also a respected and well known personality, especially in Europe and the Moslem World. His son, Prince Sultan is the first Arab astronaut, who was a prominent member with the American crew of the "Discovery" space mission. Prince Ahmad is the Vice Minister of Interior.

Fahd, the Father

Fahd grew to be a tall, handsome and towering figure. A young man full of compassion and love for his family. His children include six sons: Faisal, born in 1945, is the President of Youth Welfare. Mohammed was active in business. He was the chairman of Al-Bilad and became the Governor of the Eastern Province. Saud, born in 1950, is Vice President of General Intelligence. Sultan, born in 1951, is an officer with the Armed Forces. Khaled is a businessman. The youngest son, Abdulaziz is still attending school. Fahd is a devoted man who loves his immediate family. He is loving and dedicated to his countrymen. All Saudi citizens are considered his family. He is a brother to the elderly, a father to the young! He is looked upon as a man of great compassion with an abundance of help, love and devotion.

King Fahd showers his children with deep love and compassion that is also mingled with the traditional wisdom and disciplinary behavior.

His son Mohammed vividly recalls the love and guidance of his father. At an early age he was told: "Mohammed! You have not lived in the circumstances we lived. You should be prepared to face the difficulties of life, get used to it and do not succumb before it. You are free to define your future. But, I would like to tell you that the strong ones are those who know how to plan their future! At the end they reach what they have strived for. Their goals are not achieved if they are not supported with education, experience, good character, morality and above everything a deep belief in the Islamic religion." The King's expectations were very high, because he wanted all his children to excel in the service of their country. Many of them were educated at Universities in California, U.S.A.

Prior to his appointment as governor of the Eastern Region, King Fahd told his son Mohammed: "You are going to assume responsibility. You should consider God in all your affairs. You should be true to yourself; be careful in implementing justice without weakness. The responsibility delegated to you is an honor because it is a service to your country and the citizens of your country in a region dear to us

The loving and compassionate father King Fahd with his youngest son Abdulaziz.

all. You know the importance that the Eastern Region represents to all of us and to me personally, since the region is a treasure and a revenue source for the good of the nation. You are able to cooperate with those men to bring about more goodness and progress."

The spirit of these words of guidance applies to other members of his immediate family and other families as well. This fatherly approach and faith excites his children to the expected level of performance. They are challenged to meet their responsibilities with pride, respect, loyalty, obedience and dedication to his guidance. They strive to follow his example. In the eyes of his children, the father's strong personality is also just and generous.

Education was and is always dear to his heart; he instilled into them to strive for knowledge and to seek excellence in whatever they do. His youngest son Abdulaziz, typifies the treatment that his brothers and sisters received. Abdulaziz, who is now about fifteen years of age, is certainly a close companion to his father. He, like his other brothers and sisters, must bring deep joy to the heart of this wonderful man. Young Abdulaziz (obviously named after the great founder of the Kingdom) goes with his father to many functions, be it recreational or very official, both in the Kingdom and abroad. King Fahd's latest official visit to the United States of America included this fine and bright young man: his son, Prince Abdulaziz! His program included a visit to a Children's Care Center. The Young Prince contributed generously to the welfare of the handicapped and needy. Recently, he was a member of the official Saudi delegation to the Islamic Summit held in Kuwait in January, 1987.

King Fahd is the *head of the royal family* and this position of leadership carries many responsibilities. The Al-Saud family numbers around 5,000 people, all of them human beings with aspirations, drives and problems like any other group of people. Many problems of this large family are to be handled directly by the King and the Crown Prince; other problems are delegated to their men of trust.

Policies and principles that are applied to his immediate family carry over to his larger family. From here, it moves on to include the Saudi nation as a whole. King Fahd is truly a respected leader of his country. He is active and popular with his people. He is looked upon as a great and loving father of the whole nation.

As Crown Prince, Fahd would meet for dinner with all his full brothers and sisters, sons and daughters. His brothers-in-law Mohammed (died in 1982) and Khaled, the sons of Abdullah Ibn Abdul Rahman, are close to Fahd. They are each married to a full sister of the Crown Prince. Mohammed was close to Fahd since youth. They grew together and studied together. They studied the Qoran and acquired the latest skills from the bedouins.

Unique Qualities of Leadership

Fahd never misses an opportunity for meeting his countrymen. Talking to them from the heart and asking for their views; always seeking to solve their problems. It is of utmost importance to him. It is in his fiber to meet his people and listen to them himself to know firsthand their opinions, their desires and their aspirations. Watching and observing this great man communicating and expressing his compassion to his people, one cannot help but be deeply moved. One would truly sense his deep warmth and love for the people.

A man of wisdom and moderation, King Fahd treasures the word of truth. A word of justice from a sincere person brings deep joy to his heart. So does the opinion from a trustworthy person. Nothing disturbs him more than a fake and a liar. Truth is fundamental and supreme. It is always the strongest! False promises shall not hide it.

Fahd is gifted with great qualities of leadership, penetrating mind and top administrative experience. All these combine to help in delivering his decisions, which are characterized with wisdom, farsightedness and distinct capability to read and predict the future. His ability to initiate and to make the right decision at the right time for the right purpose brought about the great evolution of modernization in the Kingdom that is unparalleled in the history of mankind. It gave the Kingdom its rightful position of power and moderation among the family of nations. The impressive influence of the Kingdom in regional and world affairs could not have been realized without the great depth of his mind. His penetrating look into the future and his strong ability in dealing with events and circumstances with a unique flexibility, calculated study and analysis are strengthened and backed up by a vast wealth of experience earned and harnessed through nearly *four decades of public service.*

When Fahd became King of Saudi Arabia, his experience in government, along with the trust and genuine faith he received from his colleagues and predecessors, beginning with his legendary father the late King Abdulaziz and moving on to King Saud, King Faisal, and King Khaled, holding all along sensitive positions that carried great responsibilities, and performing very successfully in every task he has undertaken, all this made this unique man among the most experienced and best prepared ever to become a head-of-state!

Imagine all this trust continuing from his youth until he became a young man as he moved on in positions of power and responsibility. He represented his father in handling many tribal matters. From this he gained experience that was to become very valuable to him when he became Minister of the Interior. He was barely twenty-five years of age when he accompanied his brother, the late King Faisal, on June 26, 1945, to the founding meeting of the United Nations in San Francisco. He was thirty years of age when his father, the late King Abdulaziz, sent him to represent Saudi Arabia during the Queen's coronation in England.

The trust goes on and on! When Saud became the King, he appointed Fahd as the first Minister of Education in 1953–a landmark decision creating a position that was very dear to his heart. He truly became the father and first pioneer of the educational evolution in the Kingdom of Saudi Arabia.

In 1963 he earned the position of Minister of Interior. His contributions to the internal security of the Kingdom earned him the admiration and envy of many throughout the world. When Faisal ascended to the throne in 1964, Fahd was appointed the second Deputy Premier, while the responsibilities of the Ministry of Interior remained in his hand.

Prince Faisal Bin Abdulaziz signs the United Nations Charter on June 26, 1945. Standing directly behind is then-Prince Fahd Bin Abdulaziz.

The late King Faisal was a teacher and a father-figure to him. Admiring Fahd's leadership, deep interest in general education, good grasp of history along with current events, King Faisal kept him very close. When discussions and questions were to be settled, Fahd became the good arbiter. King Fahd has a well rounded education, keen love for books and a sharp memory. He is well read and absorbs what he reads, learning from the old and the new.

The succession of King Khaled to the throne on March 25, 1975, led to the appointment of Fahd as Crown Prince and First Deputy Prime Minister. His responsibilities were massive. The running of the daily affairs of government along with national, regional, and international policies, all rested on his shoulders, in cooperation with and under the guidance of King Khaled. He held sensitive positions and chairmanships, among them the Supreme Council for Petroleum and Minerals, the Supreme Council for Universities, Supreme Council for Youth Care, Supreme Council for Higher Education, Supreme Council for the Pilgrimage, and Royal Commission of Jubail and Yanbu.

When King Khaled died, Fahd became the King of Saudi Arabia, on June 13, 1982. He received universal national acclaim and support. His position of power and leadership was earned through decades of hard labor, dedication and devotion to the service of his people.

Be it in the East or the West, how many people in public service have earned such vast experience in the intricacies of governing a nation? Only a few leaders throughout history have earned such trust from the people and from successive Kings. One wonders how many have earned nearly four decades of experience prior to assuming this position of leadership? By any standard, from friend or foe alike, Fahd is the man who earned respect and admiration for his qualities of leadership, and for the fabulous achievements that he brought to his people.

His sharp mind analyzes the situation. He sees the need and looks far ahead, then acts. Any time spent prior to action is dedicated to the indepth study of every facet of the matter at hand. Once this is done, Fahd acts and acts decisively.

His dislike for routine and red tape is genuine, especially when it comes to the implementation of public projects.

He tells his close associates: When you have to make a decision, go ahead as long as you are satisfied with your conscience! Let your conscience and mind be your guides.

He is a straightforward man and straightforwardness means a lot to him; he likes it best!

His unique qualities are the basic ingredients for a great personality. These must be understood by the students of history; they must know him for what he is, in his own right. His story and legacy are that of a great man of our times.

King Fahd personally follows all important projects relating to various aspects of development. He possesses a talent and an obsession with a unique drive to achieve the most for the welfare of his greater family and greatest love: the people, the common man, woman and child. He personally gets involved and participates in reviewing plans, including engineering. He attends to various implementation procedures and special details. Furthermore, he does not stop at this juncture. He occasionally asks all those concerned to meet with him on the site. City planning alterations are reviewed with the people who are responsible for implementation and overall design. He frequently makes decisions after discussing various suggestions, listening to all pros and cons.

Sometimes this field review and on-site inspection are carried out under adverse weather conditions: often in temperatures as high as 110 degrees Fahrenheit and 90% humidity.

This is done in a populist approach that is very close to the heart of the people and completely devoid of the ivory-tower protocol. The manner is casual, but dignified. Fahd's burning desire and search for finding the optimum give him the inner impetus and drive to do this, and more.

Therefore it has become a natural way of life to see him among his people; guiding, exchanging views, expressing his compassion and wisdom, feeling with them and sharing their happiness or sorrow. In doing so, he fulfills his innermost desires and emotions for serving the people.

After God, people are truly his first love. They come first and foremost. Their education, guidance and welfare are supreme in his thoughts and convictions. According to him the true treasure and strength of a nation are the citizens. It is not what the land has, be it petroleum, minerals or other resources. Educating, training, guiding and developing the citizen are the positive forces which give tangible results and based on it, true development takes place with a solid foundation. His guidance to his trusted men is to make sure that the welfare of the citizen is kept foremost in the minds of planners and civil servants.

The citizen is the dynamo and driving force for progress and development. He stresses that the government should know very well that it is responsible for guarding the individual's thoughts and for protecting his life from any form of invasion. He believes the citizen should be granted the opportunity to build his nation and give his contribution in development and that the citizen should give everything within

King Fahd presenting award to a happy young man, the winner of the
annual camel race–a popular Saudi tradition. Seen with him is the Crown
Prince of Bahrain Sheikh Hamad Bin Isa Al-Khalifa.

his power in creativity, solid effort and capability for his country.
Thus, the Monarch is very careful to groom and encourage contributions from the private sector. His directives are to make sure and create
necessary incentives so the national economy will take its complete
and independent role in contributing to development. This economic
freedom has proven to be healthful and successful.

Upon ascension to the throne, King Fahd promised to work hard,
as he has done for many decades, in laying the foundations for progress
and peace. He pledged to *"act as a father to your sons and a brother
to your old. I am but one of you: what pains you, pains me, and
what pleases you, pleases me."* This came from the heart! Fahd is
truly living his promise!

In many ·of his town-meetings with citizens who come to greet
him or to submit a personal grievance, he always asserts the facts
and listens intently to their requests. As long as the demand or grievance
is between the plaintiff and the government, Fahd is more than happy
to help in solving the problem of the individual efficiently and promptly.

However, when the grievance involves other parties to the conflict, he cautions patience and reason. Many a time, a plaintiff wants a problem solved quickly right then and there! Utmost on Fahd's mind is the exercise of justice and fairness. "We have to listen to others, for their side of the story," he declares. "Other aspects must be considered in order to preserve the right of all involved in the matter."

Many times a heated discussion takes place in such conferences. Some people with grievances want a quick decision. This becomes an education for them. They are meeting a man with whom justice and compassion are supreme, a man who is concerned for the other party as well. Directives are given for proper inquiry so that responsible authorities will take the necessary just and speedy actions.

Problems or feuds that develop between families of different tribes may become volatile, but they are handled with great wisdom and efficiency. It is a unique characteristic of all the Al-Saud leadership to get personally involved in searching for every possible avenue of reconciliation. Of course, feuding parties can go to court and matters would be solved this way. However, some problems solved in this manner may lead to more division and polarization. These reconciliations are done with genuine personal sacrifices. They stem from deep compassion and basic beliefs in the family structure and the practice of fair play.

A well known Arab magazine said about the King: "He believes in the democratic openness and he has natural preparedness for democratic rule."

For King Fahd, Islam is a religion and a way of life. He said: "The religion of Islam does not distinguish between one person and another or between one sex and another, it represents heavenly justice that descended from God."

His numerous and widespread activities always include direct contact with the citizens, be it in his bureau, his court, his house, his car or anywhere he may be. This is most important on his mind. His utmost desire is to see that the citizen is always in the best possible condition. His instructions to his aides and associates are to see to it that the citizens' problems are considered as their personal problems and that nothing should stand in the way of reaching this objective. He follows their news and continues the tradition of solving their problems.

Humanitarianism and Compassion

Once, after midnight, he contacted one of the governors and ordered freedom for a jailed citizen. The King learned that a dispute between this man and another citizen concerning a piece of land led to this arrest. When Fahd realized the condition of his citizen, he ordered that a house be bought for his family and that a piece of land be given to him. He ordered that a committee should study the matter concerning the dispute and that proper decision should be made to solve the difficulty. The man was freed immediately. By early morning, he joined his family.

His humanitarianism is universal. Only a few examples are illustrated in these pages. Once, the following appeared in an Egyptian newspaper: "Save them before they lose their eyesight." A boy and a girl were threatened with loss of their eyesight if they did not receive proper treatment. It was a medical problem at birth. Doctors wanted a large sum of money for the operations.

When Fahd learned about this, he gave his directions to the Saudi representative in Cairo: "Kindly contact the parents of the children and obtain their passports to give them proper visa and airline tickets." His Majesty's instructions were to treat the two children at King Khaled Specialist Hospital for Eyes. The two children along with their mother and father were to be flown from Cairo. They would be guests of the Kingdom during their stay.

This ray of hope was conveyed to the parents. They were deeply touched and were very grateful indeed.

More recently, when a Sudanese family appealed to King Fahd to help their sick twins, the doors of mercy were wide open. The two children were successfully treated at King Faisal Specialist Hospital. The Saudi Government absorbed all expenses.

When Fahd learned about a birth defect of an Egyptian child, he ordered his treatment at King Khaled Specialist Hospital for Eyes. Two expensive operations were performed at government expense. The child regained his eyesight, and the grateful parents sent a telegram of thanks to King Fahd, saying; "This humanitarian act indicates that this blessed land that is the Mecca for all Moslems, is also their Mecca for humanitarianism and social justice."

A Tunisian with a fifteen-year skin disease was cured at King Faisal Specialist Hospital, thanks to Fahd's generosity and care. Diagnosis and proper treatment were given through the cooperation of two doctors, one Saudi and one American. This man had searched for a successful treatment in France, Italy and Germany without success.

Fahd's compassion has no limits nor borders. It covers the world! These stories are but a drop in a sea of goodness that emanates from this man of compassion and good will! A man with a great heart full of love and loyalty.

When he learned about the death of his brother, the late King

Khaled, he mourned him with misty eyes and touching expressions of deep emotion.

His love for children is heart-touching. He makes them feel at ease. His touches bring happiness and joy. He is very loyal and never forgets a friend. Once a reception was held in Mecca. One of his friends was not there to receive him. He asked about him and was told that he was ill. His majesty immediately ordered that good attention and care must be provided for him. He remembers his old teachers and inquires about them. He honors them, respects them and is always grateful for their teachings. He keeps in mind and heart the welfare and news about his aides, friends and those that tend to his Court. He asks about those absent so that he will have peace of mind about their well being.

A Saudi poet had some difficulties that led to health problems. When Fahd learned about it he was deeply moved and ordered that a house be bought for him from the King's personal account.

When he learned about a citizen who donated blood thirteen times he sent him a special message of deep gratitude and appreciation along with an award for this act of compassion and gallantry. Any similar acts were to be recognized and awarded accordingly.

King Hassan II of Morocco said: "His Majesty King Fahd Bin Abdulaziz, as usual, always, wherever and however there was an Arab dispute, tries to bring those involved in the dispute closer together. He is not only a man of peace but a majestic man of moderation and limitless energy."

The Chicago Tribune Magazine issue of October 8, 1978, wrote a special report on "The Middle East and the Personalities Influencing Events In the Region and Worldwide." The following is a quotation about Fahd who was then the Crown Prince of Saudi Arabia; "In his flowing gold-edged cloak and spotless white headdress, Crown Prince Fahd of Saudi Arabia is a vastly imposing figure–as befits a man who, though not the occupant of the throne, is the highly skilled chief operating officer of a strategically important Kingdom with an oil income of $40 billion a year. In the Kingdom's day to day affairs, Fahd energetically preaches a policy of moderation aimed at preserving the ruling House of Saud while nudging the nation along a path of cautious social progress and explosive economic and educational progress. When the late King Khaled was hospitalized for about four months in the year 1977, Crown Prince Fahd ruled as a Viceroy."

"While his interests are numerous in the various realms of Saudi government, the closest to his heart and the special interest he holds dearest is expanding the education and optimizing the use of oil revenues for importing the latest technology . . . At the age of fifty-six Fahd is in his prime," according to the Tribune.

With deep respect King Khaled once said, "My brother Fahd has a great appetite for administration."

Fahd never fails to show proper respect to his elder brothers. "This strong man" honors tradition and family ties. His relationship with his brothers, especially Mohammed, the late King Faisal and Khaled, is a witness to that.

Fahd grew to be over six feet tall, broad in the shoulder, and like his father, majestic in looks and stature.

He prepared himself well for future possibilities and responsibilities. Even in his mid-forties, he started taking some private English lessons. Certain audio-visual programs were selected and studied to broaden the scope of his education and knowledge. He took special crash courses in various topics from politics to literature. He read books of basic interest, others were summarized with background notes on the author. Such books were taped and studied by Fahd. This way he was able to cover a large number of books and widen his horizons covering regional and international histories. Books relating to such world leaders as Roosevelt, Churchill, Stalin, Adenauer, Eisenhower, Kennedy, De Gaulle and others were carefully read.

In the late sixties he met with and learned from economists and bankers. Those who met him were surprised by the sophisticated vision he already was developing about the country's future. Infrastructure was just beginning to see the light of day.

One of his associates said: "Fahd does not like men who blind him with science. But, if people do their job well, he leaves them alone to get on with the job." One of the best examples regarding this approach is building the industrial cities of Jubail on the Arabian Gulf and Yanbu on the Red Sea. In order to avoid bureaucratic red tape, a special commission was devised and created by Fahd. It is the Royal Commission for Yanbu and Jubail. Those on the commission received a 45% premium on top of their standard civil service salaries. Their top priority was to build the new cities as rapidly and efficiently as possible. Other special projects had similar agencies.

He works very hard, drawing on his abundant energies and spending long hours to clear the pressure of governmental affairs. Many a time his instructions are given to different ministries by telegram or direct contact. If someone does not live up to certain responsibilities, he is moved and the job is handled by someone else.

Fahd is known for his good humor and patience. His numerous meetings with students are a witness to that. With his wit and light spirit, he puts his audience at ease, while he genuinely enjoys the pleasant give-and-take atmosphere. His temper is very seldom exhibited, but when it is, another dormant quality of Abdulaziz comes to surface.

Fahd honors and treasures an old institution for meeting the people; it is called the Majlis.

The Majlis: A Great Saudi Tradition

A meeting between the citizens and their leaders takes place on a regular basis. This audience or get-together is known as "Majlis". Any person desiring to see a governor, or even the King, can attend a Majlis and request personal help, or submit suggestions or a grievance. This is a democratic tradition carried out from the days of Abdulaziz.

To a visitor at a Majlis, Fahd, who was then a crown prince, said; "You notice that no one here has much room for protocol, I am only Fahd to these men. My brothers are Khaled, Abdullah, Sultan etc. We are all equal under God, and such men bow to no one."

After sipping Arabian coffee and tea it was time to "share our culture and have dinner." All those present, from the highest dignitaries to the most humble of men, all would follow Fahd to a large dining room capable of seating over 200 people. Fahd would say to his guest; "Look about you! The room is full of ministers, princes, servants, drivers, clerks, businessmen. Whoever is in the Palace at mealtime joins us—without exception. It is a tradition that King Abdulaziz started and that we continue."

Prince Salman Bin Abdulaziz, governor of Riyadh and one of the righthand men for King Fahd, said to a guest at his Majlis; "Any citizen can approach any ruler asking redress for real or imagined problems. Each petitioner is dealt with carefully and patiently. Seventy-five percent of these petitioners do not need me. They come for assurance so that if they ever have a major problem, access is assured. The rest have exhausted bureaucratic procedures. They want land, or a bigger home loan, or to get a relative out of jail. We try to help. Occasionally, someone comes to the Majlis only to complain that we are moving too fast. But technology and Islam are not incompatible, as we find in the Holy Qoran—the word of God."

A more recent Majlis held by Prince Salman (known by his first name) was visited by the American Crew of the Discovery Space Mission. Everyone was deeply moved by what they had witnessed and felt through this democratic institution. The American astronauts were honorable guests of their colleague and member of the team: Prince

Prince Salman meets the people at his Majlis, where each petitioner is treated with justice, respect, care and patience—A democratic tradition pioneered by the late King Abdulaziz and practiced by Saudi leaders.

Prince Salman Bin Abdulaziz welcoming the crew of the "Discovery" Space Mission. Their visit to the Kingdom was a great memorable event. Here, the American crew briefly attended Prince Salman's open Majlis.

Sultan Bin Salman, the first Arab astronaut. Their visit to the Kingdom was a most memorable one.

Fahd's qualities of leadership were best manifested in his supreme dedication and zeal for education and massive development of the Kingdom. It is then only fitting and natural to start this parade of progress with Fahd's deep love, namely: education.

Man of Learning:
The First Minister of Education

Over a decade ago, Saudi Arabia embarked on the most daring engineering and construction projects of the twentieth century. The Industrial and Educational evolutions that have taken place are mind-boggling. They are indeed unparalleled in the history of mankind. With vast petroleum reserves, fabulous generosity, moderate and wise leadership, Saudi Arabia became one of the most notable and important economic forces in the world today. This position of prominence will remain a strong one, way into the twenty-first century.

The building blocks of education started many years ago when the first Minister of Education was appointed in 1953. The minister was Fahd Bin Abdulaziz, the present King of Saudi Arabia. He pioneered a major role in establishing the educational system of the country. Education is the corner-stone for the massive achievements that have been realized. Fahd had the foresight, determination and deep dedication to develop education in the Kingdom. He knew that without education the dream of progress and development would not be realized. Concerning the role of education and the health of the country King Fahd once said, "The human being plays the basic role in the development of his society–for wealth comes and goes, leaving the effort and sweat of man to develop a society."

Prior to establishing the Ministry of Education and heading it, a small governmental department was responsible for all levels of education. A number of years later, King Fahd described and reminisced on the status of education at the time; "I remember when I became

The Holy Qoran encourages people to read and learn.

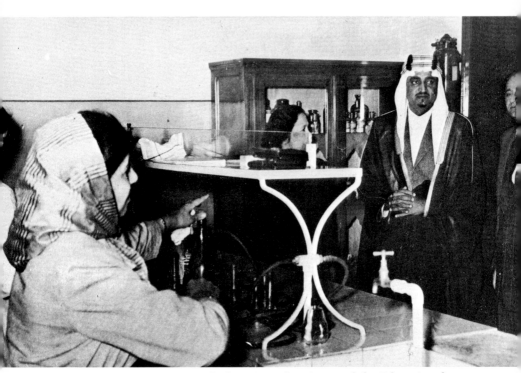

Fahd, the first Minister of Education who pioneered the Educational evolution in the Kingdom.

Minister of Education there was only one secondary school in the Kingdom, in Mecca. The total number of students attending schools in Saudi Arabia at the time was only 35,000.'' Today, the Kingdom prides itself on a fine system of education, covering the whole spectrum from primary, intermediate and secondary, to technical and vocational schools, colleges and universities.

A few years ago there was not one university in the Kingdom. In the span of a short number of years, seven major universities have been built. They are operating with standards that match the best in American universities.

Nowadays, the children in the Kingdom are getting the best possible education. Indeed, a new primary or secondary school was being opened every two weeks all year 'round. The total school enrollment is over two million boys and girls. A great leap forward! An outstanding accomplishment! What renaissance in history could compare with these achievements in the realm of education, and in such a short time?

Being the first Minister of Education, King Fahd laid the foundation for the gigantic transformation of the educational system in the Kingdom. Education for girls was one of his major concerns.

Developing the minds of men and women alike was at the heart of a success story that met the challenge of development and modernization in the Kingdom.

Technology transfer is nourished with about 10,000 students from Saudi Arabia who are enrolled in American colleges and universities.

By 1930, there were about 2,300 students in the whole country. The first secondary school that included a modern education curriculum was founded in 1937. This school prepared students to pursue their higher education in other countries, such as Lebanon and Egypt.

By 1949, the number of students reached nearly 20,000. The first institution for higher education was the Faculty of Shari'a which was established in 1949. By 1983, the number of schools reached over 11,000.

The modern educational system is structured along the following lines:

1.   Kindergarten

When the child is four or five years of age he spends a year or two preparing for the elementary school. Kindergartens are mostly co-educational and private. They receive subsidies from the government.

2.   General Education

This includes *elementary* schools. Children reaching six years of age enter at this level. They study for six years. Boys and girls have similar opportunities, each attending their separate schools.

The *intermediate* level requires three years of further study. At the end of this period the students take a general examination. If successful, they will earn a general intermediate certificate allowing them to enter into the secondary school system.

Students with practical and applied inclination are guided toward the intermediate stage with vocational technology in mind. Male students would join this curriculum after finishing elementary school. Again the duration of study is three years and the certificate received upon successful completion of the final examination will allow the holders to be admitted to schools of technical education and vocational training.

Those holding the general intermediate education certificate that is granted at the end of the intermediate stage will be admitted to schools of *secondary education*. The duration of study for this level is three years. There are secondary schools in the evening and others during the day. Those in the evening will accept adult students. Success-

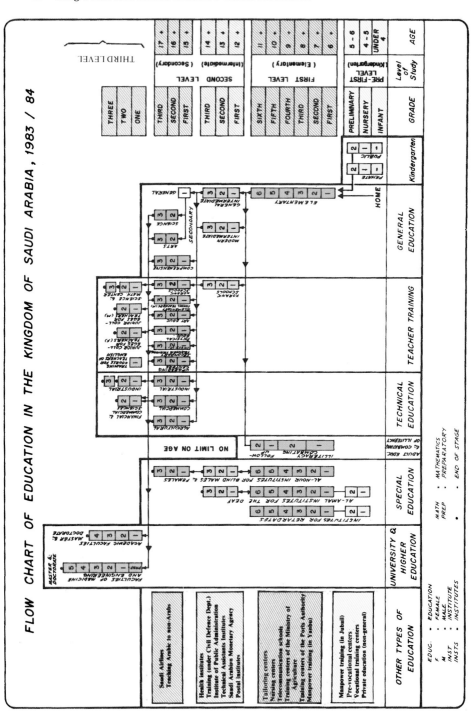

FLOW CHART OF EDUCATION IN THE KINGDOM OF SAUDI ARABIA, 1983 / 84

Saudi youth at school and play.

ful completion of this program will lead to awarding the students the general secondary education certificate, with two branches: one in science, the other in arts. Branching off takes place after the first year. One group will go into arts, the other into sciences.

There is also a *comprehensive secondary school* that was started in 1975. It uses the credit system. The school year is divided into two semesters, each of fifteen weeks duration. In addition there is an optional summer session of ten weeks. Depending on the aptitude and drive of the student, these schools require about six semesters or the equivalent of three years. Here, there are both compulsory courses and optional ones. Two branches exist, one in arts and another in sciences.

3.   Technical Education

Only males are admitted to technical institutes, secondary vocational or commercial schools and the agricultural institutes. The three major types are: Industrial education, Commercial education, and Agricultural education. Normally, the duration of study is three years after the general intermediate education certificate or the modern intermediate education certificate.

There also are secondary commercial schools and higher institutes for financial and *commercial sciences*. This line of education prepares the manpower needed for finance, business and the commercial sectors

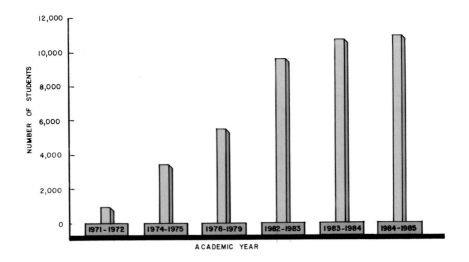

STUDENT ENROLLMENT IN
TECHNICAL SCHOOLS

of the economy. The study in the secondary commercial schools requires three years. At the successful conclusion of three years, the student obtains the general secondary education certificate or modern secondary education certificate, or their equivalent.

The following fields are covered: accounting and finance, administration, secretarial work, banking, purchasing and sales, collection and cash matters. The period of study at the higher institutes is two years after the commercial secondary education certificate. There are three such institutes, two in Riyadh and one in Jeddah. Day classes are held for regular students and evening classes for working people. Upon successful completion of this program, students are awarded a diploma in Commercial and Financial Sciences.

There is also training in the technical area of agricultural education. Such training takes place, for example, at the model Technical Agricultural Institute in Buraidah that was established in 1977. The duration of study at the institute is three years after the general intermediate education certificate or the modern intermediate education certificate.

There are in-service departmental training courses and other vocational training programs designed to prepare the necessary manpower for different trades. Some of these include:

a. Health Institutes

The level of training is between the elementary and secondary stages. These institutes train such assistants as: statisticians, nurses, technicians, x-ray technicians, surgical operations assistants, health supervisors, laboratory technicians, assistant pharmacists and nutrition assistants. The first health institute was started in 1958, through a five-year agreement with the World Health Organization. Another similar institute was established in 1962 in Jeddah and a third was established in 1965 in Safwa in the eastern region. The length of study is three years. Graduates, holding a technical certificate in various areas of speciality, work in various hospitals and infirmaries.

Nursing schools, like the Health Institutes, are for both males and females. The required minimum for admission is an elementary education certificate or its equivalent. The period of study is three years; it is between the elementary and secondary levels. Graduates are not at the level of registered nurses.

b. Technical Assistant Institutes

The Ministry of Municipal and Rural Affairs directs some Technical Assistance Institutes. They include: surveying, foremanships of construction, water and roads, architectural drawing and health supervising. These institutes admit boys holding the intermediate education certificate. The duration of study is two years. Graduating students work in municipalities or in technical and engineering offices.

c. Tailoring Centers began teaching females the art of tailoring in 1972. Females with elementary education certificates, from 16 to 25 years of age, are admitted. Duration of study is about twenty months or the equivalent of two school-years. These are run under the supervision of the Presidency of Girl's Education.

d. Postal and Telecommunication Institutes are run by the Ministry of Post, Telegraph and Telephone. Male students study for three years after the intermediate education certificate.

e. Arabic Language section at Islamic University, where Arabic is taught to students who cannot pursue their study at the university because of their limited knowledge of the Arabic language. Normally, two years are needed for this study.

f. Institute of Public Administration is an autonomous government agency mainly for training civil servants. The programs include:

- Short seminars for top executives.
- Some training programs in accounting, personnel administration, computer and secretarial work.
- Training programs for about two years duration in various fields such as computers, financial controls, typing, hospital administration and legal studies.
- Special programs to meet special needs of certain agencies.
- Certain English programs for civil servants who are sent abroad for training, or for those who need the English language in their daily work.

g. Vocational and Prevocational Training Centers

Their objective is to prepare the necessary skilled and semi-skilled manpower needed in industry. Students receive financial aid and are furnished living quarters. There are both day and evening classes. The program of study takes from one year to one and a half years. Evening courses last about five months. Vocational specialties include: auto-mechanics, auto-body repair, refrigeration, air conditioning, plumbing, painting, electricity, radio-TV, welding, construction, carpentry, metal works, etc.

The Prevocational Centers last for about ten months. They are meant for juveniles, ranging in age between 14 and 17 years, who are not able to pursue academic studies. These trades include welding, carpentry, accounting, bookkeeping, typing, secretarial work, electricity, auto-mechanics, etc.

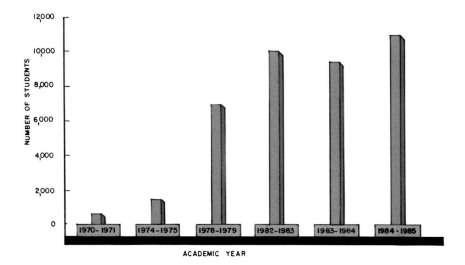

STUDENT   ENROLLMENT
IN VOCATIONAL   SCHOOLS

Vocational training

h. Instructors' Institute

It was established in 1980 to train qualified instructors for the vocational training centers including various governmental departments and agencies offering certain speciality training. These departments include: Ministry of Agriculture and Water, Civil Defense, Saudi Airlines, Saudi Arabian Monetary Agency, Ports Authority, Royal Commission for Jubail and Yanbu, and some private organizations functioning under supervision of the Ministry of Social Affairs.

4.   Teacher Training

Training of teachers is directed by the Ministry of Education or the Presidency of Girls' Education. The schools in this category include: Intermediate Qoranic schools, Secondary Qoranic schools, Art Education Institute, Upgrading Centers for Men Teachers, Physical Education Institute, Secondary Teachers Training Institute for Men, Junior Colleges, Science and Mathematics Centers and programs for training teachers of the English Language. Normally, the period of study in these schools is three years after the intermediate education certificate. Graduates are normally qualified to teach in elementary and intermediate schools.

Science and mathematics centers for men-teachers were established in 1974 to meet the chronic shortage of qualified Saudi teachers to teach math and sciences. Students holding the secondary education certificate (the scientific branch) are admitted. Those holding the arts

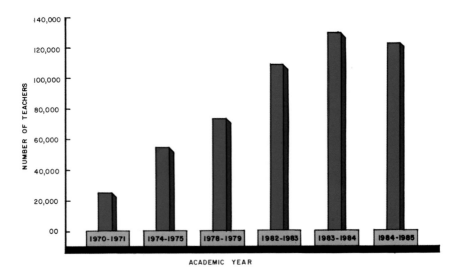

TEACHERS IN SAUDI SCHOOLS

certificate or the diploma of the teacher training institutes also may be admitted if they successfully complete the courses during the preparatory year. The first stage is finished in two years and then a diploma is awarded. After the second stage the teaching proficiency degree for teaching math and sciences is awarded. This requires the successful completion of courses in one year of study. These centers follow the semester system.

Junior colleges for men-teachers; The first two were established in 1976 in Riyadh and Mecca. Five more colleges were built the following year in Dammam, Medina, Abha, Russ and Taif. Students holding the general secondary education certificate or its equivalent are admitted to this program. Teachers working in elementary schools are admitted to improve their status and knowledge. Those with a general secondary education certificate of the scientific branch will need four semesters to graduate, while holders of the general secondary education certificate of the art branch or its equivalent will need five semesters. Students finishing the requirements of 75 semester hours receive the junior college diploma.

Junior colleges for women-teachers were established in 1979 along similar lines as the junior colleges for men teachers. Qualified women teachers are trained to fulfill the need for teachers in the intermediate schools or to improve their capabilities in the case of elementary school teachers. Thus, they become able to teach in intermediate schools. The requirements and length of study are similar to their counterparts for men.

5.   Special Education Programs for the Physically or Mentally Handicapped

These programs are established and operated by the Ministry of Education. They include:

a. Al-Nour Institutes for the Blind

Blind boys or girls receive education and rehabilitation in these programs. There are boarding sections at these institutes with room, board, clothing and recreation, all provided free of charge.

Elementary, intermediate and secondary education of the arts branch are offered. These institutes also have vocational training in handcraft areas such as: textiles, carpets, rugs, etc. Blind girls are taught in a similar manner. Subjects also are taught to help them gain admission to a university.

b. Al-Amal Institutes for the Deaf

These are cultural and rehabilitation institutes for boys and girls who are deaf or have hearing impairments. Studies are offered along with health, social and psychological care. Three stages are included in the program. They are: preparatory, elementary and vocational intermediate. Among subjects taught are: photography, photocopying, typing, electricity, sanitary installation, tailoring, knitting and embroidery.

c. Institutes for the Mentally Retarded

They are managed along the same lines as those for the blind and deaf. Programs suitable to the corresponding capabilities of the students are applied. Certain handicrafts are taught where feasible.

d. Adult Education

In 1972 a policy directive was issued to coordinate efforts in the field of adult education. A period of twenty years was set to eliminate illiteracy once and for all. An integrated plan was drawn to eradicate illiteracy within this period. The plan has four phases:

- Mobilization of manpower and financial resources needed.
- Starting the phase that would last about five years.
- Expansion of the phase lasting thirteen years.
- Finishing phase lasting two years and wiping out the last pockets of illiteracy.

Adult education studies have two stages. They are:

- *Combating stage:* The duration of study here is two years. Upon successful completion, people in this program reach a level equivalent to those who complete fourth grade and would receive a literacy certificate.
- *Followup stage:* This requires two years after the combating stage. When finishing this period, a person achieves an equivalent of the sixth grade. He is then awarded the elementary education certificate. Males receive this education during the evening, while females receive it during the day. For females, studies begin in the afternoon; they end before sunset. Most adult education and literacy schools are located in the same buildings as the day public schools.

Staffs of the day schools take the responsibility for teaching in adult education programs.

In the span of a decade, the numbers of students, schools, and those working in them have doubled many times. For example, the number of *elementary schools* in the academic year 1975–76 was 2,414; in the year 1984–85 it increased to 4,413 schools. During this period the number of elementary students was around 688,000. This is an increase of 64%, in just a decade. The number of teachers and administrators also increased from 26,361 to 45,970.

The number of *intermediate schools* for the year 1984–85 was 1,323,

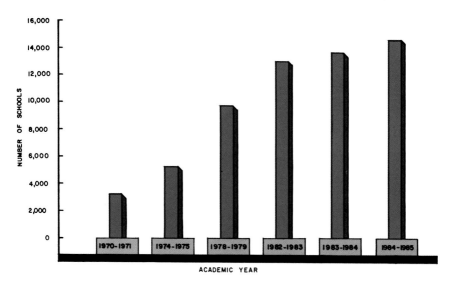

EDUCATIONAL GROWTH IN THE KINGDOM OF
SAUDI ARABIA

of which 122 were night schools. The increase during the ten years
was more than 800 schools. The number of students registering in
these intermediate schools was more than 200,000. The increase is
110,000 students from what it was in 1975–76. Around 9.4% of the
total students registered were in night schools. Intermediate schools
had 27,000 non-Saudi students. This is the equivalent of 13.5% for
the year 1984–85. Teachers and administrators numbered 16,961, while
in 1975–76 they were 9,765.

Secondary education schools increased by 359 since 1975–76. The
number reached 462 in the year 1984–85. The number of boys in day
schools was 88,000 in 1985–86. The number of girls was 70,000. Teachers and administrators were 5,878 in 1984–85, while in 1975–76 they
were 2,014.

Between 1970 and 1983 (1390 A.H.–1403 A.H.) the number of students at various levels of education increased from nearly 400,000 to
1.8 million. The enrollment of girls increased from less than 200,000
to 700,000 in that period. Schools also increased from 3,282 to 14,256.

Training institutes for teachers increased in that period by 40 institutes and the total number reached 62. The number of students reached
5,392. The total number of administrators and teachers for teachers'
training reached 1,600 compared with 1,066 only ten years earlier.

In special teaching, the number of schools for the blind was eleven
in 1985. The institutes for mental education were seven. The Institutes

of Hope were ten. Three of these were for blind girls, four were for deaf girls and three for education of mentally handicapped girls.

Gigantic steps are being taken to *eradicate illiteracy* through educational programs for the elderly. In 1985 the number registered in these programs was 7,755. Participants receive their instruction in 1,475 centers. These centers are manned and taught by 3,825 teachers and administrators. All of them are working in the day schools. Non-Saudis studying in these programs are 17.2% of the total enrolled.

Literacy educational programs are being carried out in various corners of the Kingdom in schools, camp scouts, institutes, libraries and sports arenas. Total expenditures for these programs are around two billion dollars.

One of Saudi Arabia's foremost priorities was expanding the educational system and moving aggressively to eliminate illiteracy. As an example, in one year alone (1980–1981), 370 new primary schools were opened. This is an average of one school a day. In the academic year 1984–85 a total of 1,300 new schools were opened at all levels.

Since 40% of the population is fifteen years old, or younger, the Kingdom made construction of new facilities and expanding teacher training programs among the top priorities in educational achievements.

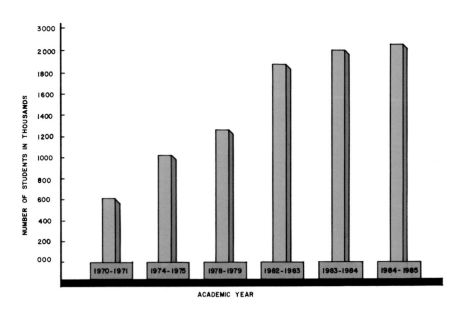

TOTAL STUDENT ENROLLMENT IN SAUDI SCHOOLS

It is noteworthy to learn that student-faculty ratio, around sixteen to one, is among the best in the world. The goal was top quality education. This was coupled with improvements in curricula, in the quality of instruction and the upgrading of the teaching and administrative staff. De-centralization and delegation of authority are practiced wherever feasible to improve efficiency.

The educational policy placed special emphasis on safeguarding religious and moral values along Islamic lines. This has been the core of educational development from a humble beginning in 1949 when the Shari'a College was established, to the great achievements in education crowned with elite universities in the four corners of the Kingdom.

Islamic teachings urge the followers to "seek knowledge from the cradle to the grave." The Saudi Arabian society is based on the teachings of Islam, which decrees a high and esteemed value for education to develop the human potential. This importance occupies a good position in community life. The parents are very much involved in the education of their children. A very good and close relationship between home life and school environment contributes to the family structure, which is at the heart of Saudi life.

Attention to girls' education has progressively expanded, beginning as far back as 1960. In the year 1983–84 the budget of the General Presidency for Girls' Education was about 1.7 billion dollars. This constituted over 21% of the total budget of eight billion dollars for education and human resources. In the span of a very few years, education for women became available in over 800 communities, covering every village and city in the Kingdom.

An *Islamic Saudi Academy* was established in Fairfax, Virginia, under the auspices of the Ministry of Education. Saudi children in the U.S. and children of American Moslems can attend. Students receive their instruction in line with cultural heritage and religious teachings of Islam. They learn the Arabic language along with math, science, history and English. While this Academy is up to the sixth grade, eventually it will include the seventh and eighth grade. A high school system will be implemented along with a two-year junior college.

About ninety percent of all the students attend pre-college schools of all kinds. Most of them (85%) attend primary, intermediate and secondary levels. Eight percent are studying in adult education programs. Two or three percent are in special educational programs. In the year 1982–83 special schools for the deaf, dumb, mentally retarded and the blind numbered 18 for males and 19 for females, serving about 2,000 special students.

Technical training is a very vital part of the educational system in developing the human resources of the Kingdom. The general education program incorporates technical and vocational training at primary and secondary levels. Training facilities are established and developed throughout the Kingdom for advanced levels in training. These institutes place emphasis on various areas of specialties such as automotive, machine tools, electrical, mechanical, and metal working. It is believed that the facilities at the Royal Technical Institute in Riyadh are among the best equipped in the entire region.

Since Saudi Arabia has the commitment for building a future based on industry and a good level of technology, nearly 70% of all foreign workers eventually will be replaced by Saudi citizens that have been well educated and prepared for their jobs. Many government agencies and companies supervise their training programs in various disciplines. Teacher training was accomplished through junior teaching colleges. Skilled professionals were prepared in other professional training institutes. The Institute of Public Administration was very active in administrative training. In the year 1982–83 nearly 9,000 people participated in the institute's various programs and seminars. Here, training service is carried out for government employees and students who are interested in joining government service. Similar programs are carried out for males and females. The fields of training covered include: computers, data processing, personnel matters, financial services and library specialties.

Along the lines of technical education, special emphasis was placed so that Saudis would master the modern technology necessary for fulfilling the needs of their gigantic development.

In the industrial sector there were five vocational secondary schools in 1983. Total enrollment was 1,511 students. Four industrial technical schools had an enrollment of 1,769 students.

In 1983 there were eight secondary schools of commerce with a total of 5,828 students. There also were two higher institutes for finance and commerce.

A model agricultural institute was established in Buraidah in 1983. In the twelve years extending between 1970–1982 the cumulative number of students enrolled in twenty-two centers of vocational training was 60,000 students. Over 200,000 participants received on-the-job training programs during the same period.

6. Higher Education

Institutes of higher learning were delegated the responsibility of expanding specialized manpower and nourishing scientific research. The Ministry of Higher Education, which oversees policies in higher learning, was allocated 31% of the 1980–1985 plan for education (2.5 billion dollars). Another 120 million dollars was shared by The Saudi Arabian National Center for Science and Technology [1] and The Institute of Public Administration. The first has activities in research grants and scholarships; the latter trains current and possible government employees. It also provides consultation to various departments of the government.

The Undersecretariat for Girls' Colleges constitutes a major division of the Presidency for Girls' Education. It specializes in handling higher education for girls. It supervises and manages *institutes of higher learning* such as the College of Education for Girls in Riyadh which was established in 1970, the College of Education for Girls established in Jeddah in 1974, Mecca 1975, and the Higher Institute for Social Work in Riyadh, 1975, the College of Arts in Riyadh, 1979, also the College of Arts and Sciences in Dammam, 1979. Three Colleges of Education for Girls were opened in 1981 in Medina, Buraidah and Abha. In 1982 another College for Education was opened in Tabouk. Scholarships are provided; they include room and board along with transportation and free tuition.

About sixty-one colleges are in Saudi Arabia. Half of these handle scientific studies and have a total Saudi teaching staff exceeding 9,000. The number of students registered at the University level increased from 8,000 in the year 1970–71 to 85,000 in the year 1983–84. In 1970–1971, male and female students attended colleges and universities of higher learning. Academic courses taught were in excess of 400. By the year 1984, the total number of male and female students graduating from these institutions of higher learning exceeded 50,000. Some students go abroad for higher education, most of them head for the U.S.A.

There are seven major universities spreading over sixteen campuses and covering the entire Kingdom. Three of these place emphasis on Arts and Sciences, three others are of a specialized type. The Ministry of Higher Education supervises six of these universities while the seventh, the Islamic University, is supervised by the Council of Ministers.

---

[1] In 1986, it was renamed King Abdulaziz Scientific City.

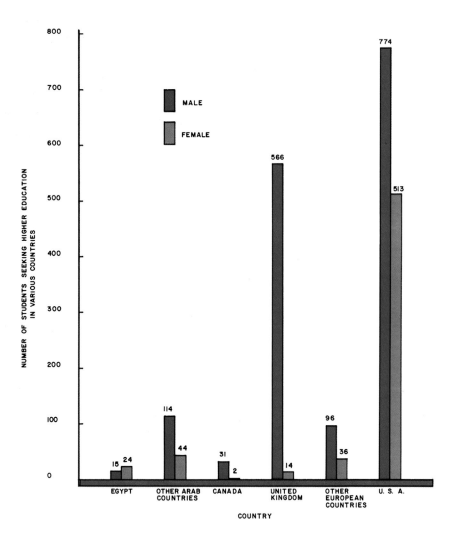

SAUDI STUDENTS BEGINNING THEIR
ACADEMIC YEAR ABROAD (1983-1984)

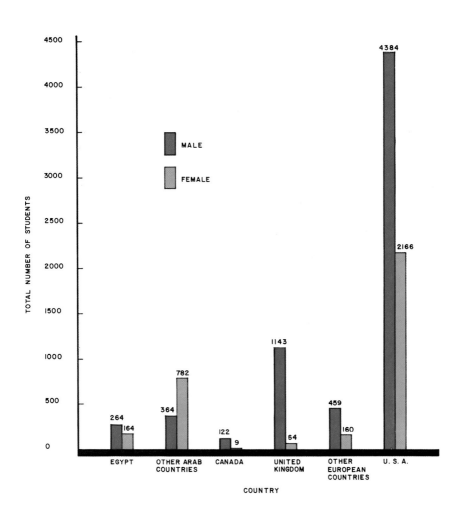

TOTAL NUMBER OF SAUDI STUDENTS
STUDYING ABROAD (1983 - 1984)

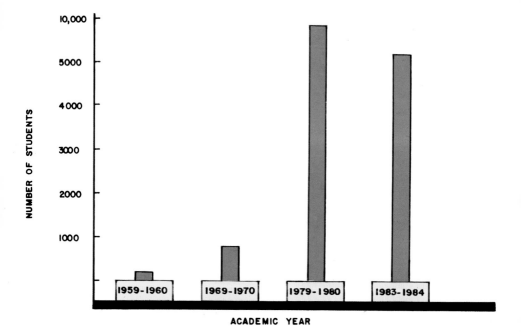

SAUDI STUDENTS SEEKING HIGHER
EDUCATION IN THE U. S. A.

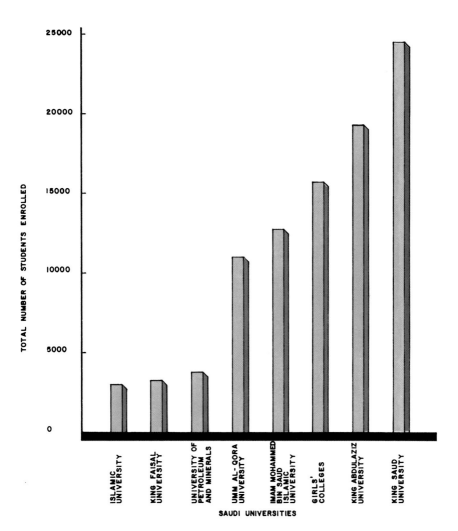

UNIVERSITIES FOR THE ACADEMIC YEAR 1984-1985

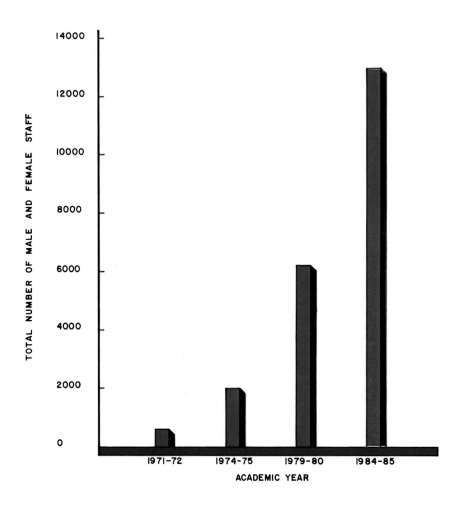

ADMINISTRATIVE STAFF AT SAUDI UNIVERSITIES

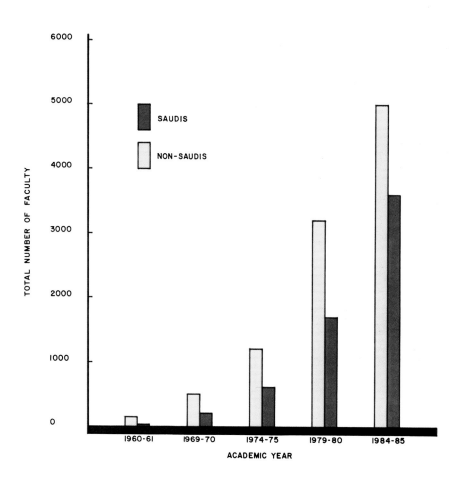

FACULTY AT SAUDI UNIVERSITIES

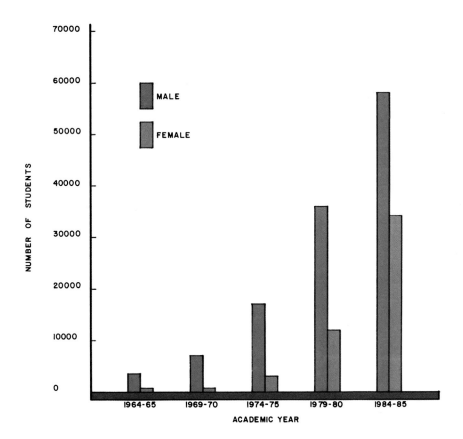

STUDENTS AT SAUDI UNIVERSITIES

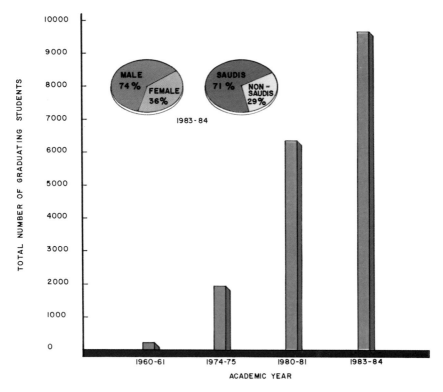

GRADUATES FROM SAUDI UNIVERSITIES

These universities are as follows:

King Saud University (KSU)

It was first established in Riyadh in 1957. It has a magnificent new campus built in the nearby community of Diriya. KSU is located on the outskirts of the nation's capital, Riyadh.

This university plays a dynamic role in education. The new campus has more than 20,000 students. KSU is a living example to the great faith in education espoused by the country's leaders, especially King Fahd. The basic mission of the university is to disseminate knowledge and build men of the future for the Kingdom. Traditions and religious heritage are intertwined in this process of dissemination.

The new campus in Diriya is ultra modern. It lies ten kilometers outside the city of Riyadh. The educational atmosphere is very inspiring and supported with good faculty from across the world. It has an excellent, modern library. The students receive free textbooks, food and lodging, along with a monthly stipend. The semester and credit hour system are adopted because of the flexibility inherent in it. There are many services that are offered by the university through its faculty.

Computer facilities at KSU

Various expertise, made available to the ministries and agencies of the government, make a valuable contribution to the development plans. Impressive large numbers of seminars and conferences are held by the university. Scientists, medical doctors, engineers and top men of learning interact with the student body and the faculty. Various sports, cultural and social activities are practiced.

In 1961 fifteen students graduated from the university. By 1981 the total number of graduating males and females was over 5,000.

When King Saud University (KSU) opened its doors, it had twenty-one students and nine professors. Within twenty-five years of expansion, culminating with a majestic piece of architecture costing over two billion dollars, the campus accommodates more than 22,000 students. The university's budget in the year 1959–1960 was 1.5 million dollars. In the academic year 1983–84, it skyrocketed to nearly one billion dollars.

In the academic year 1961–62, the number of female students at the university was only four. By the year 1983–84 this number jumped to 4,836. The number of male and female students reached 22,153 by the year 1983–84. The total number of students graduating on a cumulative basis since the founding of the university was 15,903 for the aca-

The majestic campus of King Saud University in Diriya–on the outskirts of Riyadh.

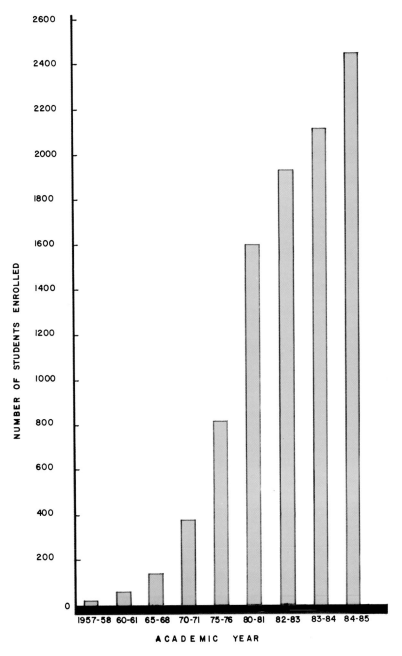

STUDENTS ENROLLED AT
KING SAUD UNIVERSITY

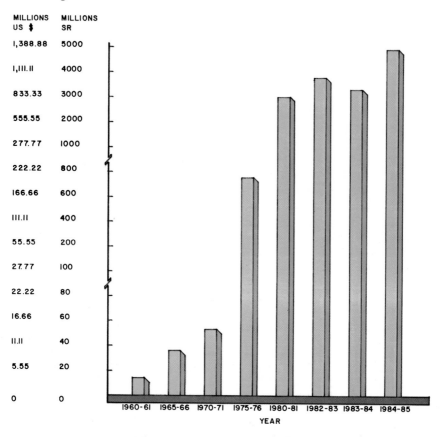

MILLIONS US $	MILLIONS SR
1,388.88	5000
1,111.11	4000
833.33	3000
555.55	2000
277.77	1000
222.22	800
166.66	600
111.11	400
55.55	200
27.77	100
22.22	80
16.66	60
11.11	40
5.55	20
0	0

1960-61 1965-66 1970-71 1975-76 1980-81 1982-83 1983-84 1984-85
YEAR

KING SAUD UNIVERSITY'S ANNUAL BUDGET

demic year 1982–83; among these were 1,943 female graduates. Faculty and their assistants numbered 2,132. The administrators were 5,255.

Now, the University prides itself with many colleges. These are: literature, science, administrative sciences, pharmacy, agriculture, engineering, education (in Riyadh and Abha) medicine, dentistry, medical assistance technology, medicine (in Abha), agriculture (in Kasim), commerce and administration (in Kasim), and the college of Arabic language. The Bachelor's degree is granted to graduates from these colleges. The Master's degree is granted in literature and sciences, administration, agriculture, education, engineering and pharmacy. The campus also includes a teaching hospital for medical students.

King Khaled University Hospital at KSU has a capacity of 870 beds. The medical compound cost more than 360 million dollars. Lodging for faculty and personnel can accommodate a population of nearly 45,000.

Islamic University at Medina

This is an international institution for Islamic studies. It was established in 1960.

Islamic University has five colleges with eleven different branches. These include: the college of Shari'a, colleges relating to the Qoran and religious studies and the college of the Arabic language. The student body comes from all over the world. Over eighty countries are represented. The faculty and assistants numbered about 400 in the year 1982–83. Between the academic years 1975–76 and 1982–83, 122 M.S. degrees and 22 Ph.D's were granted to students from dozens of countries.

All students receive a monthly stipend to cover their expenses. Also, they are provided transportation from their respective countries and later repatriated. They are furnished lodging, food, books and school supplies. A reward of nearly 300 dollars is granted to every student who graduates with honor throughout his years of study. Students can visit their country, parents and friends every year, at university expense.

The university hospital cares for the health needs of the university community. Studies continue year'round and the programs require four academic years of nine months each. Postgraduate schools offer the master's and doctor's degrees.

Islamic University at Medina

King Fahd University of Petroleum and Minerals (KFUPM)[1]

The College of Petroleum and Minerals (CPM) was established in 1963. Classes began in 1964 with 67 students, mainly Saudis. Total faculty was fourteen and the programs were progressively developed to cover a number of disciplines both in the areas of Applied Engineering and Engineering Science. The first graduation ceremonies were held in June, 1972, in Dhahran, home of the University. In 1975, the official name of the college became the University of Petroleum and Minerals (UPM). It has its board of trustees and a rector who is the chief executive officer.

The University of Petroleum and Minerals has five different colleges. These are: Engineering Science, Applied Engineering, Sciences, Business Administration and Environmental Design. Most of the students enroll in the preparatory year when they join the university. Their command of English improves here, because instruction is in the English language.

These pictures depict the beautiful campus of King Fahd University of Petroleum and Minerals—"A Jewel of a University on Arabian sands"!

---

[1] On December 25, 1986, the University was renamed King Fahd University of Petroleum and Minerals.

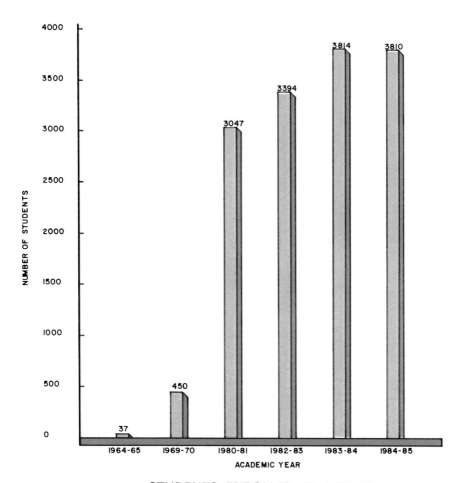

STUDENTS ENROLLED AT KFUPM

The number of students at KFUPM was 3,047 in 1980–81. By 1984–85 the student body numbered 3,810; 397 of these graduated with a B.S. degree and 77 with M.S. degree.

During the academic year 1985–1986, the total number of graduates from the University were 508. They were distributed as follows: one doctorate in electrical engineering (the first granted to a Saudi at KFUPM), 81 M.S. and 426 B.S. degrees.

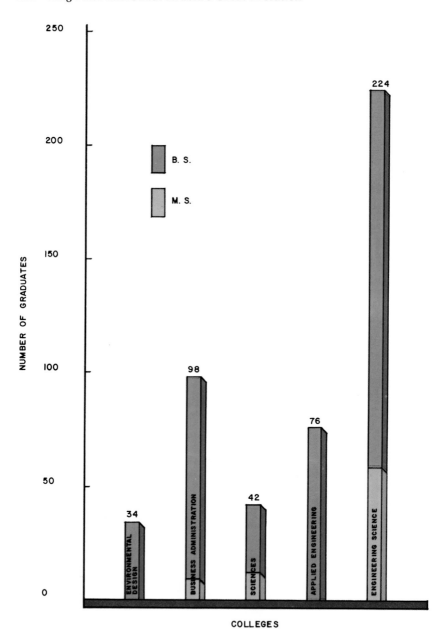

GRADUATES OF KFUPM FROM VARIOUS COLLEGES
FOR 1984–1985

The Master's degree is given in eleven specialties. It requires two years under the guidance of a qualified graduate faculty member. In 1984–85, the faculty numbered 669. Saudi faculty is 42% of this total; in 1971–72, the faculty numbered only 95. Foreign educators are mostly from the United States of America, Britain and Western Europe. There are also faculty from the Arab and Moslem countries. Saudi faculty increased during the five-year development plan of 1980–1985 until their share of the total became fifty percent. More than half of the

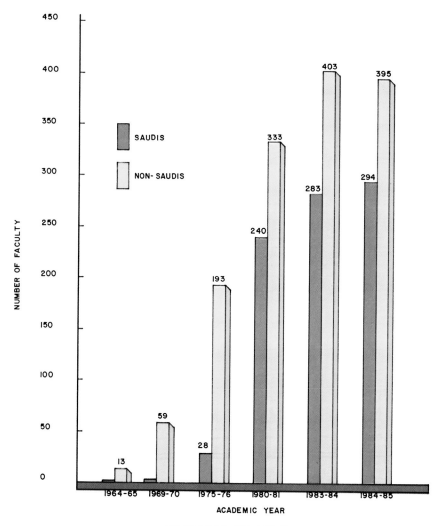

FACULTY AT KFUPM

faculty holds the Doctorate Degree. The university also sends many Saudis to study abroad; they later return to be on the faculty. KFUPM desires to be judged in comparison with other elite universities in the Western World, especially American universities. To rank well in this comparison, the university recruited top faculties and incorporated in its programs innovative techniques in education, research and public service. The university was able to attract eminent engineers and outstanding technical personnel to help in bringing the desired goal in its quest for excellence.

The university is governed by a Board, whose chairman is the Minister of Higher Education. The Board includes eight government officials and three other appointed members. The government officials include the Minister of Municipal and Rural Affairs, Governor of Petromin, Rector of King Saud University, Deputy Minister of Education for Technical Affairs in the Ministry of Education, Deputy Minister of Finance, plus three other members appointed by the Council of Ministers. Two Vice-Rectors work with the Rector. One of them is for Academic Affairs and the other for Graduate Studies and Research. The Deans of six major departments, with the directors of the preparatory year and the director of the data processing center, report to the respective Vice Rectors. The various departments have chairmen who are appointed for one year.

The Council of Deans includes the Secretary General who is assisted by a number of directors. These positions are reserved for Saudi citizens and they are essentially appointed for indefinite periods.

The university is also assisted and advised by a consortium of distinguished American universities. They are about ten in number and include such universities as: Massachusetts Institute of Technology (MIT), Princeton University, University of Michigan, California Institute of Technology, Mississippi State University, Texas A & M University, Colorado School of Mines, University of Rochester and Milwaukee School of Engineering. Each university selects its representative to the consortium committee, which acts in an advising capacity. The representatives cover a spectrum of technical knowhow that is relevant and helpful to the university's goals and mission. The consortium committee meets at least twice a year, both in Dhahran and in the U.S. It acts as a visiting-type accreditation committee which evaluates achievement and academic performance; it gives specific recommendations covering curriculum, research and laboratory work. Standards of the Accreditation Board of Engineering and Technology (ABET) are strictly observed. Engineering Programs in the U.S. and Canada are normally accredited by this board.

The Bachelor of Science, the Master of Science and Doctor of Philosophy degrees are offered in a number of disciplines. By 1986, the Master's degree is given in eleven specialties, while the Ph.D. is offered in six different areas of study. The Engineering Science programs are patterned after the American system of engineering education, except for the higher number of credits required. A Bachelor of Science degree in Engineering Science calls for 168 credit hours.

In the applied engineering curriculum, students earn the same number of credit hours after the preparatory year. Some of the credit is earned through the co-op program; The status of Applied Engineering has improved substantially through the years, so it would be up to par with the Engineering Science program.

Supporting services include an excellent library occupying a storage space of 7,000 square meters and having more than 200,000 volumes in the field of engineering, science and humanities. It has access to the latest in technology and science through its association with other international libraries. Other support services include: Data Processing Center, Central Research Workshop, English Language Center, Physical Education and the Co-op Study Program.

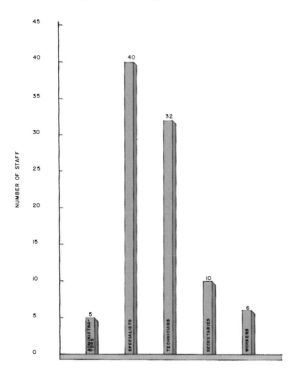

COMPUTER CENTER PERSONNEL AT KFUPM
FOR THE ACADEMIC YEAR 1984–1985

Modern Computer facilities at KFUPM

Students come from every corner of the Kingdom; also many come from other nations. Those coming from the Kingdom are brought up in a conservative family and religious atmosphere. The students' first contact with the American-modeled college community is one of caution and apprehension. The typical student is soft spoken and friendly. He graduated from high school and attended the prepartory school at the University. The students are eager to learn and cooperate with their faculty in every way possible. In many ways the students are very fortunate. They are attending a college of higher learning with excellent educational facilities. Their education is totally free. The typical student is paid a monthly salary. The books are free and so are his room and board. His quarters are very comfortable and air-conditioned.

A major branch of King Fahd University of Petroleum and Minerals is the Research Institute. Research may be carried on under contract to industry, the general public and the government. It covers various fields from petroleum and gas technology to energy resources, geology and minerals, environment and water resources, along with economics and industrial development, meteorology, standards and materials. For the academic year 1983–84, the Research Institute conducted 106 research projects.

While the Research Institute is a part of the University, its operation is semi-autonomous. The campus at Dhahran is the site for major research facilities of the institute. However, specialized establishments and test facilities are located in different parts of the Kingdom. The Research Institute has a recruiting office in Houston, Texas, U.S.A. While the research performed has direct and specific applications to the basic interests and problems of Saudi Arabia, it also has basic international application and response. The research staff comes from many parts of the international technological community.

More recently, the *American space mission Discovery*, had on board the first *Arab Astronaut, Prince Sultan Bin Salman*. From outer space, he conducted a series of experiments specifically designed by a team of engineers and scientists at KFUPM.

King Fahd University of Petroleum and Minerals, with its great mission of excellence and great achievements in education, technology transfer and human resources, has become very unique among all universities of the world, especially those in the Middle East. *Fortune Magazine called it: "A Jewel of a University on Arabian Sands."*

King Abdulaziz University (KAU)

It was founded in 1967 by Saudi businessmen who acknowledged the basic role of education in modernizing Saudi Arabia. The rapid development of the university prompted its founders in 1971 to petition the government so that operations would be under its realm.

Instruction started with the preparatory year. In 1967 there were sixty males and thirty females enrolled in the College of Economics and Administration. This was the first college at the university.

On August 8, 1971, the mission of the university was carried on by the state. The colleges of education, Shari'a and higher studies at Mecca, established in 1949, became part of King Abdulaziz University. As of 1981 (1/7/1401 A.H.), the branch in Mecca became an independent institution under the name of Omm Al-Qora University.

The university campus covers an area of 400 acres in the northeast portion of Jeddah. A mosque, planetarium, museum, aquarium and a large auditorium are included in this campus. The university has nine colleges granting degrees up to the PhD level. These include: The College of Economics and Administration, Arts and Humanities, College of Education in Medina, Physical Education Science, Engineering and Applied Science, Environmental Design, Medicine and Medical Sciences (supported by various departments and especially the university hospital with 800 beds), Earth Sciences, Institute of Applied Geology,

Entrance to King Abdulaziz University (KAU) in Jeddah

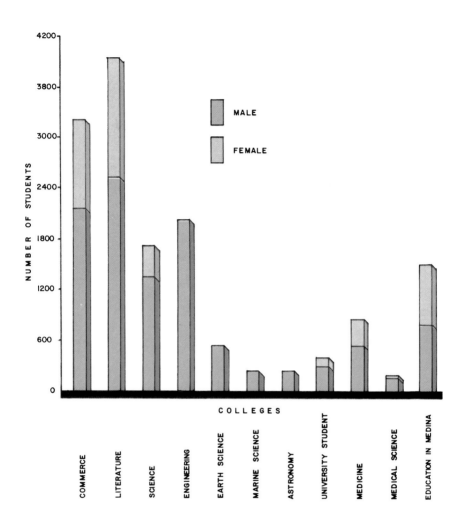

ACCEPTED AND REGISTERED STUDENTS IN VARIOUS
COLLEGES OF KING ABDULAZIZ UNIVERSITY FOR
1983 - 1984

Institute of Meteorology & Arid Lands Studies and Institute of Oceanography.

Separate and equally well-equipped facilities have been established for women. Parallel courses are taught for men and women. The colleges of engineering, earth sciences, meteorology and oceanography are not included in the women's curricula. Areas of specialty for women in-

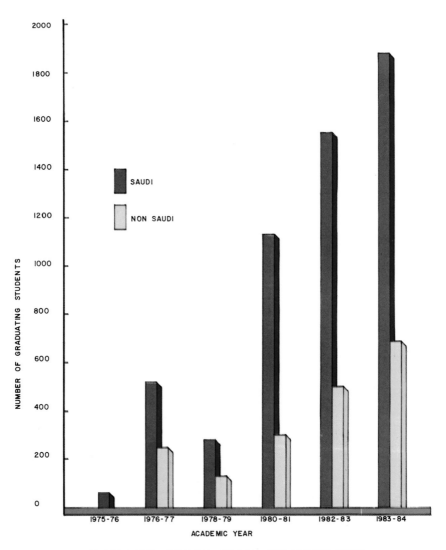

GRADUATES OF KING ABDULAZIZ UNIVERSITY

clude: Economics, Literature, Sciences, Medicine, Medical Science, and Home Economics. Also, the university's branch in Mecca has a special education program for females.

The first budget in 1967–1968 for the university was less than one million dollars. With seventeen years of progress, the budget jumped in 1983–84 to 373 million dollars. The total number of students for the same year was 14,403. Among them were 10,243 males and 4,150 females. Of these 3,255 students were non-Saudis and the balance of 11,148 students were Saudis.

The number of faculty for the year 1974–75 was 719. While for the year 1983–84, the number increased to 2,102. The number of Saudi faculty for that year was 1,019.

To increase the number of Saudi faculty, the university pursues a policy of sponsoring abroad a number of capable students to acquire higher education so they will return later and teach at the university. The number of those sent on scholarships to study abroad for Masters and PhDs were 116 for the year 1975–1976, increasing to 409 for the year 1982–83. This is an increase of 350%. By 1985, the number was 417; twenty of these were females.

The number of administrators and specialists increased from 35 people in the first year of its opening to 1,430 in 1981–82.

The total number of university graduates since 1975–76 until 1982–83 was 6,445. A quarter of these were non-Saudis. Female graduates were 26%. Non-Saudi students had nearly ten percent females among them. Students graduating in the academic year 1983–1984 were 1,840.

The university is enriched with a university hospital and many specialized centers such as computer, media educational technology, and english language. It also has a good library.

Like many other university campuses, residential quarters are made available for students, staff, faculties and their families. The future capacity for the whole campus should run as high as 40,000.

It is very fitting to conclude this section with a quotation from Dr. Rida Obaid, President of the University. *"We address our thanks and gratitude to his Majesty King Fahd Bin Abdulaziz, first education pioneer. . ."*

Imam Mohammed Bin Saud Islamic University, Riyadh

It was founded in 1974 and the Council of Ministers defined its basic rules. It became an annex to the Riyadh Ilmi Institute (scientific institute), which was built in 1950. The various faculties which were progressively added include: College of Shari'a, Arabic Language, Higher Judicial Institute, Faculty of the Basics of Religion, Institute for Islamic Call, Faculty of Social Sciences, the College of Shari'a and Basics of Religion in Abha, (and Kasim in 1976). Also, a College for Arabic Language and a College for Social Studies were added in Abha and Kasim, an Institute for Islamic Call in Medina and a College for

Modern Library at Imam Mohammed Bin Saud Islamic University.

Shari'a and Islamic Studies in Hasa. It has a branch for teaching Arabic to foreigners and also a branch for teaching English to students at the university.

Four academic years are needed for graduation. The Master's program could be finished in two academic years. The Doctorate degree could be earned in two to four years after registration of the dissertation topic.

The university has three branches outside the Kingdom: in Ras Al-Kheima, Mauritania and Djibouti. Two branches for teaching the Arabic language are located outside the Kingdom, one in Indonesia and one in Japan. The total faculty, including their assistants, were 949 in the year 1983–84. About 435 of them were Saudis. Administrators and specialists numbered 1,280. The number of students totaled 16,134. Those pursuing graduate studies numbered 2,725. For the five-year plan ending in 1982–1983, 6,232 students graduated from the university. Those obtaining the B.A. degree were 5,518, while 128 earned a high diploma degree, 548 obtained the M.S., and 38 received the Doctorate. The university granted scholarships to 1,970 students from among the Moslem nations of the world.

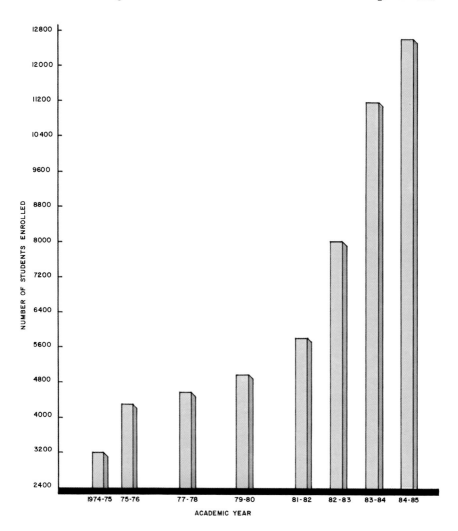

STUDENTS REGISTERED AT IMAM MOHAMMED
BIN SAUD ISLAMIC UNIVERSITY

King Faisal University (KFU)

It was founded in 1975. Instruction began in the same year in four of the basic colleges which, initially, constituted the university. These were: The College of Agriculture, Veterinary Medicine (in Hasa), Construction and Planning and the College of Medicine and Medical Sciences in Dammam. At the beginning, the number of students was

A modern building at King Faisal University (KFU)

170. A branch for girls' education and a college of Business Administration were later established.

The total number of students enrolled at the university in 1983–84 was 2,649. Among them were 1,384 Saudi males, 264 non-Saudi males, 897 Saudi females and 104 non-Saudi females. Non-Saudis constituted about 13.8% of the student body. The number of students jumped from 170 in 1975–76 to 2,649 in the year 1983–84. For the academic year 1982–83, the graduates of the university were 493. Among them 410 males and 83 females. The non-Saudi graduates were 81, constituting 16.4% of the graduating students. The graduates were as follows: Medicine, 80 male doctors and 36 female doctors; Construction and Planning, 189 engineers; Agricultural Sciences and Nutrition, 186 graduates (among them 139 Agricultural engineers and 47 female graduates in Home Economics, and 38 Veterinarians in Veterinary Medicine and Animal Science).

For the academic year 1985–1986, the total number of graduates from KFU was 321.

While the faculty and assistants numbered only 46 in the year 1975–1976, their number increased to 745 in the year 1983–1984. Among these were 293 Saudis. Academic activities in the various colleges are complemented by applied scientific centers that strengthen the educational process in the university. These include: centers for agriculture, animal science, research facilities, libraries and University King Fahd Hospital in Khobar with nearly 400 beds. The Arab Council for Medical Specialties recognized the capabilities of this hospital in training students as an advanced center for specialties in medicine. Other councils of medicine have recognized this.

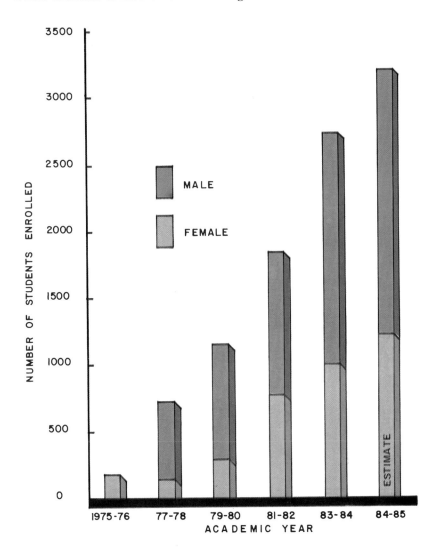

MALE AND FEMALE STUDENTS REGISTERED AT
KING FAISAL UNIVERSITY

The university has agreements with various American universities to help in the progress and development of the academic programs. Among these universities there are: Harvard, Cornell, Rice, Texas A & M and other universities that help in a secondary capacity.

Holders of the general secondary education certificate or its equivalent are accepted upon passing the admission test and a personal interview. The applicant should be in good physical condition. These requirements and conditions apply to most Saudi universities.

Umm Al-Qora University, Mecca (UQU)

This university was founded in 1981. It includes the Faculty of Shari'a and Islamic Studies which has existed since 1969 and the Faculty of Education in Mecca that began in 1952. For a period, both were under the Ministry of Education (1971–1972), then became a part of King Abdulaziz University prior to becoming part of Umm Al-Qora University.

Since 1981, the university expanded on many fronts including: College of Shari'a and Islamic Studies, Education, Applied Science

A world center at Umm Al-Qora University (UQU)

and Engineering, Arabic Language, Education in Taif, College of Dawa
and Basics of Religion (Dawa and Osoul Al-Deen).

Since 1983 two other colleges have been added. These are: College
of Social Sciences and College of Agricultural Sciences.

The total number of male and female students enrolling at the
university for the academic year 1983–1984 was 9,421. Male students
were 5,647 and female students were 3,774. Of these 7,928 male and
female students were undergraduates and 965 were at the graduate
level.

Non-Saudi males enrolled at the university were 1,792 and non-
Saudi females were 697. The total of non-Saudi students for that year
was 2,489. The total number of faculty including assistants was 1,183
for the same year. For the year 1982–83, male students receiving Bachelor's degrees were 668 and female graduates were 344. Those receiving
Master's degrees were 105 males and 37 females. Those receiving Doctorate degrees were 27 males and two females. The total graduates
were 800 males and 383 females.

Students sent on scholarships to study abroad for graduate work
leading to the Master's and Doctorate degrees were 165 for the academic
year 1982–1983; of these 119 were sent to the U.S.A. This number
included eight females. Forty students were sent to Britain and six
were sent to Egypt. Many centers for research and related endeavors
are very active at the university, including a center for computer science
and television education.

Since May 12, 1975 the government of Saudi Arabia discontinued
the income tax applied to foreign contract personnel. Thus, all individual earnings are tax-free in Saudi Arabia. The workload is comparable
to any American university and depends on other activities that are
assigned to the faculty on top of the educational load. Foreign faculty
are granted living quarters. These are very modern, comfortable, and
comparable to the nice suburban homes in southwestern U.S.A.

Universities in the Kingdom seek excellence in education in their
respective missions and endeavors. All have made great progress. Indeed, an era of renaissance is taking place reflecting giant steps forward
in reviving Arab contribution to science, technology, and society.

Education and training are the foundation for building the manpower that was at the core of the gigantic achievements in the Kingdom.
This parade of progress is vividly portrayed in a separate chapter.

Performing the traditional Saudi A'rda, from left to right: the late Kings Khaled & Faisal, King Fahd and Crown Prince Abdullah.

King Fahd with Crown Prince Abdullah, enjoying the simple life—Arabian style.

From right to left, King Fahd, Prince Salman and Crown Prince Abdullah.

King Hassan II of Morocco with King Fahd. Behind him are: Crown Prince Abdullah and Prince Sultan.

**King Fahd during a visit to Paris, France; behind him is Prince Salman.
Below, he is with the Queen of Denmark.**

The Monarch attending a school cultural activity in Riyadh.

King Fahd—the father, with his youngest son Abdulaziz during the Monarch's visit to America.

King Fahd closely reviewing plans for a public park in Riyadh.

Custodian of the two Holy Mosques, King Fahd personally directs and reviews plans for the expansion of the Grand Mosque "Haram" in Medina.

Major projects are reviewed and carefully examined by Fahd, from
inception to completion. In this photo, he is reviewing plans for diplomatic
quarters in Riyadh.

King Fahd, the supreme Commander reviewing the National Guard with
Crown Prince Abdullah.

During one of his tours in the desert, King Fahd does what he thoroughly
enjoys—meeting the people of the desert, and absorbing the peace and
serenity of wide open spaces.

Chapter 3
Fahd, the National, Regional, and International Man of Moderation

National Scene

Leadership authority in the Kingdom of Saudi Arabia follows Islamic law, the Shari'a, which is based on the teachings of the Qoran, the Holy Moslem Book. The executive and legislative branches of the government are represented by the King and the Council of Ministers. Twenty Ministries and several government agencies help in the smooth function of the government. The Moslem religion, with close ties to Christianity and Judaism, believes in one God: Allah.

The efficient, just, swift and strict enforcement of the Shari'a makes Saudi Arabia a very safe country, one with the lowest crime rate among all nations of the world. Upholding Islamic law, supporting political moderation, economic stability, and developing the God-given resources of the Kingdom for the benefit of the citizen, are basic in the national policy of the Saudi leadership.

A consensus is always sought. Compromise, moderation and a strong sense of justice are the basic characteristics of the stability of the nation. This is strongly reinforced through the teachings of Islam. The opinion of Ulema, or men of religion, is well respected.

The Council of Ministers advises the King on the formulation of general policy and directs the activities of the various departments and agencies of the government. All legislation must be compatible with the Shari'a.

Bill Tewell from New Hampshire, USA, specialized in Islamic law some years ago and spent 23 years in the Kingdom of Saudi Arabia working with Aramco. He was the counselor for Aramco in the Saudi Arabian Court system. He describes the Shari'a court as; "being very effective and efficient." Tewell, with his "tremendous intellectual interest in Islamic law", feels that it is one of the world's most sophisticated legal systems. Religious courts are manned by judges or qadis. These are appointed by the senior Ulema. The highest appeal reaches the King, who has the power to pardon. It is a well treasured tradition

King Fahd is a man of the people.

that anyone in the land has the right to petition the King directly in his Majlis. Everyone is allowed to voice a grievance, suggestion, criticism, or ask for personal favor.

A national policy of peace and tranquillity, intertwined with impressive achievements in modernizing the Kingdom, is central to the basic thought and plans of the leadership. What has been achieved in slightly over a decade far surpasses what other nations would seek to achieve in hundreds of years. The pace at which development has taken place is the envy of many across the globe. This great enthusiasm and devotion to the welfare of the citizens bring the leadership very close to the heart of the people. This commitment of personal service is a key factor in the mutual trust and admiration between the government and the governed.

A former U.S. president once said; "The Saudi rulers were able to preserve an acceptable balance between delivering the material advantages of a non-modern state and at the same time preserving the proper degree of religious commitment. They also offset their absolute authority with a *remarkable closeness to their subjects.*"

King Fahd takes deep pleasure and interest in meeting people in the four corners of the Kingdom. This way he remains very closely in touch with their feelings and aspirations. Love, affection and compassion are mutual between Fahd and the citizens of the land, who sense his genuine care and desire for their security, peace of mind and welfare.

On many occasions, King Fahd makes it a special point to meet with the students, especially those at various universities in the Kingdom. He exchanges with them his thoughts and ideas on matters of common interest. In the meantime, he listens attentively to their views and suggestions. All this is done in a friendly, casual and relaxed atmosphere which has given positive results on many fronts through the years. These encounters are unique events where the leader meets students and other members of the society. He answers their questions. He responds to their requests and desires in a loving and understanding manner like a father, a friend or an older brother. This creates confidence, hope and endears him to the hearts of all who hear him and come in contact with him.

According to "Saudi Arabia—A Country Study," by American University; "the essentially stable political system could be attributed to the absence of a history of colonization, the wisdom of King Abdulaziz and his successors and the powerful force of Islam as a political instrument."

Nowadays, Saudi Arabia is blessed with a wise leadership dedicated to prosperity at home and peace in the world. This fact coupled with its phenomenal oil reserves and oil exports that are the largest in the world, earned the Kingdom a distinguished position of leadership and moderation in the Arab world, the Moslem world, as well as the international community. Not only is King Fahd the man of achievement on the national and regional scene, he also is the man of moderation, wisdom and peace among the family of nations.

Regional Arena

Saudi Arabia is a prominent and active member of the Gulf Cooperation Council (GCC) which was founded in May, 1981. The Council includes: Bahrain, Kuwait, Oman, Qatar, Saudi Arabia and the United Arab Emirates (UAE). The purpose of the Council, as established by these friendly neighbors, is to enhance and encourage educational, social and economic cooperation. Security arrangements strengthen peace and harmony among these nations of the Arabian Gulf. GCC has become a "powerful and efficient instrument that serves as a model of cooperation."

Closeness among GCC members has been further strengthened due to the dangerous situation threatening the Arabian Gulf, especially the Iran-Iraq war, which started in September, 1980. It has been going on with vengeance. This war between two Moslem nations became a danger to the region's stability and peace. Since the 1970's, close relationships between Saudi Arabia and members of GCC have developed, based on mutual security benefits and economic arrangements.

The Kingdom is also an active and prominent member of the Arab League. Central in its policy is the non-interference in the internal affairs of other nations. By the same token, it does not permit any country to interfere in its internal affairs.

A cornerstone of the Kingdom's policy is to encourage and support peace and good will in the world community, especially in the Arab and Moslem world. Brotherhood and solidarity are supreme. They are both preached and certainly practiced by the Saudi leadership. Arab differences are considered a family affair and the Kingdom spares no effort or cost toward bringing understanding, peace and harmony among the fraternal nations of the Arab world. Prominent in this regard are the strong efforts that have taken place to bring about rapprochement between Syria and Jordan on a number of occasions. Explosive differences were defused with the great efforts of Crown Prince Abdullah under the leadership and guidance of King Fahd. When a dangerous situation was developing between Morocco and Algeria, the Saudi leadership came to the rescue; it defused a ticking time-bomb.

Anywhere you go, wherever you move across the Arab world, you sense and observe the peaceful efforts, the great moderating and economic might of the Kingdom. Saudi Arabia's contributions toward economic, political, cultural and military activities whose goal is to boost Arab solidarity, are all truly enormous! A dialogue is sought and a hand-of-peace is extended to all, no matter how difficult the circumstances may be and how deep the wounds may have become! In its search for peace and goodwill toward mankind, especially Arab brothers, Saudi Arabia pursues its efforts with zest and determination, even when the odds against harmony and peace are very high.

This cornerstone has been steadily nourished through the years, since the Kingdom's unification more than half a century ago.

The central and most important Arab issue to the Kingdom of Saudi Arabia remains the *Palestinian* problem. From the days of Abdulaziz, founder of the Kingdom, Saudi Arabia was always strongly dedicated, "steadfast, unswerving and unflinching," on the Palestinian issue. Abdulaziz explained to President Roosevelt back in 1945 the absolute dangers and tragedy that would result because of displacing Palestinians from their homeland in Palestine. Roosevelt listened attentively to the explanation of Abdulaziz; but, world events led to the

King Fahd meeting Arab leaders.

establishment of the state of Israel in Palestine and the displacement of millions of Palestinians.

The warnings of Abdulaziz back in 1945 carried with them a message reverberating through the years and guarding its authenticity until this very day. Wars, destablization, human suffering and terrorism are all the bitter fruits of this problem. The Palestinian issue remains central to all problems of the Middle East. While the Kingdom has practiced and professed moderation toward peace and harmony for all nations of the region, it has always lived up to its strong beliefs in justice and decency for mankind. It has used its economic might and diplomatic stature in support of the Palestinian people in defending their legitimate right to self-determination and the establishment of a national home.

On the heels of the Arab defeat in the Arab-Israeli war of 1967, the late King Faisal played a major role at the Khartoum Arab summit, reflecting the degree of sacrifice and support given by the Saudis toward a just solution of the Palestinian refugee problem. During the Six-Day War, the Arabs lost the entire West Bank, Sinai and most of the Golan Heights. Faisal, then representing Saudi Arabia, contributed large sums of money to the front line states. This enabled them to rebuild and strengthen their defenses. The Kingdom was always consistent in its dedicated support to the Palestinian cause, without interfering in their internal affairs. In times of difficulties and differences, the Palestinians look to the Saudis for mediation and help to bring peaceful coexistence among differing groups. The financial commitments to the Palestinian cause are substantial. They are given because of their conscience and deep conviction in seeking a just solution to the oppressed people of Palestine. The Kingdom has struggled through the years endeavoring to find a just solution to this problem.

Saudi Arabia is the only Arab country dedicating genuine effort to come up with a proposal for resolving the Arab-Israeli conflict. Fahd, then the Crown Prince, devised an eight-point peace plan. He originated a creative plan to solve a difficult problem that defied solutions and brought many wars inflicting tragedy and causing destabilization in the region. This became the well-known *Fahd Peace Plan*. In September, 1982, during the Twelfth Arab Summit Conference in Fez, Morocco, all the Arab states approved this plan. This is the only peace plan receiving unanimous approval by the Arabs.

The Fahd Peace Plan called for the following:
1. Withdrawal of Israeli troops from all lands occupied in 1967, including Arab Jerusalem.
2. Dismantling of all settlements built by Israel in Arab territories occupied since 1967.
3. Guaranteeing freedom of worship for all creeds in the Holy places.

4. Reaffirmation of Palestinian rights to self-determination, exercise of their inalienable national rights under the leadership of the PLO (Palestine Liberation Organization)–their legitimate and sole representative; and compensation to every Palestinian not wishing to return home.
5. The West Bank and Gaza Strip will be subject to a transitional period not exceeding a few months under U.N. (United Nations) supervision.
6. Establishment of an independent Palestinian state with Jerusalem as its capital.
7. The U.N. Security Council will guarantee peace among all the states of the region, including the independent Palestinian state.
8. The U.N. Security Council will guarantee the implementation of these principles.

This plan is a fine contribution befitting a peace-loving nation like the Kingdom of Saudi Arabia, which desires to live in peace and harmony among all nations of the world and especially the nations of the region. This plan became the basis for the *"Fez Declaration."* Many leaders throughout the world have hailed the Fahd Peace Plan as a basis for achieving peace in the Middle East, especially in regard to solving the Palestinian dilemma.

The Saudi Ambassador to the United Nations, Samir Shihabi said on a number of occasions, "The zionists were rejecting peace and doing their utmost to hamper all efforts seeking to settle the dispute." He reaffirmed his country's unwavering support for the Palestinian people.

Peace with justice, security and stabilization of the Middle East and the world, for that matter, will not be realized until a comprehensive and just solution to the Palestinian question is achieved. This may be realized when the Palestinian people achieve their legal rights.

The war in Lebanon, which has been raging on for over a decade, is one of the side-effects of the Arab-Israeli conflict. This tragedy received deep concern and special attention from Saudi leaders. The Kingdom was there and ready to help in every way possible to bring the warring factions to peaceful terms, and to offer humanitarian and economic aid wherever the situation permitted. A Lebanese leader said; "When hell was in Beirut in June, 1982, after the Israeli invasion, we all looked for King Fahd to stop the Holocaust." Fahd made immediate contact with the United States of America and urged President Ronald Reagan to use his power in stopping the invasion. The good offices and high regard for King Fahd helped in stopping this war and in saving Lebanon from the inferno that was engulfing large parts of the country and especially the capital city, Beirut. The brutal and inhuman invasion of Lebanon was halted! King Fahd and the Saudi leadership worked tirelessly with deep devotion and enthusiasm to help stop the ensuing civil war. On numerous occasions, he made emotional appeals to stop this war of devastation, agony and human suffering. Addressing the warring factions, he once said; "In the name of all that is Holy, all that we and they have in common, the bonds of faith and language, the bonds of blood and soul, we appeal to them to turn over a new leaf in their relations."

The Lebanese ambassador to Saudi Arabia, Dr. Zafer Al-Hasan said: "King Fahd, who played a major role in halting the bombing of Beirut during the savage Israeli invasion, has been pursuing efforts with influential, international and Arab circles to help Lebanon restore its independence, security and stability. All the Lebanese people greatly and proudly appreciate this stand." The benevolent attitude of the Kingdom toward Lebanon is strengthened by deep feelings of brotherhood. King Fahd, Crown Prince Abdullah and their men, especially Prince Saud Al-Faisal, the Foreign Minister and Prince Bandar Bin Sultan, the present Ambassador of the Kingdom of Saudi Arabia to the United States of America made all-out efforts for a ceasefire in Lebanon and toward bringing peace to this war-torn nation. On many occasions, the Kingdom worked through its good offices in Syria to help in bringing diverging views and warring factions closer together.

The Kingdom's love and great sacrifices for Lebanon and the Lebanese people stems from its deep convictions and beliefs in achieving amity and unity among the people of the nation.

Saudi Arabia continues its great efforts to bring peace and tranquillity to war-torn Lebanon. It continues to support legality and a unified, independent Lebanon free from all foreign domination. It certainly stands ready to help in the reconstruction of the country and in easing human suffering.

Next to the Arabs, Moslems of the world occupy a position of importance and religious sharing.

Moslem World, (*Custodian of the two Holy Mosques*)[1]

The Kingdom is an active, dynamic and founding member of the *Organization of Islamic Conference (OIC)*. which strives for Islamic unity in supporting Islamic causes, putting forth the effort necessary to bring about peace and harmony between Moslem brothers.

Saudi Arabia is the birthplace of Islam which is its greatest contribu-

---

[1] On November 1, 1986 a Royal directive was issued to replace the term "His Majesty" with "Custodian of the two Holy Mosques" and to avoid the words "my lord, magnificent" and other glorifying terms.

King Fahd greeting the pilgrims on arrival to Saudi Arabia.

tion to humanity. Mecca and Medina were the root places where Islam was born and began to flourish. The Prophet Mohammed, in the seventh century, generated a zealous following of believers that led to the Islamic Empire stretching from Spain in the west to India in the east. Being the guardian of the Islamic Holy cities is considered as the Holiest of missions for the Kingdom of Saudi Arabia and its leaders. With nearly two million Moslems from all corners of the globe making the Hajj, or pilgrimage, to the Holy places in Saudi Arabia, the Kingdom became the focal point for all Moslems of the globe. This position of prominence is esteemed in many nations of the world, especially the Arab countries, the developing nations and the Moslem world as well. One billion Moslems in the world today look to Saudi Arabia as a guardian of their Holy Shrines and the spirit of justice and tolerance in Islam.

The Kingdom stands against atheism as professed by world communism. Its support for the struggle and liberation of the people of Afghanistan from communist domination is very impressive, indeed. The Kingdom lends its moral, political, economic and social support to the

Pilgrims from four corners of the world praying in the Holy Mosque in Mecca

oppressed people of Afghanistan who are struggling against a communist dictatorship that has led to the destruction and devastation of innocent people. A special position of reverence and respect has developed in many Moslem nations for the peaceful efforts of the Kingdom.

The leadership continues its efforts on many fronts and through many avenues to help in bringing about peace, especially between the warring Iraqis and Iranians; both are Moslem countries. This long war is bringing destruction and agony to their people. The threat of spilling over is real. If that happens, it will spell disaster for the world community, especially American interests and the lifeline interests of the Western World.

As an oil giant, a mighty economic power and a strategic nation, the Kingdom occupies a unique role in the world today.

The International Arena–(*Wisdom, Peace, Justice and Compassion for mankind*)

The basic principles of Saudi foreign policy are:

- Safeguarding Saudi Arabia's independence and protecting it from any foreign aggression.
- Guarding the Haramein[1]; preserving and protecting these sacred places for all Moslems of the world.
- Cooperating with Arab and Islamic nations for the well-being and welfare of their people.
- Adherence to the charter of the Arab League.
- Respect and adherence to the spirit of the United Nations charter; cooperation with peoples of the world toward the establishment of peace, welfare and stability for mankind.
- Non-interference in the internal affairs of other nations.
- Peace, harmony and peaceful coexistence with other nations.

Saudi Arabia is an active member of the *United Nations*. The Saudis are especially proud of being a founding member of the United Nations charter which was signed on June 26, 1945. Among the fifty founding nations, the Kingdom takes deep interest in strengthening the organization and offering substantial help to many projects carried by it toward the welfare of other nations of the world.

King Abdulaziz eagerly supported and agreed with the American President Franklin D. Roosevelt on the urgent need for establishing the United Nations on the heels of World War II. High hopes were pinned on the UN for preventing violence and warfare that led to the

---

[1] In Arabic, Haramein means two Harams; namely the two Holy Mosques of Mecca and Medina.

Fahd, seated in center, was a member of the Saudi delegation to the founding session of the United Nations in San Francisco, California, U.S.A., in 1945.

massive destruction during World War II. Then Prince Faisal, later to become King, signed the charter on behalf of his country. On this great mission of hope and peace, he was accompanied by then, young Prince Fahd Bin Abdulaziz and Prince Khaled who became a King. Addressing the delegates, Faisal said: "In such a moment as this, we should not forget the resolute efforts of Franklin Delano Roosevelt for the cause of peace, and for his farsighted action in initiating this conference."

Upon his ascension to the throne in June, 1982, King Fahd asserted to the nation that Saudi Arabia is active "within the framework of the United Nations, its agencies, and committees. We are committed to its charter. We reinforce its endeavors."

The foreign minister of Saudi Arabia Prince Saud Al-Faisal, described the UN as "a safety valve trusted and respected for the preservation of international peace and security." Saudi Arabia, he declared, "Stands up against any action that attempts to weaken it or replace the authority of international law with the instruments of force and the means of terror." The Kingdom actively participates in various organizations and functions of the United Nations. Its generous financial contributions speak well for the Kingdom's dedication to the UN's success and welfare. The Kingdom ranks fifteenth in its contributions among the one hundred and fifty-nine member nations. It ranks tenth in terms of per capita contributions.

The goodwill of Saudi Arabia and its generous contributions cross many borders around the globe. Its compassion, generosity and help stretches from the earthquake victims of Yemen and Mexico, volcano and flood victims of Columbia, to the famine-stricken nations of Africa

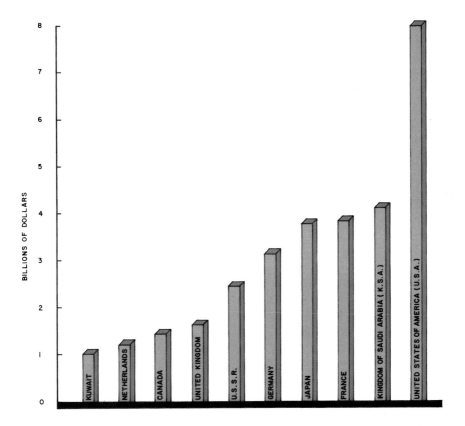

FOREIGN AID FROM TOP TEN
DONORS IN THE WORLD FOR 1983

and other peoples in need everywhere. The Kingdom strongly supports self-determination and economic development for the family of nations. The World Organization, the United Nations Educational, Scientific and Cultural Organization (UNESCO), the UN's International Children's Educational Fund (UNICEF), among other organizations, are all strongly and enthusiastically supported by the Kingdom. It certainly meets its share of responsibilities and much more for the well-being of the human race.

Saudi Arabia strives energetically toward good relations with the Western World and other peace-loving nations as well. There is deep mutual interest and strong relations with the United States of America, the European community, Japan and the countries of the developing world. The Kingdom does not have any diplomatic relations with the communist world. It is strongly anti-communist because of the atheistic ideology and stands against designs for world domination. It maintains limited economic relations with some East block nations. The gigantic oil reserves of the Kingdom and its tremendous potential in mineral resources, along with its strategic Holy position as the birthplace of Islam, all this make the Kingdom of paramount importance to Western democracies and others in the world community.

The wheels of industrial progress depend greatly on the strategic oil supplies from Saudi Arabia. Friendly relations of unique and specific importance to the Kingdom exist and are continually strengthened with the United States of America, Britain, France, Japan, West Germany and other countries of the European community, the Arab world and the Moslem world as well.

The one *special relationship of paramount importance* is certainly that between the Kingdom of Saudi Arabia and the United States of America.

William B. Quandt, an authority on foreign policy, from the Brookings Institution said; "Because Saudi Arabia sets atop the largest and most easily exploited reserves of petroleum in the world, it inevitably is being drawn into the center of international politics. What the rulers of the Saudi Kingdom do or fail to do can have many severe consequences. What happens in this little known country is therefore of concern to statesmen, bankers, businessmen and strategists throughout the world. "As far as American interest in this special relationship," Quandt continues "for Americans, the stakes involved in the US–Saudi relationship are particularly great. No country has benefited more from relations with Saudi Arabia than the United States. American oil companies have made enormous profits. American businessmen have had a disproportionate share of the Saudi market."

American-Saudi relations trace their origin back to over half a cen-

King Fahd with Mrs. Margaret Thatcher, Prime Minister of England and Chancellor Kohl of West Germany.

Then Crown Prince Fahd with Mr. James Callaghan, former British Prime Minister (above); also with King Baudouin of Belgium and the late King Khaled.

King Fahd with former French President Giscard d'Estaing (above) and with French Prime Minister Jacques Chirac.

King Fahd with the President of Venezuela, Mr. Carlos Perez.

tury, to the days of Abdulaziz, when Americans were granted the preferential right to explore for oil, water and minerals. When oil was finally produced in good quantities in 1938, a new era of Saudi-American relations began. A strong foundation for this special relationship was born from the historic meeting of King Abdulaziz with President Roosevelt.

The first was a visionary ruler of an emerging Kingdom at the heart of the Islamic world, the latter a determined leader of a nation at war. Their meeting was in February, 1945. After the historic meeting with the Allied leaders at Yalta, Roosevelt met King Abdulaziz aboard the U.S.S. Quincy in the Suez Canal.

This bedrock relationship built on mutual interest and cooperation has grown through the years and remains a strong one, despite certain differences relating to the Palestinian question.

Oil supplies from Saudi Arabia are strategically very important to the prosperity of the United States of America, as well as Europe and Japan. The Kingdom remains the largest customer for American products in the Arab world. It is the sixth largest market for U.S. products on a worldwide basis. Saudi investments in the United States help strengthen and invigorate the American economy. According to the United States Department of State, in its background notes on Saudi Arabia, this conviction is expressed in this manner: "Coupled with its vast mineral wealth, Saudi Arabia's strategic location makes its friendship important to the United States and the Middle East. Saudi Arabia's leaders value close and friendly relations with the United States."

At one time, more than ten thousand students studied for higher education in the United States and more than 70,000 Americans lived and worked in the Kingdom. The backbone of the five-year development plans is supported by the strong infusion of brain-power of Saudis who graduated from top American universities.

The Joint Commission on Economic Cooperation between the two countries was initiated in June, 1974. To implement this arrangement, a reimbursable technical assistance agreement was signed in February, 1975. Permanent U.S. representation to the commission was established in the capital city of Riyadh. Under this joint commission, cooperation grew extensively in a number of areas including education, technical training, science and technology, solar energy research, transportation, administration and industrialization.

However, this special relationship is sometimes strained by certain differences of the Arab-Israeli dispute. Despite this, Saudi Arabia and the United States of America share a basic and common concern about the security of the region and its orderly progress. Consultations on various international economic and development programs continue. Former president Jimmy Carter put it this way: "Almost invariably, when I was president, I felt that our own basic goals were compatible with those of the Saudi Arabians and that they were inclined to be helpful whenever possible." He continued by saying; "They prefer stability between existing regimes, compromises when Arab unanimity is at stake, peace in the region and political orientation toward the West."

An important meeting between President Reagan and then Crown Prince Fahd in 1981 took place during the North-South Summit in Cancun, Mexico. Saudi Arabia followed a policy of support for the international economic community within a practical mission of moderation. Its policy and leadership, toward world oil production within the Organization of Petroleum Exporting Countries, were very instrumental in protecting the stability of world industries and economies.

The Kingdom allocates five percent of its gross national product for foreign aid. It is very active in the international monetary fund and contributes extensively to the stability of financial organizations around the world.

A special relationship has been strengthened through many decades beginning with President Roosevelt and moving on to Presidents Eisenhower, Kennedy, Johnson, Nixon, Ford, Carter, and Reagan.

Harold Laskai, the British political scientist and economist, said something very profound that can be applied to Saudi Arabia. He said in essence that a country is stable when no significant part of the population feels permanently excluded. Ambassador Newman states that this is true of Saudi Arabia, and that it is the only country in the vast region which really operates that way. Newman admires the great progress achieved under the development plans. He takes special pride in the fact that the Minister of Planning and now Minister of Petroleum & Mineral Resources is Hisham Nazer, a former student and assistant of the Ambassador.

When King Fahd assumed power in the Kingdom, Newman was so impressed he declared; "I saw that his Majesty met with everybody in all the provinces in order to establish this system of multifaceted contact, that is the secret of his success." Another former U.S. Ambassador to the Kingdom John C. West, once said: "I was impressed by their warmth and hospitality and the friendly feeling that existed between the leaders of their country and the United States."

In a recent visit by King Fahd to the United States of America in February, 1985, his principal message was: "The United States of America has a responsibility to make use of its powerful influence and to make a strong effort for achieving peace between Israel and the Arab neighbors, through a just solution to the Palestinian question." King Fahd declared; "The Palestinian question is the cause of instability and turmoil in the region. I hope, Mr. President, that your administration will support the just cause of the Palestinian people."

The Fahd Peace Plan of September, 1982 is moderate and just. It carries with it many positive features. It calls for Palestinian self-government on the West Bank and Gaza Strip in association with Jordan. While the views may differ between the Reagan peace plan and the Fahd peace plan that was unanimously adopted at the Fez Conference in Morocco, the meeting between the two leaders went very well toward the betterment of relations between the two nations and toward possible solution of the Palestinian problem, a solution that has been long over-

King Fahd with former American presidents—a long lasting relationship
between America and the Kingdom.

These photos with President Ronald Reagan were taken during King Fahd's historic visit to the United States of America in February, 1985.

due. The peace plans could be a starting point for constructive dialogue.

King Fahd and President Reagan strongly agreed to keep the pressure on the Soviet Union to remove its occupation troops from Afghanistan and to continue their efforts to end the Iran-Iraq war. The U.S. remains a key figure and broker for Middle East peace. To serve its basic and genuine interests in the region and to stand for the basic American principles of justice, the U.S. should rise up to the task and to expectations, so that its moral, political, economic and military might would be put to good use toward establishing a permanent peace and a just solution to the Arab-Israeli conflict.

Despite any differences that may exist in this regard, Saudi-Ameri-

King Fahd with the American Secretary of Defense and Prince Bandar Bin Sultan, the Saudi Ambassador in Washington, D.C.

can relations continue to be very strong. This stems from sharing many basic principles that are dear to both the American and the Saudi people.

Basic economic and geopolitical interests bring the two nations closer together. Also, Saudi-American trade contributes strongly to this relationship. One Saudi economist observed that, "Until now, our eagerness to trade with America and to invest in and import American products and services has resulted in giving the U.S. the largest share of the Saudi Arabian market. But, the U.S. slice of the pie could be much larger."

In the years to come, oil, petrochemicals, mutual interests along with American and Saudi investments all will still contribute toward better relations. The twenty-first century carries with it the opportunity and hope of an even brighter era of Saudi-American relations, especially because high hopes and expectations are alive and well toward ending the Palestinian tragedy.

Prosperity, safety and security will prevail at the core of Saudi society. Preservation of old traditions, love and affection for the people will be at the foundation of national policy. A distinguished position of economic might and political leadership will leave its everlasting impact in the region, the Moslem World and International community. This eminence in wisdom, peace, justice and compassion for mankind shall remain as a bright star of Saudi policy for generations to come.

Chapter 4

Saudi Arabia Redefines Progress

If one has seen Saudi Arabia in the early 70's and again in the early 80's, he will no doubt be overwhelmed and fascinated by the mind-boggling progress and the tremendous achievements that have taken place in slightly over a decade. It is like a dream come true! If one is acquainted with Saudi Arabia, and lets his imagination take him back to the days of Abdulaziz, one will then realize the fantastic effort, blood and sweat, that were intertwined and enmeshed in modernizing this great mass of desert. Imagine the magnitude and vast impact of this progress, keeping in memory that only a few years ago, introducing the telephone and telegraph required the ingenuity of Abdulaziz to convince the populace that, certainly this machine is not "an instrument of the devil."

Abdulaziz, not only unified the Kingdom, but he laid the solid foundation for security, stability and made impressive strides toward progress, considering the meager resources at his disposal. The development process drew its inspiration from the basic tenets of Islam.

The pace of development moved at a massively accelerated rate since the mid-70's. At center stage was the dedicated support and wisdom of King Fahd, keeping the goals high and on target. His vast experience through the years materialized into actions and deeds. From the time of his predecessors to his golden era, he has been the man of long-range planning and dynamism. The progress that was achieved in every walk of life be it in the military, security, infrastructure, agriculture, health or otherwise is truly beyond imagination! What may take other nations, with good luck and good leadership, a hundred years to achieve, became a reality in the Kingdom of Saudi Arabia in a record time: slightly over a decade.

Visitors from all around the world such as Europe, Far East, America, the Moslem and Arab countries who witnessed this development process marveled at what they had seen! They wondered how these achievements have been made in such a short time and not hundreds of years! The people and the government were united in their enthusiasm to move forward, under the guidance of Shari'a, in a land that extends a hand of peace and friendship to the peoples of the world; a nation that has been generous and considered generosity as a duty to help others in need.

Technology transfer, combined with Saudi brain power that was nurtured in top Western and mainly American universities, became a well-tuned vehicle to carry and deliver Fahd's dreams and designs for modernization. *King Fahd was not only the pioneer but truly the heartbeat of this gigantic modernization process.* He made these dreams come true.

King Fahd once said: "Our goal shall always be–God willing–to maintain the equitable distribution of wealth among all of the citizens and to promote the welfare of each Saudi Arabian, no matter how remote his village or how far his city is from the centers of construction and industrial activity." In his goals and dreams, Fahd was enthusiastically supported by a dedicated team of government leaders, ambitious Saudi businessmen, competent Saudi engineers, along with a multitude of professional experts from across the world who all helped in a massive process of technology transfer and efficient use of the best talent available to mankind.

In the mid-70's, the wisdom of optimizing the use of economic opportunities brought a torrent of financial support that was sorely needed to extract reality out of big dreams. The wise decision was to produce all the oil that could be beneficially sold on world markets, to help ease the shortage of oil and in the meantime to generate hard cash for development. At the time, loud voices were strongly supporting and promoting the view that oil is more valuable underground. These voices urged that only the minimum amount of oil should be pumped and sold. If this policy was adopted, a historic opportunity would have been lost forever. As events moved on and in the present day oil glut, such theory and voices have been proven totally wrong. The foresight of Fahd prevailed and the golden opportunity presented in the oil markets was wisely seized; money was well spent for modernization and industrialization. The dream of King Fahd "to maintain the equitable distribution of wealth among all the citizens," was realized in a remarkably short period of time, truly unparalleled in the history of mankind!!! During the last fifteen years, covering three development plans, the per capita income rose twelvefold from 2,800 Saudi Riyals to 35,000. The annual compounded gross domestic product (GDP) averaged a growth rate of 10.6 percent. "This is a unique achievement in the history of development throughout the world."

Oil was not only the lifeline for the industrialized West but also the lifeline for bringing Saudi Arabia to the Space Age and for building a most modern infrastructure.

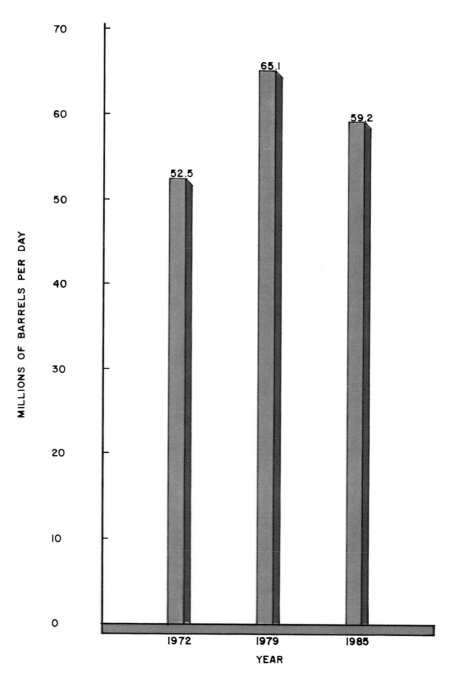

WORLDWIDE OIL CONSUMPTION

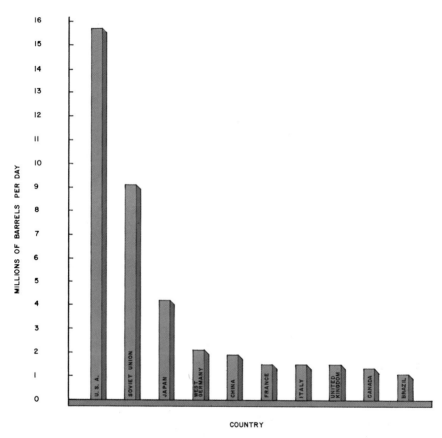

TOP TEN OIL CONSUMING COUNTRIES
OF THE WORLD (AS OF JAN. I, 1985)

In the organization of Petroleum Exporting Countries (OPEC), the Saudi voice has been a vibrant voice for moderation and stability.

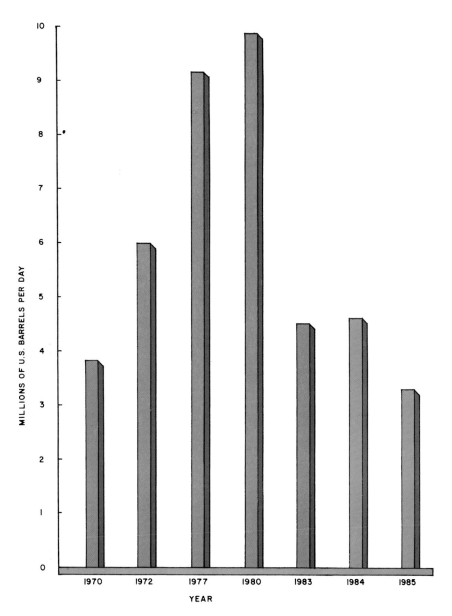

CRUDE OIL PRODUCTION FOR SAUDI ARABIA

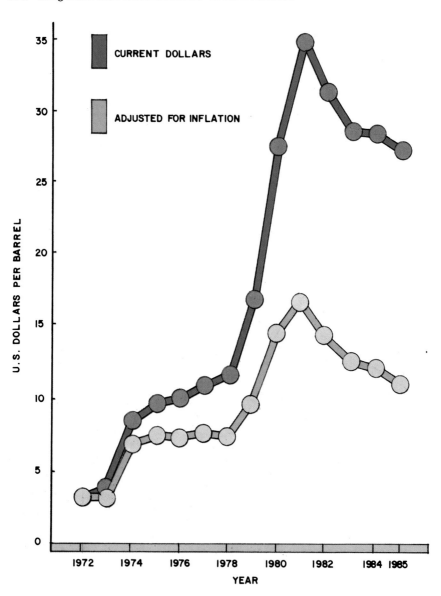

AVERAGE YEARLY PRICE FOR ALL
CRUDE OIL RECEIVED BY U.S. REFINERS

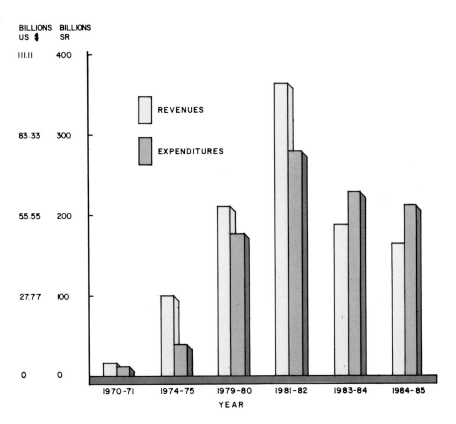

REVENUES AND EXPENDITURES OF THE KINGDOM

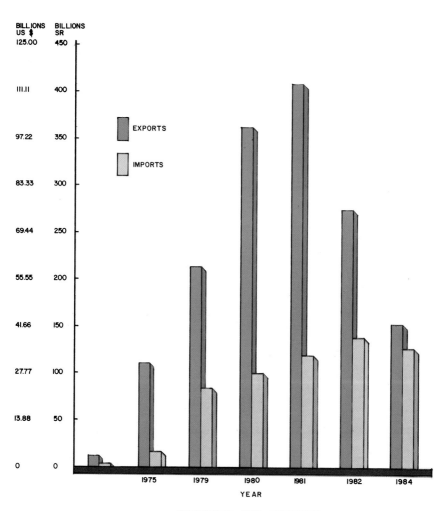

EXPORTS AND IMPORTS

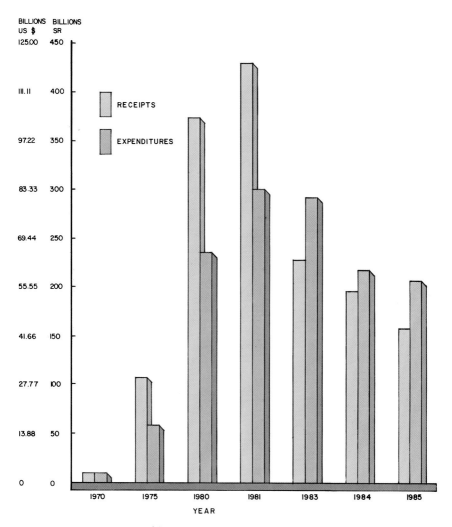

BALANCE OF PAYMENTS

Oil and Aramco

Oil discovery in 1938 became progressively important with time. When development was picking up momentum in the early 70's, oil was the necessary fuel that energized the process. With fifty-three years of operation behind it, the Arabian American Oil Company, known as Aramco, played a unique and vastly important role in the oil operations of the Kingdom of Saudi Arabia. During this time, it has exported over fifty billion barrels of oil that brought tremendous wealth to the country and its citizens. Aramco became a giant in the oil business.

Dhahran, which was a small campsite built in 1936 with a few tents and lots of hostile desert, became, in the 80's, the modern city of Dhahran that is home for about 55,000 employees of Aramco representing 57 countries. It is the home for a leading center of higher education, King Fahd University of Petroleum and Minerals. Between Dhahran and Al-Khobar, what used to be rough desert terrain is now a continuing garden of beauty, reminiscent of the most beautiful parks in Western Europe or America. The maze of bridges crisscrossing the highways would take your imagination to the modern cities of the world be it Paris, London, Washington D.C. or Houston.

The discovery of oil did not materialize as easily as one imagines. It is reported that one geologist who was very much disappointed in the search for oil said, "I will drink all the oil ever found in Arabia." The historic oil well number 7, or Dammam number 7, brought the good luck to Aramco, Arabia and the world as well. In the following years, oil was discovered in large quantities and Saudi Arabia became the oil giant of the world.

Aside from producing oil and bringing oil wealth to the modernization of the Kingdom, Aramco plays an important role in the economic development, especially of the Eastern Region. Local businessmen benefited from the technical advice, assistance and financial aid offered by the company. Oil and gas are supplied by Aramco to the industrial cities of Jubail and Yanbu. They serve as the source of energy and feedstock for the massive petrochemical industries in these two new cities. The company serves in training its employees. Presently, the Saudis account for over sixty percent of the company's employees. Also, applied research is conducted to service the special needs of the Kingdom.

Back in 1944, Aramco produced 20,000 barrels per day. The production was at a peak in 1980 when it reached nearly ten million barrels per day. It remains the world's largest crude oil producing company along with natural gas liquids. It produces 95% of the Kingdom's total oil output and manages 98% of the petroleum reserves of the Kingdom. It is noteworthy to mention that this company has been discovering more oil than it has produced.

The remaining recoverable oil reserves have reached nearly 170 billion barrels, or about 25% of the world's proven reserves. Saudi

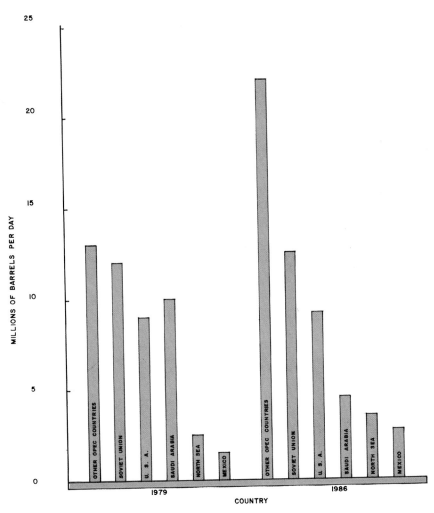

OIL PRODUCTION FOR CERTAIN REGIONS
OF THE WORLD

Arabia has more oil reserves than any other country on the face of the earth.

By early 1986, about 62% of all the managing positions in Aramco were held by Saudis. Many of the day-to-day operations and controls in the fields are conducted by Saudis. Nearly 90% of all operators' positions are filled by the natives.

Aramco is now 100% owned by the Saudi Government. It is managed by a Board of Directors made of twenty members. Six of these

Oil at Ras Tanura—a lifeline for the world.

are from the government, and each of the original U.S. oil companies that originally founded Aramco has two representatives; Aramco itself has six representatives, the president is included among them.

In February, 1975, the government requested Aramco to design, (feasibility and design work started with Petromin) build and operate a system for gathering associated gas (gas produced along with crude oil) from the various areas of Aramco's operations. This is known as the Master Gas System (MGS). It became the backbone of the industrial development program in the Kingdom. The company has completed all the gathering projects that were needed to recover and make good use of the gas. The raw associated gases are processed and fractionated for use by Aramco and various Saudi industries. The recovered ethane is supplied to the petrochemical industries in the industrial cities of Jubail and Yanbu. This is their basic feedstock. Other gaseous products that are made through fractionation such as propane, butane and natural gasoline are exported to various countries.

Associated gas was previously flared or burned just to get rid of it. Recovering it was an additional national resource that became the raw material for the petrochemical industry. It also became a good source of energy for power plants and home use as well.

The master gas system also included the building and operation of a pipeline to deliver natural gas liquids and ethane to Yanbu on

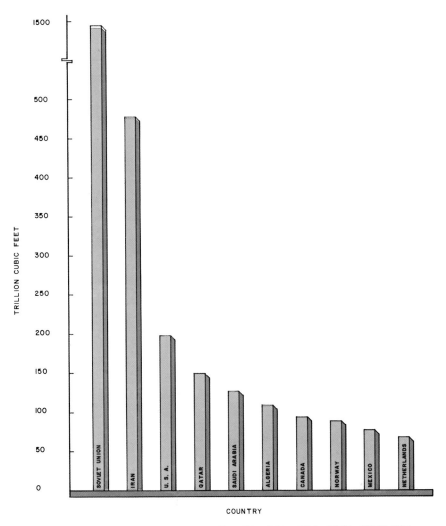

PROVEN GAS RESERVES FOR TOP TEN NATIONS OF THE WORLD (AS OF JAN. I, 1985)

the Red Sea. A fractionation plant was built there. A terminal for exporting natural gas liquids was also built. The fractionation plant made available feedstock to the petrochemical industry and also fuel gas for the Royal Commission Power Plant. It supplied the necessary gas as an energy source for the desalination plant of the Saline Water Conversion Corporation and also for the Petromin Refinery.

Aside from the major MGS gas gathering projects, Aramco developed facilities to produce and process large quantities of non-associated gas from the Khuff reservoir. The non-associated gas is used to supplement the associated gas supply when crude oil production is low.

King Fahd inaugurated the Exploration and Petroleum Engineering Center (EXPEC) in Dhahran in May, 1983. This is the number one center of its kind in the Middle East.

The Arabian Oil Company Ltd. (AOC) produces oil in the Khafji of the (divided) neutral zone between Saudi Arabia and Kuwait. It was established on February 10, 1958. All rights and concessions were granted to it from the mother-company: Japan Petroleum Trading Company, Ltd. The Kuwait government also granted AOC the concession in its one-half interest. In January 1960, oil was found at 4,900 feet at a rate of nearly 6,000 barrels per day. By the end of 1984 the number of producing wells in the Khafji field was 103 and in the Hout field there were 21. However, production from this company and the Getty Oil Company is minimal when it is compared to the gigantic production of Aramco. (57.5 versus 1435.5 million barrels in 1984).

Petromin

Back on December 5, 1962 the Kingdom of Saudi Arabia established the General Petroleum and Minerals Organization (Petromin). The responsibility of this organization covers the development of the natural resources of the Kingdom including crude oil, natural gas, minerals and other related industries. Petromin helped in increasing the gross domestic product (GDP) and also in developing human resources and diversifying revenues so that dependence on petroleum would be reduced. Thus, Petromin contributed in the diversification of the economy and found a number of partners for its operations. These include Shell Oil Company and Mobil Oil Company. The fifty-fifty joint ventures help in coupling the expertise of large international oil companies with the largest crude oil exporter. This combines financial and petroleum resources of Saudi Arabia with management, technical and marketing expertise of well seasoned companies. Among the objectives in establishing Petromin are these:

- Contribution in the various facets of commercial and industrial activity as relates to petroleum and minerals in order to improve the progress and development of the petroleum and mineral industries along with their products and other related industries.
- Control of petroleum and mineral resources.
- Execution and management of public projects relating to petroleum and minerals in the Kingdom.

- Diversification of revenue by finding substitutes for petroleum, which will gradually take its place when petroleum supplies are exhausted.
- To carry directly or through hiring other organizations, studies, theoretical and scientific research relating to petroleum and minerals.
- Training the Saudi citizen so he will contribute his share in serving the nation.
- Carry directly or through delegation to others what is assigned to Petromin by the government concerning operations for research relating to petroleum and mineral products; be it in production, purification, buying, selling, marketing, transporting or distributing these products whether in or outside the Kingdom.
- Cooperation with companies and private organizations who carry on petroleum and mineral activities so as to ease operations for exploration and exploitation, including distribution and marketing.
- Establishment of companies and projects through contributions in its capital, be it in the Kingdom or outside of it, again, in the industrial realm of petroleum and minerals.

Petromin followed a dynamic policy toward achieving these goals. It carried various activities in building petroleum refineries, storage facilities for local consumption or transport of petroleum products internally, development of refineries for export, building petroleum crude pipelines from the eastern region to the west, commercial exploration of mineral resources and marketing of the government share for petroleum crude.

Initially, Petromin established the Arabian Drilling Company, the Arabian Geophysical and Surveying company (Argas). A number of other companies started soon after. These included the Petroleum and Mineral Tankers Company (Petroship), and Arabian Marine Petroleum Construction Company (Marinco). In 1964, Petromin established the Jeddah oil refinery, and then in 1974 it formed a joint venture with the Saudi Arabian Refinery Company (Sarco).

Production of lubricants was based on a joint venture with Mobil oil for a petrolube blending plant. Luberef I refines base oils used in lubricants. It is also a joint venture with Mobil oil. Studies are well underway for building a GCC lubricant base-oil plant. On the Red sea, Petromin is working on a 350,000 barrel per day oil refinery for export.

Petromin established the fertilizer plant: Saudi Arabian Fertilizer Company (Safco) which was then transferred to the Saudi Arabian Basic Industries Corporation (Sabic).

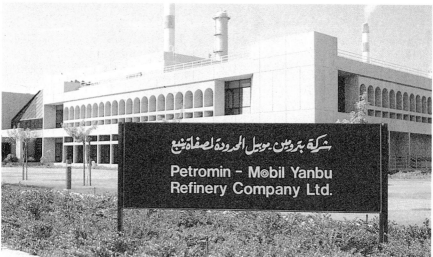

When associated gas was simply separated from crude oil and burned or flared, Petromin designed a gas collection system. This mammoth project of twelve billion dollars was then continued by a task force and Aramco's four partners who finished it. Flares of the last few decades were eliminated in the mid-80's.

Saudi Arabia has a refining capacity of 1.14 million barrels per day with six refineries. These are: Ras Tanura with a capacity of 450,000 barrels per day, Riyadh 135,000 b/d, Jeddah 105,000 b/d, Yanbu domestic refinery 170,000 b/d, Arabian Oil Company 30,000 b/d, and Petromin-Mobile Refinery at Yanbu 250,000 b/d. Top quality products are made in these refineries. A good bit of it is used for internal consumption and other products with superior quality are exported. The total number of employees with Petromin is nearly 12,000. Of these 73% are Saudis.

In the *minerals sector*, Petromin pushed onward to meet its responsibilities and to achieve its goals. The Kingdom is well endowed with minerals. In 1983, Mahd Al-Thahab gold mine was operational. It is located about 280 kilometers northeast of Jeddah; it has a production capacity of 120,000 tons of raw materials per year. Deposits of iron, zinc, copper, phosphates, tungsten, lead, and some coal have been found.

An evaluation study was made concerning the industrial projects at the southwest of the Kingdom (northeast of the city of Najran). Raw materials were estimated at 4½ million tons with a content of 1.6% copper, 4.7% zinc, 1.17 gram–ton gold and 43.7 gram–ton silver. In the Nukra project, exploration takes place in the Sukheirat region that is rich in raw materials.

The wadi Al-Sawaween area has been discovered to have large deposits of iron. Coal in good quantities was found in an area near Kasim. Phosphate has been discovered in the north part of the country. A systematic program has been devised by the proper organizations to assess and determine the quantity and quality of these deposits. Proper steps are being taken for commercialization.

Aramco and Petromin play a healthy and central role in enriching the oil sector and contributing to its productivity. The backbone of the Saudi economy and the development plans was the abundance of oil and the great wealth that came with it from the mid-70's to the early 80's. In 1984, Saudi Arabia ranked third among the top ten oil producing countries of the world, coming after the Soviet Union and the United States of America. However, when one talks about the number one country in proven oil reserves, it is the Kingdom which occupies the enviable position with nearly 170 billion barrels. Coming next to Saudi Arabia is Kuwait with 93 billion barrels and a distant third is the Soviet Union with 63 billion barrels. The United States ranked eight with 27 billion barrels in proven reserves. With nearly 50 billion barrels of oil produced to fire and finance the massive rate of development and modernization in the Kingdom, one should remember that back in 1946 Saudi Arabia had a proven reserve of only three billion barrels of oil and in 1959 the proven reserves were fifty billion barrels.

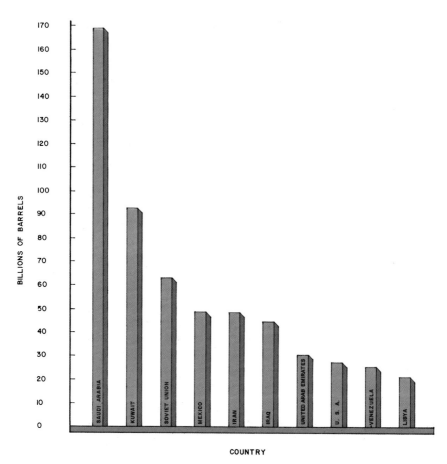

COUNTRY

PROVEN OIL RESERVES FOR TOP TEN NATIONS
OF THE WORLD (AS OF JAN. I, 1985)

The Five-Year Plans

Modernizing the Kingdom was based on scientific and well thought out five-year plans. Each of these plans had definite objectives that were defined in accordance with the specific requirements of the economy and basic social entity, so that the citizen could enjoy a prosperous and stable way of life. The first five-year plan began in 1970. While many economists and experts expressed their reservations about the practicality and viability of such a plan, the results were far beyond

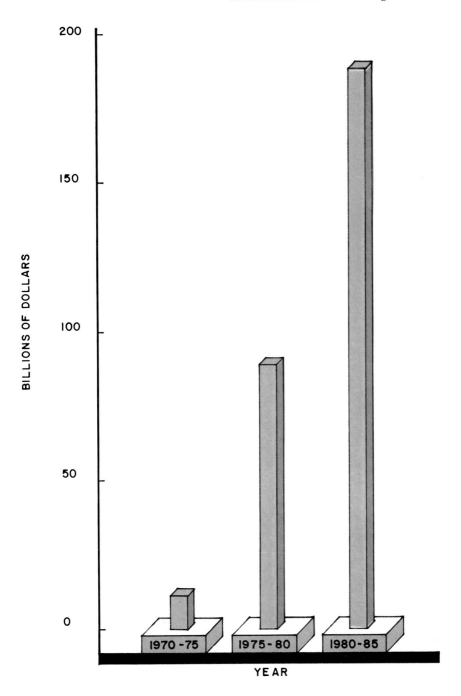

PROJECT EXPENDITURES DURING
EACH FIVE-YEAR PLAN

expectations. When the second five-year plan was initiated in 1975, similar gloom was shed over it by some international experts expressing the belief that the goals were too high and could not be reached in such a brief period of time. However, the goals were reached through dedication and hard work by the leadership and those involved in modernizing the nation. This accomplishment was repeated again in the third five-year plan of 1980–1985.

The *Ministry of Planning*, with the support of other Ministries and sectors of the economy, was very successful in implementing these plans and reaching the high goals in a record time. The abundant financial resources were efficiently used to modernize the nation and bring a higher standard of living to all the people of Saudi Arabia. The five-year plans have indeed played a pivotal and critical role in developing the country.

Certain policies were adopted in implementing the various five-year plans. The long term goals of developing the country applied the following basic principles:

- Maintaining the religious values of Islam by applying and receiving spiritual guidance from Shari'a.
- Defending the religion of the country and maintaining internal security with social stability.
- Continuing the balanced economic growth through the development of the country's resources. Increasing the income from oil over the long range. Conserving non-renewable resources. Thus, the social well-being of the citizen is to be improved and to provide the economic strength necessary for achieving the basic fundamental goals of the development process.
- Reducing dependence on the production of crude oil as a primary source of the nation's income.
- Developing human resources through education, training and increasing the standards for health.
- Completing the basic infrastructure that is basically necessary in reaching the basic and ultimate goals.

Hisham Nazer, the Minister of Planning said: "We must define what we view to be the goals of development. In brief we can say that this goal is the happiness of man. Such happiness is two-sided, the spiritual and the material . . . these two aspects of man's happiness complement each other. They are mutually reinforcing and are stressed accordingly in the development philosophy of the Kingdom."

The *first Five-Year Development Plan*, initiated in 1970 stressed a basic philosophy for successful modernization of the Kingdom of Saudi Arabia. This philosophy was based on two major principles:

developing the needed human resources through education and training and building a comprehensive economic infrastructure. Development projects were designated as a top priority in this plan. Thus, human resources development, along with infrastructure, economic resources and social resources received 58.2% of the total money allocated in this plan; while defense, loans, aids, subsidies and administration received 41.8%. The total amount of money available for this plan was 41.3 billion Saudi Riyals. The economy was essentially gearing for the massive industrial development and diversification that were to follow. The plan was very helpful in feasibility studies. This helped in the plans that succeeded it. It was also made available to the planning experts and economists. Much of the statistics and needed information were obtained.

During the *second Five-Year Development Plan* between 1975 and 1980, the economy received a tremendous boost from the astronomical income from oil. This good fortune was a great shot in the arm for the terrific boom in construction, infrastructure development and human resources as well. Sixty-four percent of the total money available for this plan was geared toward development of the infrastructure, human resources, economic resources and social resources. While the balance of 36% was geared toward other areas that included defense, loans, subsidies, aids and administration. The total amount allotted for this plan skyrocketed to nearly 500 billion Saudi Riyals. This was a very remarkable period in the history of the Kingdom.

The plan was designed with the purpose of achieving a fundamental base for massive development. The achievements reached were numerous, covering ports, airports and highways that connected the country's far corners. This was coupled with a building boom that was manifested in many parts of the nation. Also services were strengthened and improved along with development of natural resources. Building an infrastructure was an absolute necessity for modernization and development. Bridges, communications, telephone and telegraph along with developing human resources, natural resources and agriculture, all were given special attention. Ports and airports were to be developed with the quality and capacity needed to absorb the influx of material and to meet the needs of the development itself.

The *third Five-Year Development Plan*, essentially, brought about the conclusion of the infrastructure developments and made serious beginnings in the diversification of the economy, so that dependency on oil would be minimized with time. Again, development received 62% of the total money allotted in this plan, while other sectors received 38%. The total sum of money allotted in this Five-Year Plan also skyrocketed to a new record of 1,132.7 billion Saudi Riyals. While the planned expenditures for these Plans were respectively 41; 498 and 1,133 billions of Saudi Riyals, the actual expenditures were respectively 78; 688 and 1,166 billions of Saudi Riyals. The ratio of actual expenditures to planned expenditures were respectively, 190%, 138% and 103%. For these years, revenues were respectively 176, 719 and 1,379 billions of Saudi Riyals. After the infrastructure was well under way, the third development plan of 1980–1985 started to move away from infrastructure and construction activities toward the development of industry and agriculture. This plan incorporated an increase of investment in the development of human resources and in the training of manpower needed to optimize the benefits from expanding the industrial sector.

The third plan emphasized the following goals:

- Encouraging diversification of the economy so that dependency on revenue from oil would be minimized with time.
- Encouraging the building of light industries so that foreign imports would receive the proper and necessary competition from local industry.
- Increasing joint ventures with foreign companies so that technology transfer will continue to move smoothly with optimum benefits for the Saudi citizen.
- Maximizing the effectiveness of training, manpower, industrial development and housing efforts.
- Eliminating any imbalance between the various regions of the Kingdom, as far as per capita income and amount of investment.
- Completing the infrastructure activity and especially the massive industrial complexes at Jubail and Yanbu. Once these industrial giants begin to generate profits, their shares will be made public so that the people will receive direct benefits from them. This way, private enterprise and proper incentives will play their proper roles. An intergration of economic diversification with infrastructure made impressive achievements toward a self-sustaining economy.

Revenue from other sources than oil is expected to grow in the years ahead; especially, since the petrochemical industries are taking their share in the world market on a competitively healthy basis. All these plans, along with the ones to follow, encourage the free market and free enterprise system; competition is very much encouraged as an optimum method for development.

The third plan for development, 1980–1985, continued the job that was started in the previous plan so that infrastructure projects that have remained would be completed. Some of these projects are massive and needed more time than allotted in the second five-year

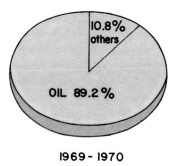
10.8% others

OIL 89.2%

1969-1970

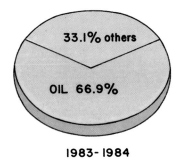
33.1% others

OIL 66.9%

1983-1984

GOVERNMENT   REVENUES

plan: as an example, during this plan the international airport in Jeddah, called King Abdulaziz Airport with an area of 65 square miles needed 10,000 men in its construction. The roof for its major hall is the largest of any airport in the world. Under the same plan, the airport of Riyadh, known as King Khaled Airport, was completed. This is in addition to another twenty airports that were finished in various corners of the Kingdom.

The fourth Five-Year Development Plan of 1985–1990 moves on in an atmosphere of security and tranquillity in the Kingdom of Saudi Arabia, despite the problems and conflicts that continue to plague the region. This plan will differ from the previous three in the fact that it will concentrate on the productive and private sectors more than it will concentrate on the building of infrastructure. It is believed that "The present rate of growth is the normal rate, and would be reached whether the oil income had risen or fallen."

Drawing on the basic principles for all the previous Five-Year Plans, the Fourth one defined eight strategic bases toward achieving these goals. They are:

1. Improving the economic standard for services and benefits that are offered directly by the government to the citizen such as education and security services, or indirectly such as electricity, transport and basic foodstuffs. This is done through a decrease in the cost of services, by optimizing the use of mechanization means and modern techniques. One of the methods for contributing to this objective is to judge the economic feasibility of projects no matter what they are, and to encourage the citizens to embark on beneficial industries that depend on raw materials and use productive techniques needing a small number of workers and using the smallest possible amount of resources, such as water.

2. Opening wide horizons and encouraging the private sector to be
    involved in many of the economic functions of the government,
    so that the government will not carry on an economic activity
    that can be accomplished by the private sector.

3. Giving opportunities to the private sector to manage, maintain
    and delete some sectors that are presently run by the government
    on a condition that this will result in a true benefit to the citizen

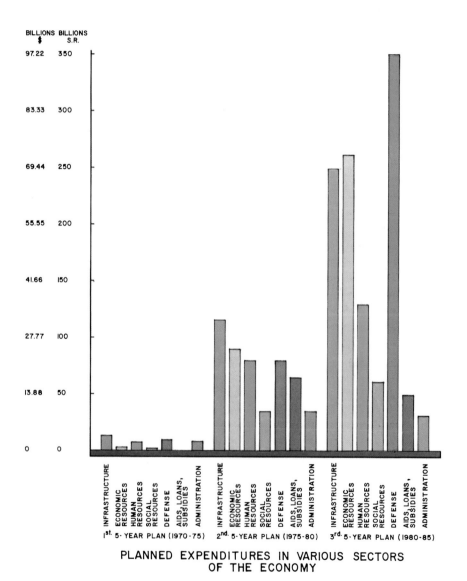

PLANNED EXPENDITURES IN VARIOUS SECTORS
OF THE ECONOMY

in decreasing the cost and giving better services and work for the people. Also by giving investment opportunity and participation of the citizen in owning and directing the basic industries through the public offering of stocks for companies such as Sabic

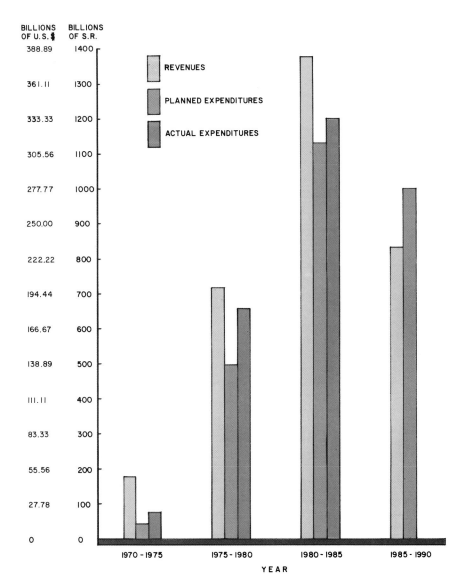

REVENUES AND EXPENDITURES
FOR EACH OF THE FIVE YEAR PLANS

and Petromin, so that the private sector will be participating and managing these organizations at the proper time.

A basic strategy in this goal called for review of policies, methods and means used by the government concerning the private sector, so that more freedom and flexibility would help it toward progress and better achievements.

The strategy also calls on banks to encourage production projects instead of concentrating on commerce and imports.

4. Improvements and selectivity in the subsidies and aids offered by the government, be it direct or indirect. The decrease in these subsidies to various items and services will be done in such a way that it will not affect to any great extent those of small income. Central in this matter will be the directive for all governmental departments who direct public services to practice the *economic feasibility* and cut waste. This is based on two basic principles:

    a. Decrease in the cost of production for these services to Saudi society in that the sale should not be less than the cost except in rare circumstances. Review of the cost should be done on a regular basis.

    b. Giving preference to the economic view in governmental decisions. This strategy is to be applied wherever possible in the decisions of governmental investment and spending. Leading in this regard would be making the production of water a basic important guide in establishing economic feasibility for governmental projects. The same applies to exploration for minerals, marine resources, development and proper use of available gas toward industrialization to the furthest extent possible. Also, proper development for the petrochemical industries and derivatives of gas and petroleum through the private sector or other companies. The increase of petroleum products to the farthest extent possible, on a condition that it is done on an economical basis.

5. Continuation of human resources development. Review of programs for education and training and assessing what this review would require for development and revision to be in conformity with the spirit of Islam, in the changing needs of society and requirements of development. Stress the need for quality training and concentration on technical development on both the middle and higher levels. Training should respond to the true needs of the economy. Concentration on training for management with special emphasis on the library, so the student will develop the habit of reading and researching. He will then gain proper general knowledge and make better use of the libraries.

6. Special attention to develop the Saudi society and to make available the proper social and health care necessary to the Saudi citizen. Help him to contribute in implementing and achieving the programs of the plan and to benefit from its fruits through educating the citizens to the goals and requirements of the plan. Stress the importance of work as a religious and social value so that the individual in society will develop and change in some ways, his outlook toward trades and technician jobs which do not receive the proper acceptance from a number of citizens. Also, spreading education by encouraging publishing, the spread of public libraries, establishment of museums and safeguarding old places of historical value. Build a national library that will contain a book depository for every Saudi author.

   Good attention is to be paid to the Saudi citizen, especially the handicapped. Introduce national programs to help them and to take care of children in various respects and on different levels. Introduce education programs and programs for military education in the secondary schools. Widen the programs for fighting illiteracy through education of the elderly. Attention is also paid to medical services, social care in the various sectors, and encouraging an increase in charitable organizations of good will. Continuation in the programs for environmental protection and development along with continuing increase in the programs for the youth.

7. Preparation of the defense and security plan. Do whatever is necessary to guarantee the protection of the nation.

8. Following a financial policy that realizes a balance between revenues and expenditures.

   Through the Five-Year Plans the Kingdom moved from the balanced strategy in the first and second plan to the stage of diversifying the productive base and to producing a true change in the economic structure for the nation via the third and fourth plans. The fourth plan has nearly 1,500 projects that are new. Additionally, it is continuing the work to finish another 1,800 projects that are transferred from the third plan. Some of these are to be continued as a whole and others need partial fulfillment.

   The Kingdom has made good use of foreign expertise whenever and wherever needed. "However, the realization of the Kingdom's targets and policies originate from the Kingdom's own will and it does not come from any foreign companies."

   "Although some biased opinions have been expressed concerning the first three plans, the achievements with these plans have been enormous. Also, despite some of the reservations expressed by biased opinions for the fourth plan, the Kingdom has made great strides in development and services extended to its citizens that are lacking in many countries that are criticizing the Kingdom's plans," according to Saudi planners. Saudization is one of the major objectives of the fourth Five-Year Plan. Over 600,000 foreign workers who are not among the experts category will be leaving for their respective countries by the end of this plan. In the meantime, the economy should absorb over 375,000 Saudis net in the work force. The fourth plan assumed an increase in productivity of the individual that will be equivalent to four percent per year. For Saudization to succeed, the Saudis should accept jobs in various parts of the economy that are normally occupied by expatriates. Many of these workers have come for a specific mission. Once the mission is accomplished they go back home.

Gigantic projects have been accomplished. The first Five-Year Plan spent about 11 billion dollars, while the Second Plan spent 89 billion dollars. The Third Plan for 1980–1985 expended 188 billion dollars for these major projects. This boom placed a heavy demand on services and brought a distinct awareness for improving them. Maintenance & service companies are counted on to deliver their share.

The vehicles for distributing wealth, raising the standard of living and energizing the development process, are the various successful Funds.

Credits by Various Funds

These funds played a central role in the various development plans. The leading ones are: the Public Investment Fund, the Saudi Agricultural Fund, the Real Estate Development Fund and the Saudi Industrial Development Fund for both projects and power plants. Up to 1983–1984, the Saudi Credit Bank gave 159,000 loans amounting to half a billion dollars. The General Investment Fund gave a total of 20.5 billion dollars in loans. The Real Estate Development Bank provided 20 billion dollars in loans. The Agricultural Bank made 284,000 loans totaling five billion dollars. The Industrial Development Fund loans for projects amounted to four billion dollars and the Industrial Development Fund loans for power plants totaled eleven billion dollars. Loans and assistance to private citizens, public and semi-public institutions were extended through these funds that played a very comprehensive role in the economic development of the Kingdom. These loans are of long duration and they are interest-free to the citizen. Building and industrialization projects could receive loans equivalent to fifty percent of the total cost for each individual. Citizens with industrial licenses are eligible to receive such loans. Their duration is up to fifteen years.

Take for example, the Saudi Industrial Development Fund that was established in 1974. Its purpose was to support and promote the development of private industry in the Kingdom. The fund contributed extensively by providing medium term loans and the necessary advisory services to many local manufacturers. By January, 1984 over 600 indus-

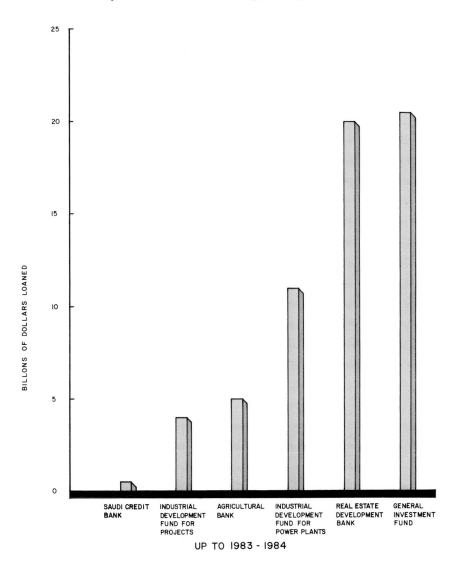

UP TO 1983 - 1984

LOANS GRANTED BY VARIOUS
FUNDING AGENCIES AND BANKS

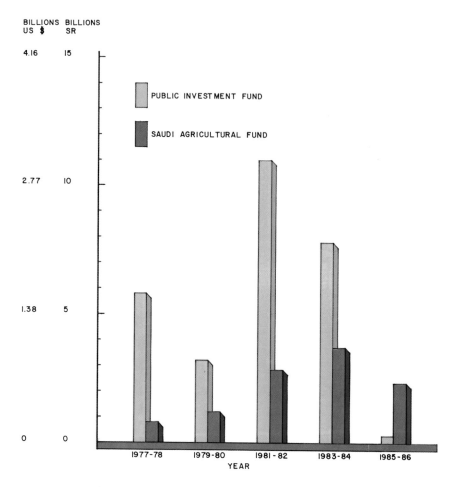

BILLIONS BILLIONS
US $ SR

PUBLIC INVESTMENT FUND

SAUDI AGRICULTURAL FUND

YEAR

CREDITS BY VARIOUS FUND ORGANIZATIONS

trial projects were operational that were supposed to be funded by the Industrial Fund.

Loans from the Real Estate Development Fund (REDF) increased from nearly one billion Saudi Riyals in 1974–75 to about nine billion Saudi Riyals in 1983–1984. For the Saudi Industrial Development Fund (SIDF), the loans increased substantially to 5.2 billion Saudi Riyals in the same period. The Public Investment Fund (PIF) gives credit to the public or semi-public corporate sector of the economy. It extended nearly six billion Saudi Riyals in 1977–1978 and the loans increased

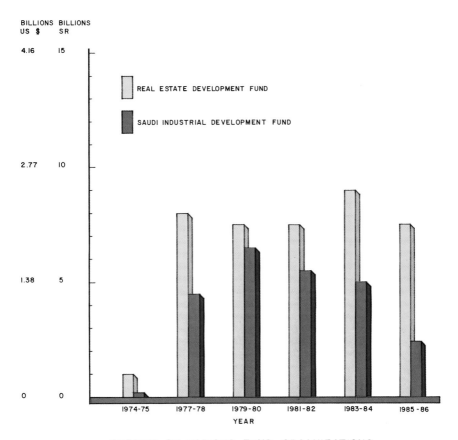

BILLIONS BILLIONS
US $ SR

4.16   15

REAL ESTATE DEVELOPMENT FUND

SAUDI INDUSTRIAL DEVELOPMENT FUND

2.77   10

1.38   5

0   0

        1974-75   1977-78   1979-80   1981-82   1983-84   1985-86
                                        YEAR

CREDITS BY VARIOUS FUND ORGANIZATIONS

to nearly 11 billion in 1981–1982 moving to 8.1 billion in 1983–1984. The credit dispersed by the various public financial institutions showed a very steep growth from a miniscule sum of 16 million Saudi Riyals in 1969–1970 to the staggering figure of about 26 billion Saudi Riyals in the year 1983–1984. Cumulative credit given by all financial institutions until the middle of 1984 totaled nearly 184 billion Saudi Riyals.

Modernization and Industrialization Boom

This parade of progress covered all sectors of the economy. The achievements speak for themselves, in numbers and diagrams. Previously on other pages, achievements in the education field and the oil sector were vividly presented. Here other aspects of this fabulous progress are portrayed.

Transport

This category includes modern highways, paved and unpaved roads, airports, seaports, railroads, bus transport, telephone, telegraph and post.

Roads

The road network connects the four corners of the Kingdom with modern expressways complete with various types of interchanges reminiscent of the most modern highways that you will encounter in Western Europe or most of America. In 1970 the total road network was about 17,000 kilometers. Now, the Kingdom has 81,881 kilometers of roads both paved and unpaved. The paved roads are in excess of 30,000 kilometers. The asphalted roads were about 8,500 kilometers in 1970. They increased at an average rate of 10.8 percent, while agricultural roads were developed at a faster pace, averaging an increased rate of 21.6% annually.

Modern highways are dotted with rest areas, trees, vegetation and manicured lawns as they approach various cities and villages. Care has been taken to protect the environment and animals of the desert, be it sheep, goat, camel or others so that they will have crossing paths at various intervals of major highways. The transportation infrastructure received special attention because of the major role it plays in the further development of the economy and the society. Cities and villages of the country are easily reached by modern roads. Maintenance of these roads continues at the proper level of efficiency and expertise. A national company was established to tend to services along these highways, so that it will build at specific designated distances modern facilities for lodging, restaurants, emergency services and industrial maintenance along with telephone communications, helicopter sites, and security zones. The company involved in this task is a public national company. The government granted them land at no cost. Also generous loans were made available. These modern roads became very useful to the pilgrims and to the Saudi citizen and his family. On the road, they find special places for rest along with modern facilities. There are gardens planted and manicured in various parts of this network of highways. Like many other projects, results in these areas were sought and realized at a rapid pace.

The rural road network continues to develop and make progress. Nearly eight billion Saudi Riyals were spent on this network of asphalted roads. They were built in difficult terrain and bridges were

Modern highways and modern traffic.

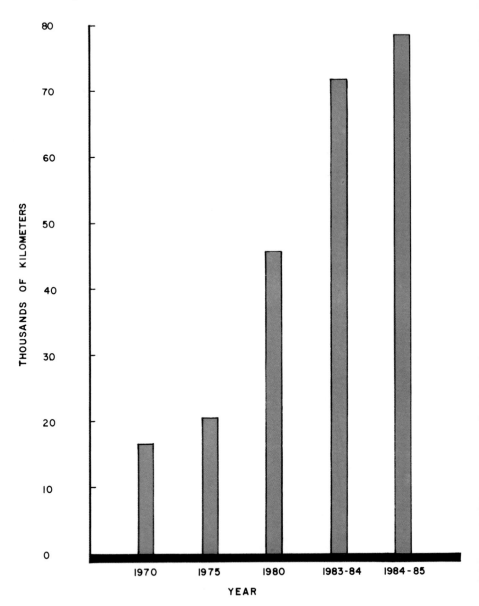

HIGHWAY NETWORK CONSTRUCTION
(PAVED AND UNPAVED)

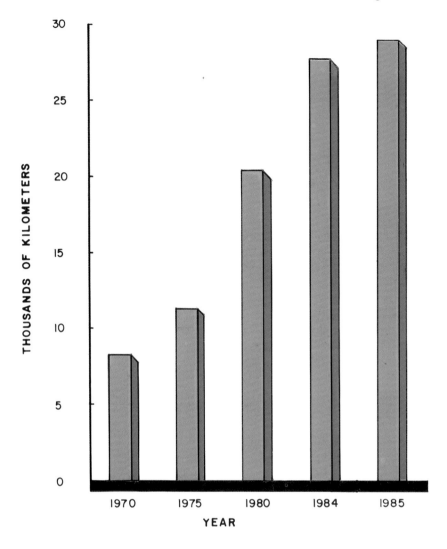

PAVED ROADS

used where needed. Traffic jams around major cities were solved via bridging or bypassing through city belts. Also there are modern roads connecting the Kingdom with its neighbors, such as the Arab Republic of Yemen and the road connecting the Kingdom with Kuwait. Two roads connect with Jordan. One road connects with Qatar; it extends to the United Arab Emirates and the Sultanate of Oman.

The giant bridge or causeway connecting the Kingdom with Bahrain has been completed. A joint company supervises the operation of the mammoth causeway. On November 11, 1982, the cornerstone of the bridge was jointly placed by King Fahd and the ruler of Bahrain, Sheikh Issa Bin Salman Al-Khalifa. It is considered as one of the major projects built by the Kingdom of Saudi Arabia. It is, essentially, a four-lane highway; two lanes in each direction with one lane for emergency in both directions. It is 25 meters in width and about 25 kilometers in length. This causeway has many bridges; their total length is 12.5 kilometers. Presently the bridge is being connected with a network of major highways. At one time 2,000 workers, specialists and engineers worked on it. The bridge cost 800 million dollars. This sum was entirely paid by the Saudi Arabian government in accordance with its policy of increasing cooperation and welfare among the Gulf Cooperation Council (GCC). This project will increase trade between the Kingdom and Bahrain. The bridge was technically finished on April 26, 1986, after nearly five years of work. A commentary by the Saudi State Radio said; "It is a dream come true! It will have economic and social benefits to the entire Gulf region that will dwarf all the money spent on it." The fifteen minute drive across the bridge shortened the commuting distance between Manama in Bahrain to Riyadh in Saudi Arabia, Kuwait city in Kuwait and Doha in Qatar to a trip of three hours. After negotiations that went on-and-off for many years, this project is finally a reality with important social and political implications.

Airports

The Kingdom built 23 airports connecting various regions of the Kingdom and giving easy access to various countries of the international community. Three of these airports are international in nature, competing in size, modern services and quality with the best airports in the world. The three international airports are: King Khaled International Airport on the outskirts of Riyadh, King Abdulaziz International Airport near Jeddah, and The International Airport in Dhahran in the eastern region.

In 1976 the airports had less than four million passengers. In 1982, over eight million international passengers were handled. While in the year 1969–70, the arrivals to Saudi Arabian airports were about two million passengers, in 1982–1983 they were around 12 million.

The Kingdom's National Carrier is called Saudia. It was established in 1945 with a gift of one Douglas DC-3 Dakota. This was given by President Franklin D. Roosevelt to His Majesty King Abdulaziz. From this tiny nucleus, the leading airline in the Middle East was born. It is well known for its efficiency, safety and punctuality. In 1986, the airline carried twelve million passengers, compared to only a meager

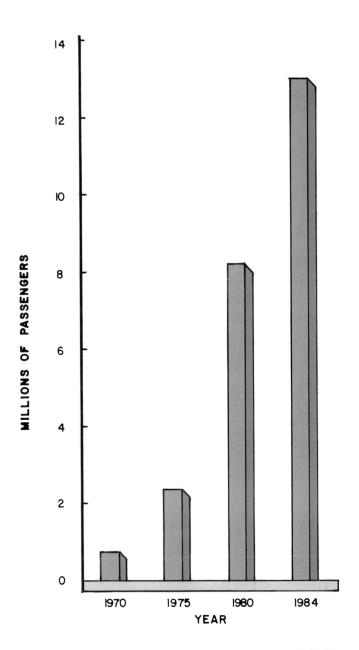

ARRIVALS AT AIRPORTS

number of 53,000 in 1953. Saudia is a pride of the Kingdom of Saudi
Arabia. It has one of the most modern fleets in the airline industry.
By the end of 1985, sixty-two of these were large bodied aircraft. Ten
of them are Boeing 747. Saudia's fleet was 28 planes in 1975. By early
1986 it had 103 aircrafts.

Seaports

They play an important role in opening gates to the outside world
through import and export. In order to respond to the vast needs of
the various development plans, especially in handling the necessary
cargo, development of seaports was a basic necessity. A tremendous
volume of goods and products coming to the country made it imperative
to develop and expand seaports. The leading ones are: The Jeddah
Islamic Port, King Abdulaziz Port in Dammam, Jubail Commercial Port,
King Fahd Industrial Port in Jubail, Yanbu Port and Jizan Port. These
ports have 133 piers. The largest two being the Jeddah port and the
port in Dammam, having respectively 45 and 39 piers. The expansion
of seaports was extensive, having the capability of handling 135 ships
at one time. It is possible to unload 65 million tons of dead weight
per year. This competes with the largest seaports in the world. The
cost was about 43 billion Saudi Riyals.

Seaports in the Kingdom are among the most modern and sophisticated in the entire world. They serve as a major corridor for the nation's
active trade with the outside world.

Concentrated attention is given to human resources, especially on-
the-job training for the Saudis, who are presently managing seaports
in the Kingdom. Some of the major seaports have modern locomotives
that are equipped with specially designed features making them capable
of anchoring ships, controlling fire hazard and pollution of the sea
by oil along with rescuing stray ships. These locomotives also have
the latest in telecommunications, equipment and technology.

While the overall handling capacity of seaports in the Kingdom
was around two million tons in 1970, it had risen very sharply to 49
million tons in 1984. The number of piers increased from 27 in 1975
to 133 in 1984.

Railroads

A major railroad connects Riyadh and Dammam. It is 562 kilometers
in length. The railways system is being expanded and made more
efficient through the General Railway Organization. The new dual line
connecting the Eastern Region with Riyadh has been built. It reduces
travel time from seven hours previously, to three and a half hours.
While the number of passenger-kilometers was about 39 million in

1970 it has increased to 76 million passenger-kilometers in 1984. This represented an average annual growth of about six percent. Still the number of those traveling by railroads is modest, increasing from 117,000 to 187,000 in the same period. The railroad freight in ton-kilometers increased from 34 million in 1970 to nearly 1,100 million in 1984. This represented an average annual growth of about 26%.

Bus Transport
A Saudi public transport company was founded in 1979. It carried 146 million passengers in 1982–83. This is compared to 119 million passengers in the previous year. A fleet of seven hundred buses gives a needed service to the commuter and helps in reducing traffic jams and congestion in major cities. It also provides efficient transport facilities for the pilgrims visiting the Holy places in the Kingdom.

Telephone, Telegraph and Post
From a very humble beginning in the late 60's and early 70's, the Kingdom made miraculous achievements in this area of communication. Telephone services have received fantastic improvement in quality and reliability. Not only are you able to call anywhere in the Kingdom, but, essentially, the world is at your fingertip. In a matter of seconds you can connect with both major world centers and small towns. The service is so good that in many instances it far surpasses the best telephone systems anywhere in the industrialized nations of the world. In 1985 the number of working telephones in the Kingdom reached nearly one million telephone lines. The expansion of telephone lines in Saudi Arabia has truly been phenomenal. While the exchange capacity was about 77,000 in 1970, it was over 1.2 million in 1985, with an average annual growth of over 26%. The cities and villages served are over 300. The countries linked with the Kingdom are 154. The number of mobile telephones is over 8,000 and their capacity is 20,000. These are served by 50 wireless stations.

The network of local communication is supplemented with an advanced international network of communication including four earth stations for communication via satellites for the International Organization of Space Communication (Intnsat). Two of these stations are in Riyadh and the third is in Taif. The total capacity of these stations is about 3,000 telephone circuits through which communication is facilitated with most countries of the world. Also, through these, television programs are broadcast by the Kingdom to the outside world, especially to the Islamic countries on special religious occasions. It is connected to brotherly nations with a network of cables and microwaves. It absorbs about 30% of the cost for the Arab satellite (Arabsat). It has built an

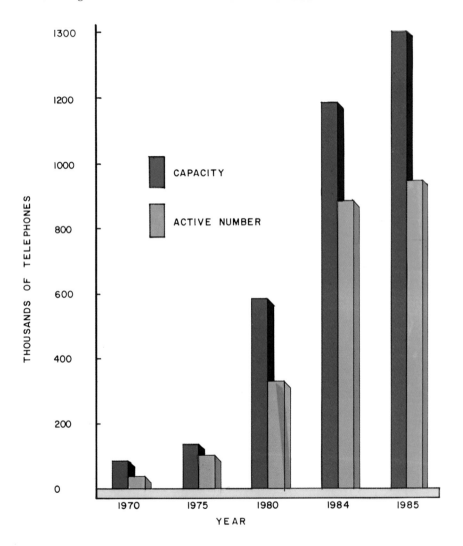

TELEPHONE COMMUNICATION

earth station to receive and transmit from the Arab satellite which was put into orbit in 1985. The same year, it was used to transmit the Hajj procession to the Islamic world, live on the air.

Telex services have also expanded and a network is now in operation with 30,000 lines serving 129 cities and villages. Subscribers are around 17,000. The incoming telegrams increased from 43 million words in 1970 to over 100 million words in 1984. The outgoing telegrams increased from nearly 50 million words in 1970 to 145 million words in 1984.

The expansion rate and modernization of the telecommunication system is truly unmatched anywhere in the world. Local and international services are excellent. The Arab communication satellite (Arabsat) improved the telecommunication between Saudi Arabia and the Arab World.

The postal service realized tremendous improvement both in quality and reliability since the early 70's. A giant leap forward was realized by introducing the most modern methods and equipment; especially automatic handling and separation of mail, including the zip code for a number of Saudi cities. In line with other modern nations, the Kingdom added the special postal service where a letter would be received in the same day. This is similar to what one would encounter through an express service in the United States of America. The growth of the postal service is very impressive, making services available to over six hundred centers of population. Riyadh, Jeddah and Dammam have major post office complexes.

Information (Television, Radio and Press)

Impressive strides have been made in the mass media sector. The television studios in Riyadh are among the most modern in the world. The television tower graces the majestic and huge marble building of the Ministry of Information. The government operates two major television stations, one in Arabic and another in English. News is televised in Arabic, English and French. The Eastern Region of the Kingdom is capable of receiving several stations from the neighboring Gulf countries, including stations from as far away as Iraq and Iran. The Kingdom has 37 radio transmission stations with ten television relay stations and nine mobile television stations, along with five temporary television stations.

A good number of daily newspapers and weekly magazines are now published throughout the Kingdom. At least three major newspapers are in English. Some of these have a wide circulation on the international scene, especially Europe and the Arab World. Tremendous progress in this sector gave the Kingdom a good capability for disseminating and gathering local and international news and information. One should remember that television was introduced to the Kingdom just over 20 years ago. Its impact on the people is wide and universal.

It is only fitting and natural for the Kingdom of Saudi Arabia to be in the *forefront of exhibitors at the World's Fair* for communications and transport, Expo 86 held in Vancouver, Canada. The Kingdom's pavillion is a reflection of its fine achievements in this sector. It is the only Arab country represented alongside 54 other nations.

Visitors to the Fair were very much impressed with the spectacular progress. Among them were Prince Charles and Lady Diana of England, who inaugurated the opening of the International Fair.

Around the same time, the Kingdom was well represented at the International Paris Fair in Paris, France. The Saudi pavillion was a great success. Among its first visitors was Jacques Chirac, the French Prime Minister, who inaugurated its opening. He expressed his admiration for what he saw as testimonials to formidable progress.

The Kingdom takes pride in sharing the story of its modernization and culture with the rest of the world community.

Agriculture

Agriculture and water supply received special attention in the development plans. Recently the Kingdom of Saudi Arabia gave 50,000 tons from its local production of wheat to help the hungry in Sudan and Bangladesh along with another 50,000 tons of foodstuffs, medicine and clothing. Special attention given to agriculture is in line with the policy of diversifying the economic base. About half the Kingdom's population lives in rural areas. Many of them work in agriculture. It is strategically important to increase good production for the increasing numbers in the population.

The government encourages the farmers by granting agricultural land and giving interest-free loans. The Agricultural Bank contributed extensively in this regard. The General Organization for Grain Elevators and Flour Mills buys the wheat from the farmers with an encouraging price that is subsidized by the government. The agricultural sector achieved an average increase of 8.7% during the Five-Year Plan 1980–1985. For the same period, the non-petroleum sector increased by 5.1%. Generous support by the government for the agricultural sector materialized as follows:

• Payment up to 50% of expenses for fertilizer.
• Payment up to 50% of the animal feed.
• Supporting potato production by allowing the farmer to have five tons free and after that paying 1,000 Riyals for every ton with a maximum of 15 tons.
• Equipment for poultry and dairy absorbed up to 30% of the cost.
• Equipment and pumps up to 50% of the cost.
• Transport of animals by airplanes absorbing 100% of the cost.

The Agricultural Bank, the Saudi Credit Bank and the Agricultural Development Fund provided finances to the farmers. For the period 1975–1985 the small and medium term loans to the farmer exceeded

Irrigation, wheat production and green fields, are vivid pictures of a changing landscape.

42 billion dollars. In the Five-Year Plan 1980–1985, the government allotted twenty one billion dollars to agriculture which became a fast growing part of the economy. The total number of loans granted by the Agriculture Bank back in 1984 reached 278,000 with a total value of seventeen billion riyals. Between 1970 and 1984 the government distributed 559,000 hectares of land to the populace.

Fertilizer production has risen very steeply from 24.4 thousand tons in 1970 to 863.2 thousand tons in 1984. The average annual increase is 19.4%. A good portion of fertilizer production is exported to other countries.

The government encouraged the production of wheat, paying two riyals per kilogram, beginning in 1985. Previously the payment was 3.5 riyals per kilogram. In the four years between 1981 and 1985, the government spent four and a half billion riyals in agricultural aid.

In the decade between 1975 and 1985, the land under cultivation increased by over 1,300%. In this period wheat production increased by 400 times. One of the shining achievements in the third development plan is the production of wheat. It reached nearly two million tons in 1986. This is almost twice the amount needed for local consumption. Saudi Arabia, basically a desert land, became an exporter of wheat. Also, poultry and meat production increased threefold. Egg and dairy production doubled. Thus, the Kingdom became self-sufficient in meat, poultry, eggs, dairy products and began to export to the international market: wheat, dates, certain vegetables and fruits.

The silos' storage capacity increased from 40,000 tons in 1977 to nearly 900,000 tons in 1984. Advanced irrigation systems and modern mechanization were used. The tremendous increase in the production of vegetables, fruits and cereals led to exporting a good portion of it. Citrus production registered a good increase from 13,000 tons in 1969–1970 to 48,000 in 1983–84. In the same period, grape production increased from 24,000 tons to 60,000 tons. The main product of the Kingdom, namely dates, increased very remarkably from 240,000 tons to half a million tons.

As far as livestock is concerned, red meat production increased from 14,000 tons in 1979 to 28,000 tons in 1982. White meat production increased from 58,000 tons to 108,000 tons in the same period of time. The government continues its subsidies to private agricultural projects with equipment and machinery, so that more land will be brought under cultivation.

The generosity of the Kingdom extends far beyond its limits. It has granted 260 million dollars to the International Fund for Agricultural Development (IFAD), so that 130 projects in nearly 80 developing countries would be financed. In the decade between 1975 and 1985 over 210 million dollars were donated to the international food program.

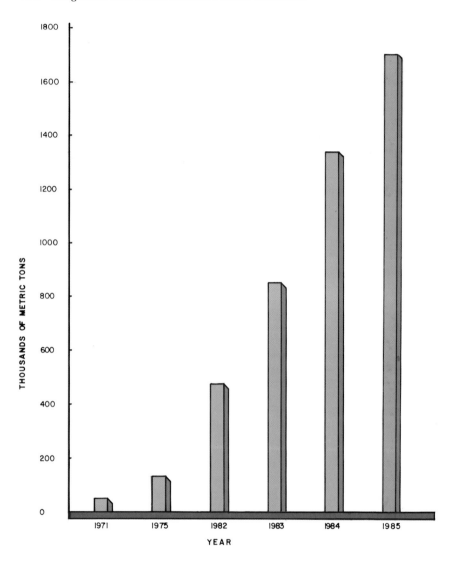

WHEAT PRODUCTION

About 42,000 tons of dates were given in the last three years, and thousands of tons of wheat were given to other nations in need. In the summer of 1986, Egypt was grateful for receiving 200,000 tons of wheat surplus from its sister country, Saudi Arabia.

On November 9, 1984, the Food and Agricultural Organization in Rome, Italy, acknowledged these achievements in agriculture by giving an award to the Kingdom's Ministry of Agriculture and Water.

Water

A desert-land like Saudi Arabia would place prime importance on the availability of water without which cultural or industrial progress could not be made. The government worked diligently to make drinking water available to all the population. It gave a position of priority to the distribution of water to the various regions of the Kingdom. The Kingdom occupies a prominent position in water desalination. It is a

King Fahd inaugurating a water desalination plant.

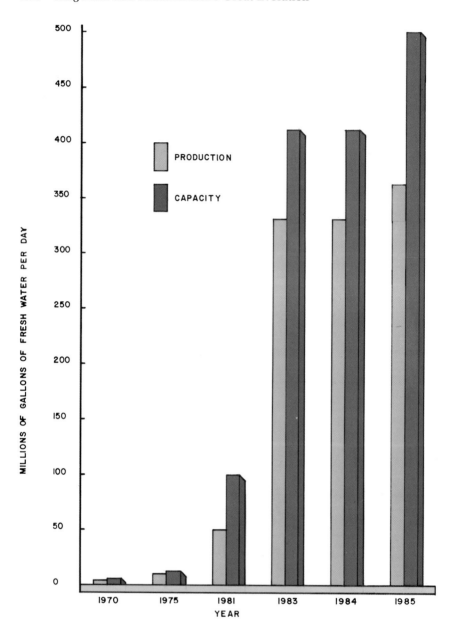

SALINE WATER CONVERSION

world leader in producing fresh water from saline water. It has over thirty desalination stations on the shores of the Arabian Gulf and the Red Sea.

Scientific studies show that nearly two-thirds of the Kingdom's surface is of sedimentary rock-beds that contain a number of acquifers. These acquifers complement other sources of water.

The Kingdom built many dams. One of these is the biggest in the Middle East, built in the region of Bisha in the southern part of the Kingdom. These dams collect water from the occasional rainfalls. The capacity of the dams is 650 million cubic meters. Under consideration are three large dams with a collective storage capacity of 56 million cubic meters. These are to be built at Wadi Aradab, Wadi Bisha and Wadi Khulays.

The water distribution network had 2,200 kilometers in 1975. It increased about tenfold by 1984 to 20,000 kilometers. Water desalination capacity was about ten million gallons per day in 1975. In a decade, it increased to five hundred million gallons per day by 1985. This is a jump of fiftyfold. Again, while there were sixteen dams in 1975, by the end of 1984 there were 170. This is an increase of more than ten times, a staggering growth and a record achievement never matched in any other nation in the world!

Certain urban areas receive water from very distant places. The capital city of Riyadh receives substantial amounts of fresh water, nearing 300,000 cubic meters per day, from the Jubail Desalination Project on the Arabian Gulf. Underground water supplements this source. The

A typical dam in the Kingdom.

city of Jeddah relies heavily on water desalination projects that supply the city with 350,000 cubic meters per day. This represents about 90% of the total supply. Taif and Mecca are supplied with 152,000 cubic meters of fresh water per day. The Eastern Province has desalination plants. The Asir region receives a supply from the Red Sea. The Ministry of Agriculture and Water implements projects for serving distant villages and towns in the Kingdom.

Industrial Development

The Kingdom embarked on gigantic projects for massive industrial development. Basic to an industrialization boom are the availability of reliable sources of energy, mainly electrical energy. When oil and gas are abundant and within easy reach financially and when a coupling of the latest in international technology is made with long-range planning, wisdom, dedication and the technology acquired by the natives, then all the ingredients are there to succeed. That is exactly what is behind the success story in industrialization for the Kingdom of Saudi Arabia and in diversifying the economic base.

Electrical Energy Supply

Aside from the basic need for industrialization, electrical energy is a public utility that brings comfort and services to the basic needs of the citizens. Thus, the Saudi government generously supported this sector of the economy with a goal of having an abundant supply of electrical energy for industry and all Saudi citizens everywhere.

The Saudi Industrial Development Fund was very generous in its loans to the various electrical companies. This gave the impetus for building the necessary power stations. The availability of abundant sources of cheap oil and gas also were a great incentive.

General electric power increased seventeenfold from about 1.8 billion kilowatt-hours to 31 billion kilowatt-hours in a decade. The number of electrical subscribers increased from nearly 400,000 in 1976 to over 1,500,000 in 1984. Essentially, electrical power was within reach for all Saudis. Total loans by the Saudi Industrial Development Fund for power generation reached 38.9 billion riyals by 1983. The phenomenal growth of installed electric capacity increased by an average of 32% per year from 418 megawatts (MW) in 1970 to nearly 14,600 megawatts in 1984. The amount of electric power used increased along the same rate from 344 megawatts in 1970 to over 11,800 megawatts in 1984.

King Fahd renders special personal attention to development projects, especially electrical power generation because electricity is a service of great importance touching the lives of average citizens

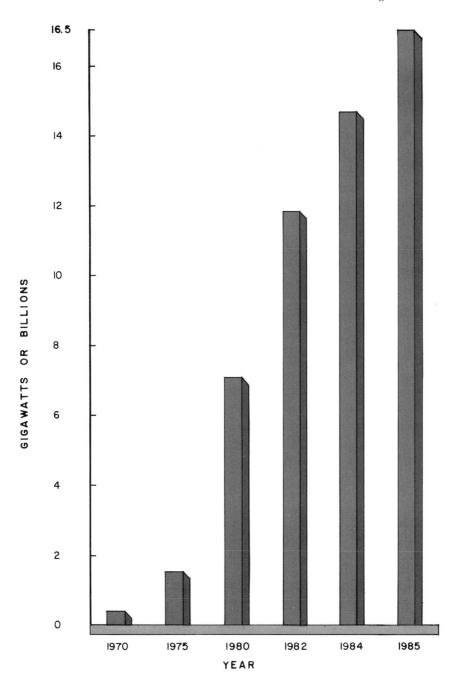

ELECTRICAL ENERGY SUPPLY

everywhere. His directives were to make electricity available everywhere in the cities, villages and far away settlements. Recently he ordered a decrease in the cost of electricity to the ordinary citizen so that every Saudi will derive optimum benefit from it with minimum cost. A push toward power generation and rural electrification continues. As early as March, 1986, King Fahd inaugurated the eighth station in the capital, Riyadh. It is considered among the biggest electrical generating stations in the world with a production capacity of 800 megawatts, which will increase to 1,000 megawatts. The station covers an area of nearly 600,000 square meters. The cost is nearly one and a half billion Saudi Riyals.

Manufacturing Plants

The industrial expansion of the non-oil sector was remarkable. The government played a key role in developing the basic hydrocarbon industries and the private sector has done its share in building other industrial projects. The number of licensed factories was 207 in 1970. It increased to 3,252 in 1984. In the same period, operating plants rose from 207 to over 1,600. This number reached over 1,800 by 1986. The decade between 1975 and 1985 witnessed the fastest rate of growth for the industrial sector of the economy.

The Saudi Basic Industries Corporation (Sabic) expanded its global distribution network to improve its marketing strategy and wide reach in service to customers around the world. It is a backbone of the Kingdom's industrialization drive and diversification of the economic base.

Sabic was created as a basic umbrella having joint ventures with various companies on a 50–50 basis. Possible partners were recruited based on established expertise. Many American firms such as Mobil, Shell, Exxon, Cales, and Texas Eastern were all recruited along with a consortium of Japanese firms led by Mitsubishi.

Sabic brought into reality eleven basic industries since it was first formed in 1976. These industries include massive projects in the metal sector, fertilizer and petrochemicals as well. It leases eleven warehousing facilities in five countries overseas for its liquid and dry product exports. It also has three domestic warehouses and leases some others. Two additional dry storage facilities are to be leased in Europe and for the first time, one will be leased in the United States of America, with one new liquid product warehouse in the Mediterranean and two in the Far East. Sabic exports manufactured products in the Kingdom to its affiliate companies around the world and covers a wide range of products including: polyethyene, urea, methanol, ethylene dichloride, crude industrial ethanol, styrene, caustic soda, ethylene glycol, melamine, steel rods and bars. Also, polyvinyl chloride (PVC) and

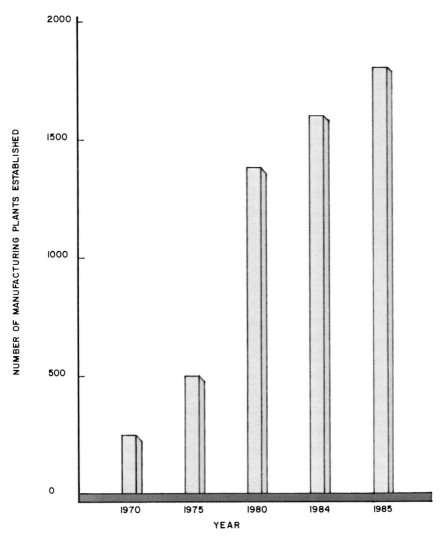

MANUFACTURING PLANTS

polystyrene. Sabic competes on equal footing with major chemical companies of the world. Its main arsenal is providing excellent service to customers while selling top quality products. Its wide international distribution network is the result of hard labor that began in 1980. A maze of joint-ventures with American and Japanese companies help in transporting Sabic's products to world markets.

The revenue from petrochemical exports during the first ten months of 1985 was two billion Saudi Riyals. When all the plants are operational at full capacity, they are expected to add to the national treasury a sum in excess of ten billion Saudi Riyals each year. This will achieve one of the main goals of establishing this industry by adding credible value to the crude hydrocarbon resources.

In the span of a decade, the industrial output increased over thirty-fold. While 1970 production was worth 85 million dollars, Saudi industries in 1983 sold goods worth more than four billion dollars. This was realized because of the tremendous support received from building the basic infrastructure in the First and Second Five-Year Plans. Also, because of the commitment and deep involvement of the government in many ways, especially, with the Saudi Industrial Development Fund. This fund financed more than one thousand projects in that period at a cost exceeding ten billion dollars. Industrial centers were built near a number of Saudi cities, among them Riyadh, Jeddah, Kasim, Dammam, Hofuf and Hasa.

To encourage domestic products, contractors were required to buy locally-produced goods and services that would be worth at least 30% of their contract. This guaranteed that 30% of the value of all contracts given by the government would be put back into further development in the Kingdom. Sabic, through joint ventures, made available partners

One of over 1,800 plants now operating in Saudi Arabia.

with advanced technology and management practices for such capital intensive industries as petrochemicals, steel and fertilizers. In the industrial cities of Jubail and Yanbu, Sabic ventures were built from ground zero.

The Industrial Cities of Jubail and Yanbu

The Royal Commission for Jubail and Yanbu is truly the moving force behind the realization of these massive industrial sites of the twentieth century. King Fahd said, "If it wasn't for the Royal Commission for Jubail and Yanbu, we could not have had these gigantic industries that were built in these two cities." The commission was established in 1975 and it was delegated the responsibility to carry forward the development of the two cities and industries in Jubail and Yanbu. A major function was to support investments in the industrial sector and to help light industries as well, along with developing departments and organizations that would furnish civil services. It also carried the responsibility of developing and accomplishing training programs so that Saudis will be better prepared for these jobs. The headquarters for the commission is in Riyadh. It operates as an independent agency directly under the chairmanship of King Fahd.

These two industrial cities encompass some of the most important industrial complexes in the world today. Jubail is a city with an area of 900 square kilometers. It was designed to accommodate 350,000 people. Yanbu, on the Red Sea, has an area of 150 square kilometers. It is designed to accommodate a population of 150,000. Many basic industries are in operation in these cities; others are in the building stage. The Royal Commission spent over eight billion Saudi Riyals for infrastructure projects that included the construction of roads, housing units, hospitals, schools and water networks. A number of other projects for the two cities will be completed at an additional cost of several billion Saudi Riyals.

The two cities are indeed a shining example of the tremendous industrial progress achieved by the Kingdom of Saudi Arabia. "Undertaken during the last decade, the projects of Jubail and Yanbu stand as landmarks to Saudi Arabia's transition to the industrial age and toward international competition. They were constructed on what was essentially waste land, using the most advanced concepts in urban planning and employing the most efficient production technologies."

Industrialization in Jubail and Yanbu turned the waste gas that had accompanied oil production operations into a very useful source, instead of being wasted and burned just to dispose of it. Gas fueled the industry and was the major source of feedstock for the petrochemical industry. Prior to that, burning this gas in the atmosphere was a big waste and an environmental health hazard.

Transforming the Kingdom from a nation merely extracting and exporting oil, to a nation producing high quality finished products, helped create jobs and boost the income of the workers. Complete factories were built in Japan and Europe, dismantled and then shipped to the Kingdom for reassembly. A gigantic building process was under way. At one time, the mammoth project of the twin industrial cities was employing a skilled labor force in excess of 100,000 people. By any standards, it is a Herculean task and a gigantic accomplishment!

The industrial city of Jubail was chosen to be on the Arabian Gulf close to the mineral resources of the Kingdom in the Eastern Region. The industrial city of Yanbu was located on the Red Sea to be closer to western markets. It is supplied by gas and oil through 1,200 kilometers of pipelines that run across the country from east to west. Eleven industries were founded by Sabic, using feedstocks of liquid gas for the production of petrochemicals. A host of other industries will use petrochemicals to make other finished products such as paint, detergents, cosmetics, plastics, insulation materials and more.

The industrial sector includes many small industries that cover a wide spectrum from pipe and pipe coating companies to the fabrication of modern plastic packaging.

The cement industry is an important one for the construction sector. There are eight cement plants that are producing at a total capacity of 9.2 million tons versus half a million tons in 1970. Other projects came on stream in 1985. In early 1986, production capacity has reached over fourteen million tons per year.

The Kingdom has a great abundance of solar energy and extensive research is being done in this area. Also, environmental protection is practiced during this massive industrialization.

The Royal Commission for Jubail and Yanbu was launched September 21, 1975. This event remains unparalleled and unmatched in the annals of industrial development and economic diversification. It was headed by then Crown Prince Fahd. Members include the Ministers of Finance, Economy, Industry, Electricity and Planning.

The commission was assigned the responsibility for the planning, construction and management of the two industrial cities. It immediately established three major objectives. They were:

- Promotion of investment in the industrial sector.
- Development of institutions for providing needed urban services.
- Implementing the training programs so that Saudi youth could develop the needed modern technological skills for the advanced industrialization at Jubail and Yanbu.

Ambitions and dreams became two words intertwined in the Saudi long-range planning and objectives. Ambitions and dreams that came true! The massive development of the infrastructure that grew by leaps and bounds matched the word ambition and the wildest of dreams. The first development plan in 1970–1975 called for only 80 billion Saudi Riyals (21.9 billion dollars). Nowadays, the budget for the Fourth Development Plan, 1985–1990 is one trillion Saudi Riyals (274 billion dollars).

In 1982, government expenditures were 282.3 billion Saudi Riyals which is 26 times higher than it was in 1972 (10.8 billion Saudi Riyals). This is 130 times larger than it was in 1962 when expenditures were merely 2.17 billion Saudi Riyals.

The first implementation of the master plan for the two cities in 1975 set a goal to establish 17 primary industries, 136 secondary, and 100 tertiary by the year 2,000. By the end of 1985, eleven of the primary industries were operational.

When the Jubail industrial project was inaugurated in 1977 it heralded a new era in the modern and industrial history of the Kingdom of Saudi Arabia. But visions, dreams and ambitions become truths as the Kingdom reaches and approaches its goal of industrialization and diversified economic base.

Research

Applied and scientific research is carried on in many sectors located at various Saudi Universities. In November, 1977, the Saudi Arabian National Center for Science and Technology (Sancst) was founded. It has the responsibility of directing and formulating Saudi Arabia's national science policy to promote scientific research. The Kingdom's technological and scientific needs are supported by scientific research developed by these research centers. Joint projects also are carried on with other international scientific centers in the world. The main objectives may be defined as:

- Conducting applied scientific research programs that will serve the social economic development of the nation.
- Establishing and maintaining an information center that collects and disseminates data on scientific and technological manpower resources in the Kingdom.
- Awarding research grants and scholarships to individuals and institutions conducting applied scientific research.
- Providing assistance to the private sector, so that agriculture and industrial research would be further developed.

- Supporting joint research projects between the international scientific community and the Kingdom of Saudi Arabia. Great cooperation was achieved between Sancst and American scientific organizations. One such program was the Saudi Arabian–United States program for cooperation on solar energy. About thirty separate projects have been undertaken since 1979, for conducting solar energy experiments in the U.S. and the Kingdom.

In 1986 this was renamed King Abdulaziz Scientific City.

A major Research Institute (RI), which is an independent center affiliated with King Fahd University of Petroleum and Minerals (KFUPM), has conducted solar research since 1977. This Research Institute carried on a variety of other research projects responding to the needs and long range goals of the Kingdom. This impressive institute has the most modern scientific equipment and latest in computer technology. It has about one hundred laboratories. Since the late 60's, KFUPM scientists have been investigating water desalination, hydrogen production and solar cooling.

An agreement was signed in 1983 between the National Aeronautics and Space Administration (NASA) and Sancst for cooperation in space related research. This cooperation helped in mapping programs, ground water exploration and sand drift monitoring. The General Electric company was granted a contract to supply and install a remote sensing facility station for the reception, processing and analysis of space photos sent by satellite. Joint research agreements are made. Notable among these is the one with the Canadian National Research Council.

Cooperation on scientific research and technology between the United States of America and the Kingdom of Saudi Arabia led to the Discovery Space Mission that included the first Arab Astronaut ever into space. On June 24, 1985, the U.S. Space Shuttle Discovery landed at Edwards Air Force Base in California after completing its seven-day successful mission into space. Among the proud crew was Prince Sultan Bin Salman Bin Abdulaziz. As the world rejoiced, Saudi Arabians marked the day with great pride as a milestone in Saudi Arabia's cooperation in science and technology. A scientific team led by the director of the Research Institute from King Fahd University of Petroleum and Minerals worked very closely with Prince Sultan to prepare him for the experiments that were conducted in the space shuttle Discovery. The results of the experiments will provide a wide range of new knowledge, especially in the fields of geology, aerodynamics, oil refining and physiology.

King Fahd called Prince Sultan aboard the shuttle Discovery and said, "We are proud of your mission. It is a great achievement!"

Prince Sultan Bin Salman is the first Arab and Moslem astronaut. He is among his colleagues of the American Discovery Space mission.

Social Justice and Development

The welfare of the Saudi citizen is utmost on the minds of Saudi leaders. The enormous efforts exhibited and the great brain power used in the massive modernization and industrialization of the Kingdom have been basically inspired by the inner drive to realize the most benefit for the Saudi citizen; to bring happiness and peace to him and his family.

With the great leap forward in industrialization and the increase in employment opportunities, employees are protected through a social insurance or employment insurance. The number of those insured in 1973 was 145,000. It jumped to over three million in 1984 and three and half million in 1985. The total number of establishments that were

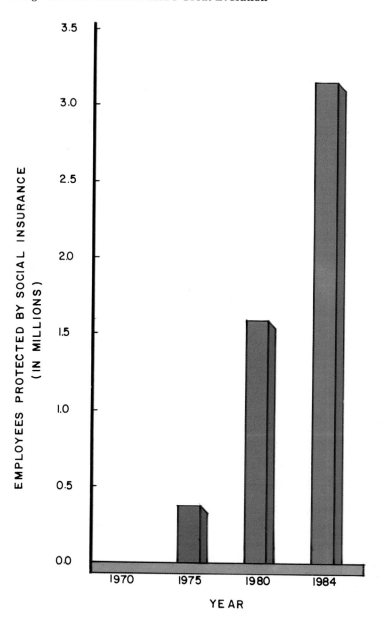

SOCIAL INSURANCE

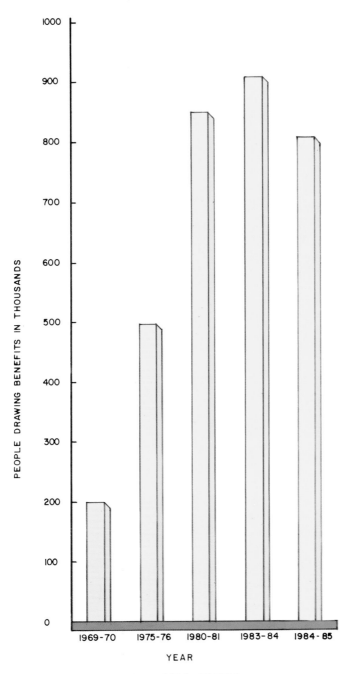

SOCIAL SECURITY

covered by this employment insurance was 1,064 in 1973. It jumped to 12,594 in 1984.

The government guarantees the proper income in case of disability or retirement. In case of death a proper income should be given to the employees' dependents.

Persons suffering from temporary disability or difficult social circumstances, and those stricken by disasters, are afforded a decent standard of living by the government. Pensions are disbursed to these people. The rehabilitation programs for the physically and mentally handicapped are offered along with various other social services. The social security system fills in a basic social need. The total amount given to recipients increased by 33.7% on an annual average, from 41.7 million Saudi Riyals in 1969–1970 to one and a half billion Saudi Riyals in 1983–1984.

The average amount paid per family or case increased from 652 Saudi Riyals in 1969–1970 to over 5,000 Saudi Riyals in 1983–1984.

Housing, Urban and Hajj Developments

Providing adequate and proper care for Saudi citizens has been a central goal of the Saudi government. Large sums of money have been invested in the construction of homes for low income groups. Also, soft-term loans are granted to citizens so that they can build their own homes. Apartment buildings are built by investors. Loans are interest-free and for a long number of years. From 1975 until 1984, 403,000 units were built; out of which 287,000 were built by the private sector, with loans from the Real Estate Development Fund. The Ministry of Public Works and Housing along with the Royal Commission for Jubail and Yanbu, both have built a large number of units. Housing projects specifically built for employees were carried by other government institutions, leading among these are: the National Guard, various universities, Ministry of Defense, Ministry of Interior, and some other ministries. The Real Estate Development Fund extended over 64 billion Saudi Riyals, up to 1984.

Government ministries and many public buildings are among the most majestic and most beautiful in the world. Their unique architecture blends Arab traditions and makes ample use of marble.

Maintaining the Haramein, or the Holy sites in Mecca and Medina, is considered as an honor and a duty. One of the King's official titles is: Custodian of the two Holy Mosques. Since Saudi Arabia is the focal point for all Moslems of the world, special attention has been focused on large and comprehensive expansions of the Holy places. To make the pilgrims' journey to Arabia a safe spiritual experience, large projects requiring substantial sums of money have been accom-

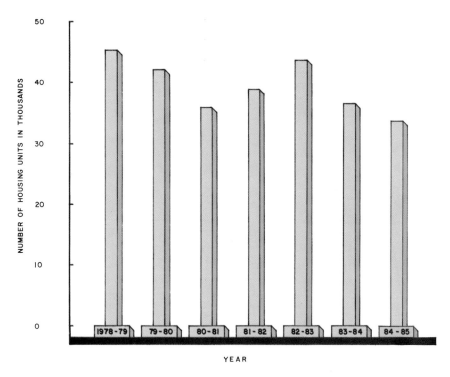

HOUSING FINANCED BY THE SAUDI
REAL ESTATE DEVELOPMENT FUND.

plished in order to bring the proper services to those making the pilgrimage or Hajj. With the expansion of governmental services, an increase in the number of pilgrims was realized from one million in 1970 to two and a half million in 1983. Those coming to Hajj from outside the Kingdom were 431,000 in 1970; they are now over a million. The number of pilgrims increased at an average annual rate of 6.3 percent.

    Those performing the Hajj will be on the increase worldwide due to the increase in Moslem population and also to the continuing economic development in the Moslem world. The Kingdom has done everything possible to bring comfort and peace so that the Hajj would be a memorable experience. Hajj is considered the largest single human gathering in the whole world.

    In accordance with the policy of providing needed services and facilities, twenty tunnels have been dug into the mountains, nineteen bridges and fly-overs for pedestrians were built, along with the construction of one hundred kilometers of multi-lane road network to ease traffic in the Hajj area. Large reservoirs were built to store the water needed by the pilgrims. About forty pilgrim cities were built in various parts of the Kingdom to help accommodate the guests.

The sites at Muna were enlarged to ease the movement of pilgrims. This was done at a cost of six billion Riyals. Enlarging the two Holy Mosques or Haramein, in Mecca and Medina was also done at a cost of seven billion Riyals. Further expansion of the two holy Mosques has begun in 1986. Those expansions will eventually increase the capacity of the Prophet's Mosque in Medina from 28,000 to 170,000 worshippers. The great Mosque in Mecca will be enlarged to accommodate one-and-a-half million worshippers.

Urban Development

The Ministry of Municipal and Rural Affairs, along with supporting agencies, made impressive strides and large investments in the public utilities sector. Water and electrical networks along with sewage and rainwater drainage systems have been built. Municipal services, construction of beautiful public parks, market centers and streets were completed. The total sum of money spent on these services during the first four years of the Third Development Plan was in excess of

Construction of Yesteryears

Modern buildings dot the desert landscape.

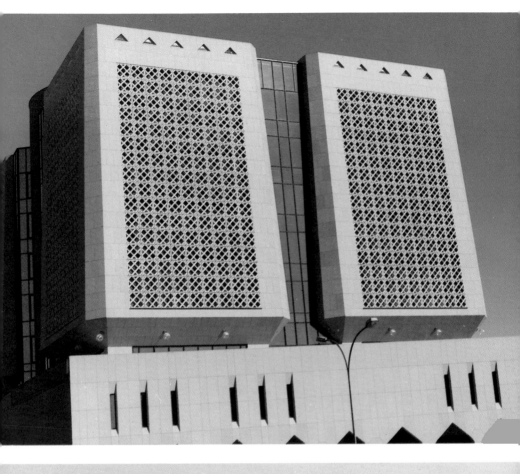

The modern city of Riyadh, capital of Saudi Arabia.

500 billion Saudi Riyals. This development money made the Kingdom's cities and towns flourish and experience an extensive urban development. One travelling across the Kingdom will witness such superb achievements in these cities. This makes them rank among the most modern cities in the world. If one had the chance of visiting these cities, say ten or fifteen years ago, chances are he would not recognize them today. Parks, trees, modern streets, modern buildings and modern services are everywhere.

What a great and dynamic change from just a few years ago! One witnesses progress everywhere: going from Hail, the bride of the north, to Jizan in the south, or from Jeddah, the bride of the Red Sea on the west, to Riyadh, the bride of the desert in central Najd and on to Dhahran, Khobar and Dammam in the east! The procession of progress and great achievements is self-evident and mirrored in the beautiful gardens and polished marble buildings that dot the desert landscape.

Take for example, the city of Riyadh, capital of the Kingdom of Saudi Arabia. It has undergone a profound transformation since the days of Abdulaziz. This is a city with great achievements in development and modernization. Its population is one and a half million served by the largest airport in the world and a marvelous infrastructure. It is truly befitting the stature earned by the Kingdom of Saudi Arabia! A stream of dignitaries and world leaders come and go, witnessing how Saudi Arabia redefined progress for the history of mankind. In 1986 it finished celebrating its fiftieth anniversary as a municipality. It is also fitting to remember that the word Riyadh in Arabic means gardens. Who would believe that Riyadh truly became a garden spot in the heart of the desert? The transformation that has taken place here is exemplary for similar transformations that have been witnessed in many cities covering the four corners of the Kingdom. Much more is yet to come.

Health

A high priority was given to medical services. A very advanced and comprehensive health care system has been developed. Specialized hospitals have been built and equipped with the world's most up-to-date equipment. Some of the specialty treatments are for the eye, heart disorders, kidney, burns, tuberculosis and cancer, along with a host of other diseases.

Take for example, King Khaled Eye Specialist Hospital in Riyadh. It is considered as one of the best equipped hospitals for eyes in the world. It has the most advanced technology for the diagnosis and treatment of eye diseases. It is also the largest. This hospital has 44 doctors, 30 ophthalmologists, 12 camera-equipped operating theatres, a cornea eye-bank and 263 beds. The resident physicians are pioneers in the eye treatment area. Patients come to this hospital from many corners of the world including Spain, Egypt, England and the United States of America.

The American Joint Commission for Accreditation of Hospitals, commended and approved in 1985, the high level of medical performance that is provided by King Khaled Eye Specialist Hospital.

King Faisal Specialist Hospital and Research Center is considered among the most competent and best in the world. An expansion brought its capacity from 240 beds to 450 beds. With a commitment to provide the best medical care for the citizens, the Ministry of Health arranged a surgery exchange program between the well known Baylor College of Medicine in Houston and the hospital in Riyadh. The hospital is managed by the Tennessee based Hospital Corporation of America. The famous heart surgeon, Dr. Michael Debakey, helped in making this arrangement possible. A team from Baylor College of Medicine comes on a rotating basis every three months. By 1984 about three hundred Saudi doctors had gained vast practical experience in cardiovascular surgery.

Many Saudi students come to the United States for training in medical care. Also a number of medical schools exist in the Kingdom. The universities having medical degrees include: King Saud University in Riyadh, King Abdulaziz University in Jeddah and King Faisal University in Dammam. The Abha district also will have a medical college.

King Khaled University Hospital is a teaching hospital within King Saud University Medical School. It has a capacity of 870 beds and 29 specialist clinics. It is staffed with an approximate number of 1,700 medical doctors, nurses and technicians.

King Fahd Medical City in Riyadh is a massive medical complex that includes four major hospitals. These are for: Pediatrics, Maternity, Psychiatry and General care. An estimated staff of 3,000 is housed in a specially built complex. Also included are a burn treatment center and a kidney transplant center.

Another unique feature of the Saudi Arabian health system is the Flying Medical Corps. In this manner health care is made available to people in remote areas of the Kingdom. The flying hospital fleet provides medical care not only to the Armed Forces as it was initially intended, but to all citizens who need it in remote areas of the nation. This fleet includes four helicopters, two Grummans, six C-130 jets, converted into mobile hospitals and a long range DC-8. The transport of operating facilities, modern laboratories, hospital beds and a pharmacy, along with quarters for the doctors and nurses, are features of this program.

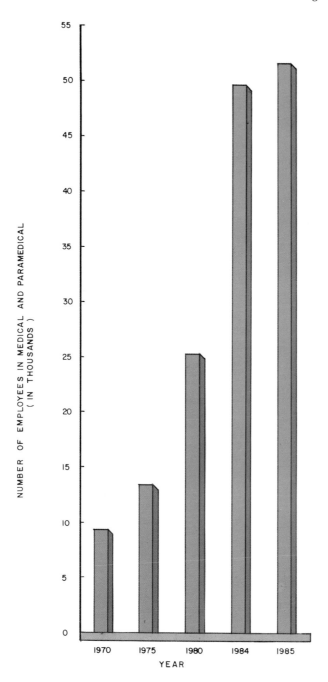

HEALTH SERVICES

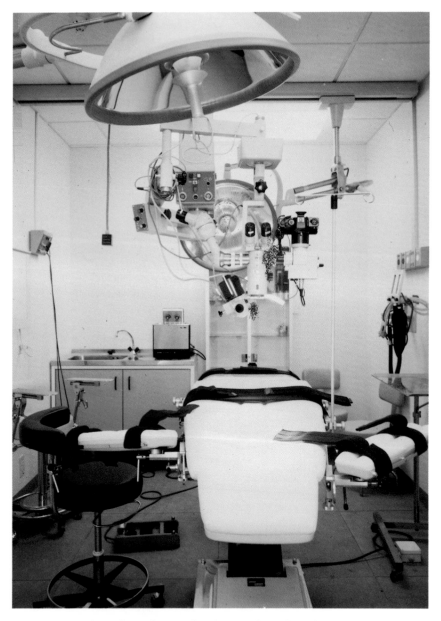

Hospitals with modern technology and good medical services.

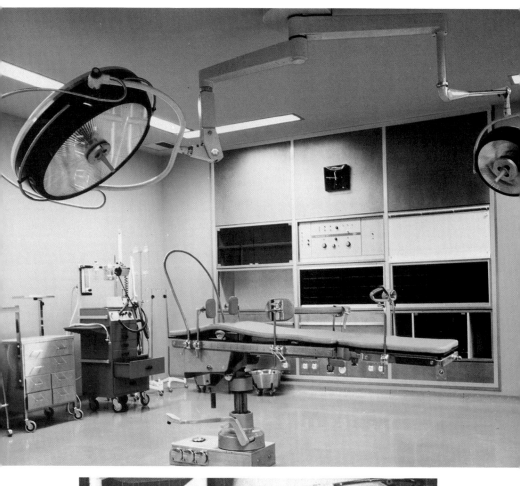

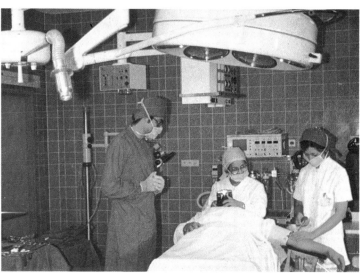

A number of government agencies and ministries provide medical services for their dependents and also for other citizens. These are: the National Guard, Ministry of Interior, Ministry of Defense and some other agencies that run modern hospitals and health centers for their own personnel. Many good hospitals are available across the Kingdom.

The Saudi Red Crescent Society complements the Ministry of Health in first aid, accidents and other emergencies. During the Hajj period, health facilities are made available in cooperation with the Red Crescent.

During the Hajj season of 1985, eleven hospitals were available with a capacity of 2,880 beds, along with 158 health centers.

In the fourth Five-Year Plan, the private sector will play a larger role in the medical field. Twenty more hospitals will be built, along with 1,000 health centers and 100 diagnostic and obstetric centers. The number of professionals and technical personnel will increase to 63,452. There will be at least one physician to serve each 1,000 people.

Hospitals run by the Ministry of Health had 7,165 beds in 1970. This number increased to 15,000 beds in 1984. Total hospital beds in the Kingdom were around 19,000 in 1984. There are 4,000 beds for private hospitals. Health centers increased from 520 to 1,830 in the same period. These are in addition to 120 specialist health centers, such as mother and child care, tuberculosis and quarantine centers.

By 1984–85 the Kingdom had 145 hospitals, 26,410 beds, 2041 primary care health centers and a medical staff of 49,641. The number of physicians was 14,267. The number of hospitals operated by the Ministry of Health was 93. The medical staff increased from 6,174 in 1970 to more than 56,000 in the various categories that include doctors, pharmacists and technicians.

Early in 1988, a unique charity hospital is to be opened on the outskirts of Riyadh. It is especially designed for treatment and research of leukemia and lymphomas in children. It is known as *King Fahd Children's Medical Center and Research Hospital (KFCMC)*. The cost will be 250 million Saudi Riyals or nearly seventy million dollars. The hospital will have an intensive care unit of forty beds and will be equipped with the best and latest specialized medical technology. The most modern laboratories, support facilities, staff housing and engineering support will be provided.

Children will be admitted to KFCMC without regard to ability to pay. KFCMC will guarantee payment of the cost of treatment for any child without other means of support.

Much of the plan for KFCMC was modeled after the well known St. Jude Children's Research Hospital in Memphis, Tennessee, USA.

It will be the only institution in Saudi Arabia devoted exclusively to the treatment and research of childhood leukemia and lymphoma. As such, it will ensure that these children will receive the best care available in the world while, at the same time, participating in the universal search for a better treatment and cure.

The hospital is designed so that most clinical services are centered around an Outpatient Treatment Center. It is estimated that the workload of the medical support units will reach the equivalent of a 600-bed hospital. This charity Research Hospital was founded by Dr. Nasser I. Rashid, co-author of this book, entirely at his own expense after one of his sons was stricken with leukemia.

Specialized major hospitals will be linked to the far corners of the Kingdom. Satellites coupled with the latest computer technology will bring closer to home the latest in medical science and practice.

Youth Welfare

Under the leadership of Faisal Bin Fahd who is the president of Youth Welfare in the Kingdom, great efforts have been made to meet the needs and aspirations of the youth.

The well being of youth in Saudi Arabia is strongly protected by the leaders of the country and especially by King Fahd, who is President of the Higher Council for Youth. His deep interest in their guidance and upbringing is a natural extension of his love as a father and educator. Programs were designed to strengthen the minds, morals and spirits of the young. Basic principles of good behavior, adherence to traditions and respect for fellowman are inherent in many youth activities. In this manner, youth will make a positive contribution to the social and economic development of the Kingdom. In the meantime, religious teachings will strengthen their moral and social traditions. Many creative and sporting outlets were designed and implemented. Sports arenas and athletic programs have been established throughout the nation.

The most modern recreational and sports complexes were built in Jeddah, Dammam, Abha, Hail, Kasim, Riyadh, Al-Khobar, Tabouk and other Saudi cities. Swimming pools, cultural libraries, literary clubs, dormitories, science centers, game centers, arts and crafts also received special attention. The ultra-modern stadium built in Riyadh has a capacity of 100,000 spectators. Sports are popular, especially soccer and basketball.

The General Presidency of Youth Welfare orients young people and supports their interest. It designs an overall global policy to cope with and gainfully use the free time of the youth so that they will be able to take advantage of their talents and potential. Strengthening the bodies and imparting in their souls the profound teachings of Islam along with Arab traditions, are given priority attention.

Every five-year plan incorporated in it an important segment for youth. The first plan mobilized their efforts and concentrated on sports, culture, artistic and social activities. Sports teachers were trained. Many gymnasiums and sports fields were built. The government gave financial support to the various youth clubs. In the second five-year plan the amount of money allotted to the General Presidency for Youth Welfare increased dramatically from 22.3 million Saudi Riyals in 1973–1974 to 142.9 million Saudi Riyals in 1974–1975. In 1976–1977, the numbers jumped to 1,500 million Saudi Riyals. By 1981–1982 the numbers again skyrocketed to nearly two billion Riyals. Thus, recreation and education of the youth were very much strengthened through 192 social and cultural athletic clubs.

National championships are organized by the Sports Federation. The Kingdom is also active on the international scale. Saudi athletes are dynamic and very much inspired to perform well.

In order to enrich the youth with knowledge about their nation, fourteen youth hostels have been built in various regions of the nation.

The Gulf Cooperation Council has Deputy Ministers for Youth and Sports who meet on a regular basis to discuss ways and means of

Sports are popular, especially soccer and basketball.

cooperation and competition. Prince Faisal is very active in this regard both nationally and internationally. From time to time he makes special visits to get better acquainted with what other youths are doing on the international scene. The latest approaches are sought, studied, sometimes adapted and adopted. Faisal Bin Fahd responded to an invitation by the chairman of the Nobel Peace Prize to visit Norway and the city of Stockholm. He met with top leaders of the country and visited sports and recreational facilities along with other youth centers. He closely observed the various programs and sports centers, always seeking to find the best, improve, innovate and implement.

Saudi youth are the Kingdom's treasure and its bright hope for the future.

Conclusion

King Fahd continues his mission for progress and modernization. The procession of miraculous achievements goes on. Today Saudi Arabia is a modern nation in every sense of the word. What has been achieved is unmatched, certainly in this century, and for that matter, in the history of man. The speed with which it has been achieved and the high standards that have been applied gave fantastic results that one would normally see in dreams, not reality.

The Kingdom continues to seek the best talent in the world. It actively seeks joint ventures with a number of experienced and proven companies, be it from Japan, West Germany, Europe or the United States of America. In doing so, the Saudis are not looking for capital injection, because capital is available in the Kingdom. What is really sought is more know-how and the best technology.

On a recent visit to the Kingdom the Japanese Foreign Trade and Industry Minister said, "This is my first visit to the Kingdom of Saudi Arabia, and I am very impressed by the steady efforts to turn the country into a modern state, which it already is, beyond our wildest imagination." The crew of the space shuttle Discovery, on their historic visit to the Kingdom, expressed bewilderment and admiration for what has been achieved in the Kingdom in such a short period of time.

Scores of dignitaries, journalists, politicians, members of parliaments, planners, scientists and engineers all around the globe are astounded by this massive modernization. Progress has been truly redefined in Saudi Arabia.

What has been achieved by the Kingdom through these Development Plans is, indeed, a great achievement by any standard. This is recognized and admired on the international scene or anywhere one measures words and matches them with deeds.

The Saudi experience in modernization and progress became a model for other countries around the globe.

Diversifying the economic base, modernizing the Kingdom, making most impressive progress in industrialization, all these are a reality for everyone to see. There also is a reality that needs to be pondered and never be forgotten by leaders around the world. It is that Saudi Arabia sets atop the richest oil reserves in the world. It is the largest holder and explorer of oil with 25% of all the world's proven reserves. After nearly half a century of oil production that fueled this gigantic development process, Saudi Arabia did not deplete its oil resources. On the contrary, they skyrocketed from about 3 billion barrels in 1949 to nearly 170 billion barrels today, and more is on the horizon to be found.

Oil! A great gift from God will continue to play a central role in the economy of the Kingdom and the economies of the entire world. Oil prices may fluctuate from time to time; all they can do is fluctuate! What remains a fact of life and an absolute reality is mankind's need for oil. This basic need will go on for many decades to come. It is a non-renewable resource, but with the massive reserves of Saudi Arabia it will take more than a century before it is depleted. It is only a matter of time before demand for this precious commodity will be on the rise again. The strategic importance of the Kingdom of Saudi Arabia will certainly continue into the 21st century. With their wise and deeply dedicated leadership, all they have to fear, after God, is "fear itself!"

Chapter 5

Defense

A Mission of Peace Demands Strength in a Turbulent World

On the footsteps of Abdulaziz, the founder of the Kingdom, King Fahd and his predecessors have contributed to the bedrock foundations of national safety and security since back in 1962, when Fahd became Minister of the Interior. A nation that was a sea of lawlessness and disorder among warring tribes prior to the time of Abdulaziz, became the *safest country on the face of the earth*. This safety and security net that engulfs the land is a wonderful gift from God. It was earned through a long struggle, dedication to justice and the application of the Islamic legal system, the *Shari'a*, that is based on the Qoran, the Holy Book of the Moslems.

Law and order are well enforced. Justice is strict, fair and swift. All this is at the core of the priceless atmosphere of safety and security that one feels, sees and lives, once he touches Saudi soil. Crime is certainly minimal. It is the lowest among all nations of the world. This is truly the envy of many; especially those who are true to their conscience; those who treasure the good inner feeling of security that mankind longs for, but much of the time is deprived from experiencing or harnessing. Since Saudi Arabia has a large expatriate population exceeding three million people, the crime rate in the Kingdom will decrease substantially, once this population leaves.

A western writer said, "The crime rate remains relatively low and would be considerably lower if there were no foreign workers in the country. *Violent street crime is almost nonexistent.*" The Saudis are law-abiding citizens. They live their religion.

You can travel the four corners of this land without fear of anyone attacking you, robbing you, or stealing whatever you may have left in your car while you are gone to have a cup of coffee. This is a land where you seldom if ever hear of robberies, car theft, murder, assault, rape, or whatever most likely and deeply troubles most men and women around the globe. You smell in the atmosphere that sense of loyalty, deep religious traditions and the genuine respect for law and order.

Departments of justice in Riyadh–justice through Shari'a is at the heart of Saudis' security and their enviable position on law and order.

One would only sense how great this achievement is by allowing his imagination to take him back only a few years, when travel was not safe at all. Even going to the Hajj (pilgrimage) was a dangerous mission, because robbers, thieves and murderers were everywhere. Once safety and security were well established, the visionary and wise leadership was able to embark on the most daring projects of the twentieth century, all for the betterment and welfare of the people. Certainly, the deep sense of justice that prevails and the education of the masses have contributed to the spread of good religious virtues, that directly established law and order and brought about stability to the land. Law, order, security and peace are phenomenal and truly exceptional in Saudi Arabia.

King Fahd, as Minister of the Interior, as Crown Prince, and later as Sovereign of the land, has extensively developed the Kingdom's security agencies. He always kept education as the foundation of his pioneering actions. He established a Security College which was later named after him. Saudi men would acquire a university level education, based on scientific principles. Thus, security men will be well prepared for the various functions and responsibilities of the Ministry of Interior.

The officers' college comprises units for traffic control, civil defense, coast guard, border patrol corps, flying squads, administration for visas, marksmanship, cavalry, languages, physical education and a few more. This was done along with the development of the various agencies and modernization of arms and techniques necessary for the Ministry of Interior to carry out its important mission. The best and most modern equipment and techniques were adopted, including the use of computers. This, coupled with the dedication of those responsible in the Ministry, contributed extensively to the safety and security that are among the most prominent in everyday life in the Kingdom.

King Fahd Security Academy prepares officers for internal security. The duration of study is three years. Graduating officers receive a degree in internal security science.

When Prince Naif Bin Abdulaziz became the Minister of Interior, he built on the achievements of his predecessor and contributed in his own right to the modernization and substantial improvements in internal security.

Naif was born in 1933. He received good training in various political, diplomatic and security matters. Prior to this position he was the Vice Minister of Interior. He has been very active with the Arabian Gulf States regarding security arrangements for the region. He traveled abroad and was a member of several official Saudi delegations, under the leadership of the late King Faisal and King Fahd. He founded the National Information Center, which uses modern computers for carrying out many security functions and services such as: registration of foreigners, control of borders, passport-issuing and renewal, civil records, organization of entry and exit of the pilgrims and other related duties.

The National Public Security Forces, supported by local police and various units of the religious police (Moutawa'a), all these are accredited by various observers as being capable of maintaining order and internal security in the Kingdom.

Responsibilities of the Ministry of Interior cover public security, investigation, special forces, the coast guard along with immigration and naturalization. Security duties are shared by the National Guard, the public security police and the coast guard, frontier forces, investigation and special forces. All governors of the regions report to the Minister of Interior.

King Fahd Security Academy, built about twenty kilometers northeast of Riyadh on the road to Dammam, was designed to serve and accommodate about two thousand students. This is much more than the number which could be accommodated by the Security College, thus allowing the curriculum to be expanded and more university

Law and order moves hand in hand with modernization.

courses to be included. Prince Naif stated that fraternal Arab States
would be welcome to send some of their students to the new Academy
when its doors open about 1987.

Modern police operations include the latest technological developments in modernization and equipment. New vehicles outfitted with
the best communications gear permitted the police directorates to operate sophisticated mobile units, especially in the major cities. Helicopters
were acquired by the security police for use in many urban districts.
The *Police College in Mecca* has been training officers for the public
security police since 1960.

According to Prince Naif, Minister of the Interior: "Under Saudi
law, it is illegal to mistreat prisoners. *We have fewer prisoners, political
or otherwise, than any other state. Our prisoners are treated humanely
in the spirit of Islam.*" All people in Saudi Arabia are equal before
the law. Strict law enforcement serves as a strong deterrent. The low
incidence of crime is a source of genuine pride to the Saudi citizen
and the leaders of the nation. "The bedrock beliefs and allegiances of
the Saudis have produced popular attitudes supportive of an orderly
society. Each aspect of a person's day-to-day activities can be catego-
rized as being within bounds of acceptable behavior or outside those
bounds. Despite all of the new wealth and the influence of foreign
workers and foreign ideas, the Saudis want to hold on to an orderly
society, as they define it, and to hold on to a basic respect for law
and the forces of the law."

Large oil reserves and the important geographic position of the Kingdom, along with the turbulence that exists in the region, especially around the Arabian Gulf, all this deepens the attention and awareness to security matters. Thus, the public security forces, in cases of emergency, receive the substantial and efficient support of a unique force called the National Guard. In extreme cases the regular armed forces energize their might to quell any threatening situation.

The National Guard and Crown Prince Abdullah

Crown Prince Abdullah and the National Guard have been truly intertwined for decades. Abdullah took special interest in various internal affairs. He has been head of the National Guard from 1963 until the present day. His keen interest in developing and making it a potent force, truly essential to the security of the Kingdom, was achieved through his deep and total dedication to the Guard. Considerable precious time is spent with the traditional groups of the Saudi society, especially tribal leaders who help in providing the capable troops for the National Guard.

Crown Prince Abdullah Bin Abdulaziz is the next man in line to the throne, the first Deputy Prime Minister and top right hand man to King Fahd. His birthplace was Riyadh, and the year was 1924. His primary education from a number of top religious scholars and intellectuals helped in broadening his knowledge and basic beliefs. At an early age, Abdullah received proper training in politics, religion, and chivalry, from the founder of the Kingdom, his father the late King Abdulaziz. He is pleasant, sincere, and possesses a towering figure like his father. His scope of knowledge has widened through personal education and extensive readings on various topics relating to government, politics and history.

Under the guidance of King Fahd, Crown Prince Abdullah played a very impressive role in strengthening Saudi-Arab relations and improving inter-Arab understanding. He is a distinguished leader in establishing peace between members of the Arab family. His successful mediation efforts and good will missions helped in promoting peace and harmony to the far corners of the Arab world. Some efforts led to the pullout of troops and tanks back from tense borders. Many times the ghost of war vanished due to his good efforts. More recently in the latter part of 1985, rapprochement between two Arab leaders was entirely due to the good efforts of Abdullah. Based on his sincerity and peaceful efforts, visits were exchanged between the leaders of the two countries, and a stronger basis for common understanding was developed.

King Fahd is the Supreme commander of the Armed forces.

Around August, 1962 when turbulence in the Middle East was reaching dangerous proportions, Abdullah's voice of wisdom, justice and good political sense prevailed.

Upon the coronation of King Khaled, Abdullah became Second Deputy Prime Minister; but he always remained commander of the National Guard. In his new position he chaired numerous sessions of the Council of Ministers. During these meetings he showed special qualities of leadership and organization in many facets of government and political life. On June 13, 1982, he became Crown Prince and first Deputy Prime Minister, as well as Commander of the National Guard.

His hobbies include hunting and chivalry (he founded the chivalry club in Riyadh). He is tall in stature with an impressive physical look

King Fahd, the Supreme Commander, receiving high ranking officials of
the Army. Also appearing behind the King is Prince Turki Bin Abdulaziz.

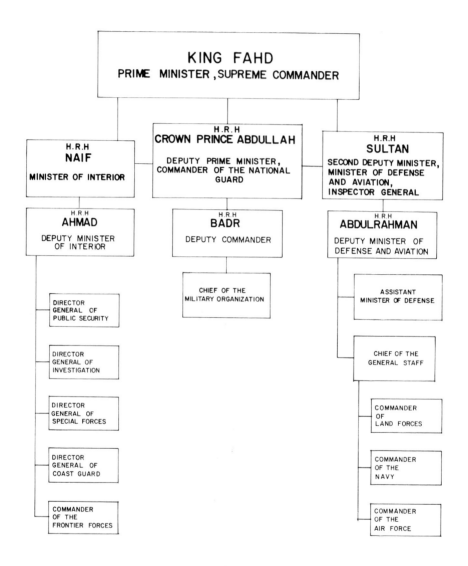

STRUCTURE OF NATIONAL SECURITY
IN THE KINGDOM OF SAUDI ARABIA

**H.R.H. Prince Abdullah Bin Abdulaziz, Crown Prince, First Deputy Minister
and Commander of the National Guard.**

reminiscent of his legendary father, Abdulaziz. He is generous and friendly when dealing with people. The Crown Prince is an *ardent advocate of justice*. His sharp intelligence, quick observation and deep religious belief make him well loved and respected by his colleagues and subordinates. Abdullah has been the efficient righthand man to King Fahd in his drive for massive industrialization and modernization of the Kingdom.

In the last decade, the National Guard became highly trained and modernized. This made it a strong force in internal security matters and a power to be reckoned with in case of serious emergency. The National Guard traces its origin to the Ikhwan that were founded by the late King Abdulaziz. The Ikhwan fervently responded to the call of Abdulaziz to carry the long struggle for unifying the land. There was a time when their excessive enthusiasm, independent military actions and excesses had to be curbed or controlled by Abdulaziz. Once this was done, the Ikhwan were allowed to reappear as the white army, which later became known as the National Guard. This is not a reserve force like its American counterpart. Most of the National Guard personnel are on active duty. It is a parallel and separate force from the regular armed forces. It remains the most powerful internal security force. Due to extensive training and modernization, it became very valuable in reinforcing the regular armed forces in case of a major emergency or an invasion. Except for anti-aircraft defense, defending the oil fields remains a major task of the National Guard.

Modern facilities were built to insure the comfort of the National Guard and their families. These were built at Khashm Al-Aan which is also the center for *King Khaled Military College*. This is an institution of higher learning. Its main mission is to train officers for the National Guard. Its doors were opened in December, 1982. The program at this college takes three years and leads to a Bachelor of Military Science degree. The capacity of the college is about 416 students. Subjects are balanced between academic and military.

Aside from the active duty component of the National Guard, there are tribal battalions that operate under the command of local Sheikhs. Personnel in this category report for duty about once a month and they receive a monthly stipend for their services. This way the central government helps the National Guard and militia battalions by distributing wealth to bedouins that may happen to be in remote areas of the Kingdom. The support of the bedouins and their tribes helps in maintaining a structured reserve that can be mobilized when the situation warrants.

King Fahd, being the Supreme Commander, has paid special attention to the National Guard. He initiated many large projects such as

Crown Prince Abdullah greets the U.S. Vice President, George Bush during his visit to the Kingdom in April, 1986.

King Khaled Hospital for the National Guard in Jeddah, King Fahd Hospital for the National Guard in Riyadh, and King Khaled Military College. Living quarters, schools, hospitals, modernization projects, are all given special attention by Crown Prince Abdullah. He, himself, oversees and follows various stages of implementation for these projects. He gives his special attention to speedy execution, so that the best is made available.

The *Cavalry of the National Guard* is a crack regiment that carries with it an emotional and historical appeal. Being the descendents of those men who swept out of the desert of Arabia in support of Abdulaziz, their presence always brings cherished memories of the long struggle for unifying the Kingdom. Aside from the Cavalry, the motorized battalions are equipped with modern tanks, half-tracks, and mobile artillery designed for desert conditions. The guards serve a minimum of three years. Some of them continue in the Guard and make it a lifetime career. Others go back to their towns and villages and become the "eyes and ears of the King" according to Prince Abdullah.

However, the great expanse of Saudi Arabia, a country as large as the United States of America east of the Mississippi River, requires a strong deterrent to any potential aggressors. The Ministry of Defense commanding under its realm the army, navy and air force, and in cooperation with other security forces, sees to it that any potential aggressor is doomed to defeat.

The Ministry of Defense and Prince Sultan

Sultan Bin Abdulaziz was born in Riyadh in 1925, where he received his religious studies and general military education. From his youth he exhibited impressive intelligence and a dynamic physical presence. His outspoken personality is coupled with activism befitting the Kingdom's prominent role in the Middle East. He has occupied important positions, among them was his command of the Royal Guard that was assigned to him by his late father, Abdulaziz. In 1953 he was governor of Riyadh. In 1955 he became Minister of Communications and supervised the first railway system in the Kingdom of Saudi Arabia.

When he was Minister of Agriculture, he initiated the Haradh project that was designed to resettle many of the nomadic tribes. In 1962, he was appointed Minister of Defense and Aviation. Since June, 1982, *Prince Sultan* became the second Deputy Prime Minister, always keeping his post as Minister of Defense and Aviation. He is also the chairman of the board for Saudi Airlines, (Saudia). *His support and valued advice are both instrumental in helping King Fahd achieve his goals for progress, industrialization and education.* Prince Sultan chairs the Supreme Committee for Administrative Reform; he is also vice-president of the Supreme Council for Higher Education. He is an articulate and well seasoned politician who has made many important visits to various Arab and friendly countries in the West. His contributions to international and regional conferences is well known and respected. His son, *Prince Bandar Bin Sultan,* is the distinguished Ambassador of Saudi Arabia to the United States.

Military training is modern and sophisticated. It made strong headway in improving Saudi military capabilities, thus boosting self-confidence. The primary mission of the Ministry of Defense is to defend the nation through the military forces. When the situation warrants,

H.R.H. Prince Sultan Bin Abdulaziz, Second Deputy Prime Minister, Minister of Defense and Aviation, and Inspector General.

military personnel are also active in agriculture, construction, development, teaching in schools, fire fighting, emergency aid and medical assistance. Prince Sultan said, "These military cities in the country are not just military garrisons in a desert land, but cities for health, science, education, and the training of generations who help in the progress of the nation by giving it a healthy push forward in military and civil domains."

Prince Sultan makes it a point to criss-cross the country and visit the armed forces in all corners of the Kingdom. He follows personally the various projects designed to strengthen the defense capabilities of the nation.

Modernization and upgrading of the military forces was greatly supported by the oil revenue and the determination of Saudi leaders to establish a strong deterrent against any aggressor. Training and modernization depended heavily on top talent from within the Kingdom and the Western World, especially the United States of America, Britain, France and West Germany (also a special Saudi-Pakistani military relationship exists). From the early 1950's until the mid 1980's, the Kingdom of Saudi Arabia spent about 75 billion dollars for American goods and services. Nearly sixty percent of this sum was spent on modernization of military services and military equipment. Buildup of defense forces and infrastructure were strongly emphasized from the days of King Faisal onward.

After the October war of 1973, and because of the resulting tensions, U.S. Secretary of State Henry A. Kissinger met with then Prince Fahd in Washington D.C. in June, 1974. The meeting dealt with Saudi security needs for the ten-year period beginning in 1975. This resulted in a buildup of Saudi defenses which surpassed even the great strides of the previous ten-year period. Although the United States of America has no formal treaty commitment with the Kingdom of Saudi Arabia, every president beginning with Roosevelt has underlined and acknowledged the importance of the Kingdom to the basic strategic interests of the U.S. Despite a massive campaign by the Zionist lobby, a historic transaction for the sale of AWACS (Airborne Warning and Control System) and F15 airplanes was made in 1981. "For the Saudis the purchase request became a test of the firmness of the relationship, but for the Americans it became a political nightmare as Israel and its supporters in the United States raised strenuous objections to the sale." Hostilities across the borders and around the Arabian Gulf make it imperative for the Kingdom to seek the most modern equipment and best training techniques for its military forces. There is the constant worry of a possible spread of the Iran-Iraq war. A report, prepared by the U.S. Congress research service of the Library of Congress for the

House of Representatives Committee on Foreign Affairs, described the evolving special relationship between Saudi Arabia and the United States. The introduction to the report stated:

"The United States and Saudi Arabia have established a special relationship, that had its genesis in the major role of U.S. companies in the development of Saudi petroleum resources in the 1930's. More recently, the relationship has been fostered by government to government assistance and cooperation. It has become apparent that officials in the governments of both countries consider that the preservation and enhancement of this relationship could provide a basis for resolving political, security, economic and energy issues facing the United States and Saudi Arabia. From the U.S. perspective, decisions on the part of the Saudi Arabian Government potentially affect the U.S. balance of payments, the future of the dollar, the U.S. and world energy equation, the rate of world economic recovery, U.S. interests in the Middle East and the Persian Gulf region and the objective of an overall resolution of the Arab-Israeli conflict."

Saudi Arabia does not wish for the "Arabian Peninsula to become an arena of contention between the United States and the Soviet Union." Because of this and also due to the tremendous opposition pressure in Washington, Saudi Arabia follows a policy of *diversification* in its acquisition of armament and drive toward modernization of its military forces. Instead of being completely dependent on a single supplier, Britain and France have become major recipients of various military contracts from the Saudi government. This covers weapons, modern equipment, maintenance, construction of facilities and training. Certain military contracts have included West Germany, the Netherlands, Italy and South Korea. Pakistan, a friendly Moslem country, plays a supportive role in the military forces.

The French signed a contract with the Saudis in January, 1984 for supplying mobile anti-aircraft missiles for guarding Saudi airfields and other sensitive targets. The contract was for nearly five billion dollars. The missile system is reportedly to be a version of the Crotale (known as Shaheen in the Arab World). Of course, such a large arms deal gave a boost to the French workforce and their armament industry. Also, in 1980, the French and the Saudi governments agreed to a contract of nearly three billion dollars for helicopters, navy ships and installations.

In 1985, when the Saudis intended to buy American military equipment to the tune of nearly five billion dollars, the opposition *lobby* with its strong influence on Congress vehemently promised to block the deal. Prince Sultan and the Saudi leadership turned to the British for this gigantic purchase. When a British politician was asked about

Israeli opposition he answered, "We work in light of our convictions without regard of what others say," adding, "The Jewish American lobby has done us a special favor when they placed political strings on the export of American arms to the Arab world and we accept this with thanks." A moderate and truly peace-loving nation like Saudi Arabia poses no threat to anyone. In fact to help American interests in the region, such sales should be strongly encouraged. They serve a dual purpose of safeguarding the peace of a very friendly nation and also the creation of thousands of jobs for the benefit of the average American. It seems as if the American administration gave the hint to go elsewhere for buying the British Toronado after realizing the impossible task of gaining approval from Congress.

The recent proposed sale of missiles to Saudi Arabia was again fought by the opposition lobby in the U.S. Congress. However, President Reagan's veto won the battle and the sale prevailed, in June, 1986.

In a response to a letter written by an American supporting the sale, the U.S. *Vice President, George Bush* said, "Thank you for your letter regarding the sale of arms to Saudi Arabia.

It was thoughtful of you to write, and I appreciate your having taken the opportunity to express your support for this important sale. The friendship between the United States and Saudi Arabia is a lasting one and is of great importance to the security of this vital region. As you may already know, the Senate was unable to overturn the President's veto of a bill that would have prevented the sale of arms to Saudi Arabia. It is because of the strong support of Americans such as you that enabled this sale to be approved."

On the same subject, *Senator Richard G. Lugar, chairman of the Foreign Relations Committee* said, "Moreover, the predictable result of blocking such an arms sale to a friendly Arab state is to have the state turn to another supplier, one that is glad to have the business and that makes no effort to impose the policy cautions that routinely accompany American arms. By refusing to sell these weapons, we would be driving the Saudis, and probably other friendly Arab states, to purchase more of their military equipment from the Europeans, or even the Soviets—a decision they clearly do not want to make but may feel compelled to if we isolate ourselves from the problems of the region. It would be an invitation to the Soviet Union to play a more active role in the area.

Although this sale is primarily proposed for security and political purposes, we cannot ignore the economic benefits to the United States. The United States is currently running the highest trade deficits in its history. This proposed sale would bring capital directly into the U.S. economy. It is a direct cash sale involving no U.S. financing, credits, or subsidies." He continues to say, "it makes no sense to reject this sale which would provide hundreds of Americans jobs."

Army

The army has become a strong force in size and deterrence. It includes mechanized armored infantry and airborne brigades. A number of artillery battalions and anti-aircraft artillery batteries, along with surface-to-air missile batteries, also are a major part of the army. The *Royal Guard Regiment* is part of the Saudi combat units.

About forty kilometers from Riyadh, *King Abdulaziz Military Academy* is the major source for second lieutenants for the Army. It replaced the Royal Military College. This facility was designed for accommodating 1,500 cadets. It is a self-sufficient small city, having family housing for staff and faculty. Military and academic subjects are taught. The duration of study is three years. Graduates earn a Bachelor of Military Science upon completion of the program. The newly commissioned second Lieutenant officers attend advanced school for further specialization in armor, artillery, infantry, airborne, air defense, engineering communications, maintenance or military administration. Competition is keen for students to attend the *Command and Staff College in Riyadh.* It offers a Master's Degree program in military science. It is patterned after its counterpart in the U.S.A. Officers are chosen to be sent for higher military education in the United States, France, Britain, West Germany and other friendly countries.

The Royal Saudi Navy

A Saudi Naval Expansion Program (SNEP) brought about dramatic changes in capabilities, numbers of trained men and numbers of military ships. Thousands of Saudi naval personnel received training abroad, mainly in the United States, Britain, and France. Naval equipment is built and supplied from various sources: some come from America, at the yard of the Tacoma Boat Building Company of Washington, and the Peterson Builders of Wisconsin. Certain torpedo boats were built in West Germany along with other patrol craft. Some coastal patrol craft was built by Cnim of Cherbourg, France. Other craft was built by Halter Marine of New Orleans, U.S.A.

The Saudi Naval expansion program provided for the establishment of a deep water port in Jeddah on the Red Sea and Jubail on the Arabian Gulf, along with the construction of various major Naval bases at both Jeddah and Jubail. Like other military cities built around the country, these two bases will have all the necessary facilities for family housing, schooling, shopping and recreation for all the Naval personnel and their dependents. The *United States Army Corps of Engineers* was assigned to oversee this construction in its capacity as the provider of engineering and construction management services to the government. Smaller naval bases also exist at Ras Tanura, Ras Al-Mishab, Yanbu and Dammam.

The Royal Saudi Air Force

It was established in 1950 by order of the founder of the Kingdom, the late King Abdulaziz. Prior to that period, air operations were under the realm of the army. Initially, the British helped in providing aircraft and training. As British influence declined in the region and U.S. interests increased, American aircraft and training personnel were used by the Royal Saudi Air Force (RSAF).

King Faisal Air Academy in Riyadh carried the mission of training the Air Force personnel. It will be moved to a new area at the huge air base that is being built at Al-Kharj. Training in the Air Force takes twenty-seven months of instruction. Initially, the students are taught an intensive course in English that is followed by primary flight instruction on Reims Cessnar aircraft. Along with Saudis, top faculty from Britain and the U.S. engage in training at King Faisal Air Academy and the *Technical Studies Institute at Dhahran*. In the latter, technicians for Saudi aircraft receive their instruction. Primary training is followed by several months of advanced training that takes place in many top air facilities in friendly nations. Leading among them are the United States and Britain.

The Taif Air Base trains helicopter pilots. Saudi pilots for the F-15 fighters were sent to Luke Air Force Base in Arizona. Major air bases used by the Royal Saudi Air Force are located in Dhahran, Riyadh and Hafr Al-Batin (near the Kuwait and Iraq borders). Others include Tabuk that is located in the northwest corner of the Kingdom, closer to the Israeli-Jordanian border and the Khamis Moshait in the southwest of the Kingdom. *King Khaled Military City*, a huge facility accommodating nearly 70,000 military personnel and their dependents, includes the air base *at Hafr Al-Batin*. This major military city has been recently dedicated.

Squadrons of F-15 planes and British Lightnings along with F-5's carry an impressive combat punch. The AWACS give early warning and provide a reliable umbrella of safety and protection. Jet interceptors, air defense radar, SAM missiles from the British and the Americans, along with Maverick air-to-ground missiles help in making the Air Force a deterrent to be reckoned with in the Middle East.

A foundation for developing Saudi Arms manufacturing recently was established. Already in the Kharj a small defense industry produces American and West German rifles and machine guns, under license.

The modern Armed forces of the Kingdom are a force for peace.

More production under license will take place, along with the assembly
of military vehicles and aircraft. A general agency for military industry
was recently formed. This is considered as a first seed for the Arms
industry, whether in the Kingdom or in association with the Gulf Cooperation Council. This agency will be under the realm of the Ministry
of Defense and Aviation. Like other agencies it will also have an independent board of directors. Among those on the board will be members
such as the Minister of Finance and National Economy, the Assistant
to the Minister of Defense and a number of capable personnel.

Saudi Arabia pursues a basic and *genuine policy of peace and
friendship* toward other nations of the world. The strengthening of
its defenses is at the heart of carrying out such a policy. They are
strongly against the interference in the internal affairs of other nations
and they certainly practice what they preach. *Their military deterrence
is truly a force for peace in the region.*

Chapter 6

A Look into the Future

Overview

One cannot help but marvel over the spectacular achievements realized by the Kingdom of Saudi Arabia in its quest for modernization and industrialization. This is a blessed land, indeed! *The birthplace of the Prophet! The Mecca for nearly one billion Moslems around the globe who cherish it and face it five times every day. This great land is a vast mass of desert floating on a sea of oil;* with proven oil reserves of 169 billion barrels that would last over a century. The massive infusion of capital from this God-given resource brought the most modern technology to the Kingdom and truly made the desert bloom . . .

While other nations in the world have substantial oil reserves, they did not succeed in achieving even a fraction of what the Kingdom has achieved. On the contrary, instead of having billions of dollars in reserves like the Saudis, they harnessed and reaped billions of dollars in debts. The debts of many of these oil producing countries became an international monetary dilemma that could develop into a nightmare. The Saudi government, under the dedicated and wise leadership of King Fahd with his farsightedness, deep devotion to the people and supreme determination for bringing welfare and progress to his land, provided the basic ingredients of success and completed the perfect equation for massive development and improvements on all fronts.

Private Sector and Joint Ventures

After the construction of a gigantic infrastructure, the most modern in the world, the Kingdom gears itself for the future. With a period of consolidation, emphasis is being placed on the private sector to be actively involved in industrialization and services. A prime intention of the government is to encourage the private sector to take initiatives. It will continue to provide basic incentives for development and progress through the various funds.

Saudi Arabia is on the road to becoming the Middle East's industrial high-tech center. It is to become the region's center for the aviation industry. The *"Offset program"* is a novel approach for generating industrial investment. This policy requires contractors to reinvest back into the Kingdom a portion of the value of their major contracts. The Saudi government will require the large foreign owned consortiums that may be involved in defense projects to reinvest up to 35% of the value of their contracts back into high technology service industries in the Kingdom. Also, foreign contractors must subcontract 30% of the value of a government contract to local subcontractors and thus help in revitalizing the local economy.

Diversifying the economy is one of the major policies of modernization and industrialization. "We must stop being just an oil-based economy," says a senior official from the Ministry of Industry. A broad industrial base has been established. It is on the road to becoming much healthier with time. Income from this sector will be on the increase and thus, will lessen dependency on oil. While oil will continue to play a major role in the economy, other sectors will do their share. Any lack in technology will be rectified through the tremendous effort

King Fahd thrives on giving care and compassion—his way of life for years to come.

King Fahd Children's Medical Center is designed to be the best in the world for the treatment of leukemia and lymphomas. When finished, it will be the first of its kind outside the U.S.A.–Private enterprise investing in the future of the Kingdom.

of the government and the citizens toward attracting American, European and Japanese companies for joint ventures and for setting operations in the Kingdom, so that technology transfer will be more accelerated in the years ahead. The private sector will play a major role in all the joint ventures. For example, contracts with the Boeing and General Electric companies will lead to "Offset Ventures" that will help in creating a major aviation industry in the Kingdom, an industry designed to service not just Saudi requirements, but also the needs of their allies in the Gulf Cooperation Council (GCC). This may include Iraq and Jordan. The large contract, signed with Britain to the tune of 4.2 billion dollars, carries with it an Offset program, much of which will be based and geared toward the aerospace industry. These high-tech areas will increase the need for highly skilled workers who will help in operating these projects and the Offset ventures that are derived from them.

King Fahd has called upon Saudi businessmen to rise to the challenge and generously invest in the future of the land. As revenue from oil and funding from the government both level off or decrease, the private sector could become a major partner in future development. The fourth Five-Year Plan stresses the importance of this sector's involvement and serious contribution to fueling the nation's economy through diversification. Free enterprise has been a close kin to Arabia from the myrrh and incense days way back into the beginning of history. Early traders of Arabia linked the Arabian Peninsula to the outside world.

Saudization will be proceeding with vigor. Nearly 600,000 expatriates of the lesser skills will be heading for home since the basic infrastructure would have been finished. The health of the Saudi economy will continue to affect positively the economies of many nations around the world, extending from the Philippines to America and beyond.

Mineral exploration, solar energy, desalination and more *research and development* will lead to many improvements across the entire spectrum of Saudi life and economy. Free market and the free enterprise spirit that are very dear and basic to the Saudi way of life will add more health to the national welfare and economy.

The population will progressively and surely become more educated and sophisticated, but always guarding basic traditions and values. The increase in education and development of better skills and knowhow will be a positive element in improving services, making the economy more diversified and enriched with better returns for the good of all.

The Saudi scientific team designed and analyzed space experiments carried on by Prince Sultan Bin Salman during the Discovery Space Mission. Prince Bandar Bin Sultan, Saudi Ambassador to the United States of America is fifth from left on the back row.—More research and development are on the horizon.

Employment and Saudi Women

For many decades unemployment has been alien to Saudi society. With large numbers of graduates from Saudi centers of education and universities, a higher plateau of competence and requirements will develop to fit the needs and fill the many jobs that will be generated. Nearly 400,000 will be on the market before the dawn of the 1990's. Saudi girls are attending schools in record numbers, nearing a million. Those attending universities are impressive in both number and competence. The time is here when Saudi women will play a major role in shaping their society within the bounds of Shari'a and the true spirit of Islam. They will certainly make great contributions to the Saudi family as they have done for centuries, and more recently to the Saudi economy as well. They are progressively becoming an important factor to be reckoned with in the work force. The employment of women in certain sectors, such as nursing, teaching, medicine and other related professions, will certainly help in the process of Saudization that is one of the basic goals of the Fourth Plan. Since the early 60's, Saudi women reached new heights and milestones in education, care and compassion.

Security

Security, peace and tranquillity along with law, order and justice were at the core of the success story in the development process. Without security there would have been no progress. Fahd follows the footsteps of Abdulaziz in treasuring and implementing all the necessary steps for creating an *atmosphere of security and absolute justice*. The position of the Kingdom in this regard is an envy of many nations around the world. Despite the endemic turbulence in the Middle East, the seasoned and moderate leadership in the Kingdom of Saudi Arabia will continue to steer a steady path avoiding conflict and practicing peace and friendship everywhere. While this is not an easy task, King Fahd and his capable team shall rise to the challenge and steer the ship to safety! Security, justice and order will always be the cornerstone for harnessing the benefits from the progress achieved and also creating the right environment for many more achievements to come.

Fahd, the Man of Peace and Achievement

Saudi Arabia will continue to be the great moderating force in a turbulent world riddled with violence and terrorism. The Saudi voice for justice and moderation will be loud and clear. Their oil policy, in the past, present and future will remain moderate and stable. It is based on keeping an equilibrium between the interests of producers and consumers. They seek to stabilize world markets of oil for the benefit of mankind. Their contributions to world peace will always be accomplished with dedication and dynamism. They will continue to be truly the peace makers, not only among the Arab nations and Moslem world, but also among the family of nations as well.

What has been achieved in the Kingdom under the wise and peace loving leadership of King Fahd, who was supported by a dedicated team and inspired by his predecessors, is truly a source of pride not only to the Kingdom of Saudi Arabia but the entire Arab and Moslem world as well. *Saudi achievements are a shining example for the world community to see, admire and emulate! This genuine Arab Renaissance brings to mind Arab contributions to history during the height of the Arab Empire.* No nation in history made such gigantic steps towards progress in a matter of a decade! Since the early 70's the astronomical jump in per capita income rose over twelvefold reaching 35,000 SR by the end of 1984–85. The massive changes that have taken place with the spectacular pace at which this happened, anywhere else could have caused disruption in society and behavior that could have been impossible to contain or maneuver. In Saudi Arabia positive change was realized bringing with it the best in development that could compete with the elite in the world, while traditions, religion and basic values remained at the heart of Saudi society and stability.

If all these achievements are not enough, rest assured! The best is yet to come.

Appendices

Appendix	Title
A	Profile: The Saudi Today
B	A Brief History of the Arabs
C	Simplified Diagram for the Government of Saudi Arabia
D	Major Battles Fought by Abdulaziz in his Arduous Struggle to Unify Arabia
E	Abdulaziz and His Companions in the Winter of 1901, on Their Way from Kuwait to Recapture Riyadh
F	Sons of Ibn Saud
G	Brothers and Children of Ibn Saud
H	The Moslem Calendar
I	Glossary of Arabic Words
J	Worldwide Energy Demand By Sources
K	Estimated Proven Recoverable Reserves of Crude Oil and Natural Gas of the World
L	References
Index	

Appendix A

Profile: The Saudi Today

From the cradle to his resting place, the Saudi citizen is endowed with care and compassion. Prior to his/her birth, the mother receives good health care. The infant most likely is born in a hospital where medical care and medicine are free.

If the mother was employed, she would have been receiving full pay for two months during her pregnancy.

The infant will receive *free medical care* from top medical doctors and excellent hospitals for the rest of his/her life. In this, they will be joining the ranks of their elders before them.

As the newborn grows and reaches five years of age, he/she will go to kindergarten for a year and at six years of age will start their formal *education*. He or she will spend six years in elementary school, three years in intermediate school and three years in the secondary school. All their education, books and supplies are free. Schools in the Kingdom adopt the modern approach to teaching. Stressing Islamic values begins at an early age.

The education evolution in the modern Kingdom of Saudi Arabia is truly miraculous. The scope of its achievements was engineered through pioneering actions taken by King Fahd, who was the first Minister of Education.

Boys and girls have equal opportunity to acquire the ultimate in good education. Both have their separate schools that are well equipped and properly staffed.

Those who do not succeed in school may choose to work in an enterprise compatible with their capabilities and interests.

Once the young men or young women graduate from high school they may choose to be among 100,000 students attending seven universities in the Kingdom. Both have equal opportunities for higher education.

The universities listed below adopt the latest techniques and cover a wide range of specialties from medicine to engineering. They are spread over sixteen campuses covering the four corners of the Kingdom.

The Saudi today enjoys a modern Kingdom, under an umbrella of care, compassion and deep religious traditions.

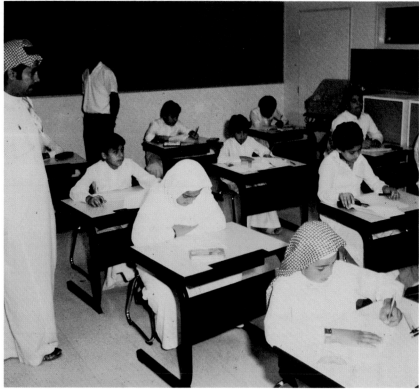

1. King Saud University in Diriya (near Riyadh), established in 1957.
2. Islamic University in Medina, 1960.
3. King Fahd University of Petroleum and Minerals, in Dhahran, 1963.
4. King Abdulaziz University in Jeddah, 1967.
5. Imam Mohammed Bin Saud Islamic University, in Riyadh, 1974.
6. King Faisal University, in Dammam and Hasa, 1975.
7. Umm Al-Qora University in Mecca, 1981.

Students receive various allowances, including free housing, books, scientific trips, clothing, over $300 per month for expenses, as well as complete medical care.

When pocket computers became readily available in the market, King Fahd University of Petroleum and Minerals became, perhaps, the first university that distributed such computers to its entire student body, free of charge. Later the students had terminals in their dormitories which connected to the main computer center of the University. This is the second largest computer facility in the Kingdom.

A student may apply for a scholarship to study abroad, especially for certain rare specialties. Those working for some organizations, agencies or ministries, may improve their status and know-how by studying abroad at their employer's expense. Through his studies overseas, the student, at one time, was joining about 10,000 students studying in the U.S.A., over 5,000 in Britain, over 1,000 in West Germany, and a few more throughout the western world.

Benefits include: monthly salaries, book allowances, expenses for scientific trips, yearly repatriation transportation to the Kingdom and complete medical care. Superior achievements are rewarded by extra bonuses.

If illness befalls the Saudi citizen, he or she will be treated with care. A student studying abroad receives $1,100 every six months for medical care. A couple will receive $2,200 every six months. In either case the government will pay for such extra medical attention as operations or other emergencies.

Of course there are private and public medical services. Those who desire private medical attention can receive it. However, most of the public health services are of superior quality. For example, King Khaled Eye Specialist Hospital is the best in the Middle East and is considered to be among the most prominent in the world. The number of hospitals in the Kingdom more than doubled between 1970–1985. During 1984 alone, nineteen hospitals and over 100 health care centers were opened. King Fahd Medical City in Riyadh will be the largest hospital complex in the Kingdom.

If a Saudi becomes gravely ill in a remote area of the country and needs quick medical care, arrangements may be made to use one of a fleet of C-130 planes equipped as flying hospitals. The patient is taken to the proper medical facility, where services and medical attention are free of charge.

Many young Saudi women today seek to enrich their knowledge and study for higher degrees. If they are employed, say with the Ministry of Education as an example, their studies will be sponsored by the Ministry. They will receive their full salary while seeking higher education. Young women are honored, respected and encouraged in their search for better education.

Several separate educational institutions exist for women. Institutes of Commerce and Banking, Teacher's Education, College of Pharmacy and Medicine are among the few we name here. However, women tend to shy away from disciplines normally dominated by men, notably civil engineering, mechanical engineering and the like.

After high school, many young men decide to continue their education in one of the several technical institutes. Students normally graduate from the universities with a college degree in four to five years and from a technical institute in the equivalent of about three years. Some extra time is needed to improve their working knowledge in the English language, which is the language of instruction for some technical subjects.

Upon graduation from the university or the institute, the horizons are wide open for the young graduates. They may work with the government in numerous agencies, departments, and ministries or for the private sector in one of the nearly 1,800 manufacturing facilities that exist nowadays in the Kingdom. Some choose to study for graduate work either in the Kingdom or abroad. Some may work awhile, then go back to do graduate work. Again, those qualified will receive scholarships to cover all expenses.

Once ready to settle down and build a home, all the graduate has to do is apply to the Real Estate Fund to receive an *interest-free loan* of up to nearly $85,000 that is repaid over a twenty-year period.

If the graduate is unable to purchase a piece of land to build his home, he may apply for a plot large enough to be used as a homesite.

A young Saudi with an *entrepreneural mind* may wish to invest in a real estate project. Again the Real Estate Fund makes it possible to receive an interest-free loan for ten years, covering 50% of the cost of the building project (The maximum is about four million dollars).

Interest-free loans are available to the citizen through organizations such as the agricultural bank and the industrial fund, to help in setting up agricultural, industrial and social projects.

For example, the applicant may present a study to the agricultural bank; the loan will cover fifty percent of the cost. The other 50% may be borrowed from other financial institutions.

Those graduating from a technical institute receive loans to start their business and buy needed equipment. They are assisted in securing visas to acquire the technical know-how that may be needed for successful operation of their business. Those going into agriculture, like many others, receive interest-free loans and a good subsidy for equipment– all to serve the welfare of the citizen and protect his product.

Agricultural equipment is heavily subsidized by the government. In the late 1970's government assistance went as far as transporting cattle by air to Saudi Arabia at no expense to the Saudi entrepreneur. Those interested in industrial enterprises receive advice from the Ministry of Industry. Complete economic studies are provided. The optimum and most viable industrial enterprise is suggested. Once a project is selected, an application is made to the Industrial Fund. An interest-free loan covering 50% of the cost is secured. With this starting boost, the entrepreneur is almost destined to certain success.

All doors are open for employment, that essentially is guaranteed for every Saudi citizen. Those who join the military make over $1,000 per month, just upon entry. Their status improves as their experience increases and as they are promoted both in rank and income. In the meantime, they are given living quarters for themselves and their families.

Once they are working for the government or the various companies that exist in the country, continuing education and training are available and encouraged. While an employee is in training he receives full pay and can, essentially, quit anytime he so desires.

When the young Saudi is ready to get married, those needing it receive a loan of more than seven thousand dollars to help them get started.

As young men and women grow, they face life's problems like everyone else. Obviously they have received a very good head start. Horizons are open to them on many fronts.

Others soar in their climb and achievements. Their limit is the sky. But *all claim their share of the "pie," earning the fruits of their labor and rewards of their imagination, determination and drive.*

Saudi citizens live under an umbrella of secure defense in a compassionate society stressing religious values, law and order. They live their religion. It is their way of life!

Appendix B

A Brief History of the Arabs

Introduction

Black gold, with its great impact on global energy needs, brought strategic importance to the Arab land. Although the Arab world accounts for a big share of world news, it still is least understood among other nations.

Stretching from the Atlantic Ocean to the Arabian Gulf, Arab land occupies more than five million square miles (thirteen million square kilometers), and is the richest in oil and gas compared to any country in the world. Twenty-eight percent of this land lies in Asia, and the other seventy-two percent is in Africa.

Nearly eighty-five percent of this great mass is desert, under which lie massive quantities of oil and gas that awakened the recent increase of interest in the Arab world. The next decade should witness a continuation of this interest, coupled with better understanding of the Arabs as a whole. The impact of their oil and natural resources is being felt throughout the world. That interest probably will continue for decades into the Twenty-First Century.

What Are the Arabs?

Some of the Semetic tribes who inhabited the Arabian Peninsula were known as the Arabs. Two different groups of Arabs lived in this Peninsula. One was mainly nomadic, roving the huge deserts that extended between the Euphrates River and the center of the Peninsula. The other group were the inhabitants of the southern portion, namely, Yemen. Largely the nomadic group were referred to as the Arabs.

Prior to the birth of Islam, and during the epoch of Jaheeliyya[1], the Arabs were the nomads of Jazeerat al-Arab, meaning the "island of the Arabs," a great portion of which is nowadays Saudi Arabia. Many of these people moved northward into the Fertile Crescent that includes countries such as Syria, Jordan, Palestine, Lebanon and Iraq. The migrants mingled with the old civilizations of the Babylonians,

---

[1] From jahl, meaning ignorance; during this period the Arabs were nomads worshipping many gods, rocks, trees, waters, springs, etc.

THE ARABIAN PENINSULA
A stylized view. By Don Thompson.

Assyrians, Phoenicians and Hebrews. This interaction was of great significance in history, especially after the birth of Islam.

The wide horizons of the great deserts provided the nomadic Bedouin with a romantic sense of liberty. However, the harsh environment brought about its own strong laws that characterized the structure of tribal lives. Mere survival depended on the unity and protection of the tribes. A system emerged where a family or a tribe were held responsible for acts of anyone belonging to the family or the tribe. The judgement was swift and severe: life for a life, tooth for a tooth, eye for an eye.

The individual crimes were restrained because of the harsh punishment that followed and the lasting vengeance that took place. Tribal disputes were settled from time to time by an arbitrator being a "wise man" or an authority. At times these disputes provided a good excuse for a raid or "ghazou," which is aimed at the enemy and his possessions.

With the harsh life of the desert, the Bedouins depended heavily on the camel, drinking its milk and using it for transportation. The major diet came from the dates, fruits of the palm trees.

Prior to the birth of Arab civilization, the Fertile Crecent was the cradle and crossroads of civilizations. This area has been a strategic path and a great center for learning. It has known conquerors and immigrants from both East and West. The traces of its civilizations go as far back as fifty centuries. The Neolithic man learned here to cultivate crops and domesticate certain animals. He found permanent sources of water and began building permanent dwellings.

Prior to 3000 B.C., the people of this region had learned to write and work with copper. They had developed towns, trade, government, and a society of small ruling class and large peasantry. Great civilizations rose in the valleys of the Tigris, Euphrates and along the Nile River.

About 4000 years ago, the Egyptian engineers dug a canal between the Nile and the Red Sea, to bring boats carrying the riches of Arabia, the Sudan and Somalia to the Nile Delta. This early civilization made Egypt a center for learning and wealth for nearly 3000 years, until it was conquered by Alexander the Great in the year 332 B.C.

Throughout history and until the mid-Twentieth Century, Egypt was under the control of many foreigners. The Fertile Crescent, known as the great arc of semi-arid grassland, has provided a way around the hostile desert. From the earliest times it was a route for trade, migration and invasion. Some sixteen centuries before Christ, Abraham followed the Fertile Crescent from Iraq to Palestine.

Marco Polo also traveled the Crescent on his journey to China in the Thirteenth Century A.D. and noted something that is of great focus and attention in the world today. He wrote: ". . . a fountain from

Gigantic oil reserves of the Arab World are a lifeline for worldwide industry.
Oil is the basic ingredient for progress.

which oil springs in great abundance. This oil is not good to use with food but is good to burn."

Between big palm trees and the hostile desert land, the fighting mood was a chronic mental condition for the Bedouins and raiding was one of the few manly traits. During the Jaheeliyya Period, some tribes practiced the "ghazou" without any mental anguish. The ghazou was sort of national sport and no blood was shed except in very extreme circumstances. The weak tribes could buy protection by paying the stronger tribes a certain fee called "khouwwah."

Despite the many evils of ghazou, the Bedouin within his laws of friendship was a loyal and generous person. The poets of the Jaheeliyya time, and the writers as well, continually sang the praises of *hospitality* "addiafa." They also praised "alhamasah," meaning *enthusiasm*, and the "murouwwah," meaning *manliness*. These were *supreme virtues of the race*.

Severe competition for water and pasture was the main cause for conflict that split the desert people into fighting tribes. However, the consciousness and helplessness in the face of a very stubborn and rugged nature gave the feeling of need for the duty of hospitality. To refuse a guest the courtesy, or to cause him harm after being accepted as a guest, was considered a very serious offense, not only against the mores (customs) and honor, but also against God himself, who is, after all, the real protector.

There were Arab Jews and Christians before the rise of Islam. They still form a minority in the Arab land. With the spread of Islam and the great Arab conquests, the Arab Empire became a melting pot in which was formulated what may be called the Arabic character. An Arab may be short or tall, white or black, blond or brown, dark or blue-eyed. He may be of Assyrian, Berber or Phoenician origin. The Arabic language and the Moslem religion are both strong unifying factors. In modern times an Arab is defined as any person whose native language is Arabic.

The Arab world stretches from the Atlantic ocean to the Arabian Gulf. It is endowed with fabulous wealth, and it is the cradle of old civilizations. It is here where three great religions of the world were born: Judaism, Christianity and Islam.

Although the Arabs have been mentioned as far back as the Eighth Century B.C., they were propelled to prominence with the birth of Islam.

Birth and Great Conquests of Islam

With the rise of Islam, the Arabs built a large empire and a fascinating culture as well. They were the heirs to an ancient civilization that flourished on the banks of the Tigris and the Euphrates Rivers and along the land of the Nile at the Eastern shore of the Mediterranean Sea. The Arabs excelled in using and improving on the Greek and Roman cultures.

They in turn played a dynamic role in transferring to the European nations the newly-born civilization, that benefitted from all the ancient ones preceding it. This transfer ultimately led to the awakening of the Western world by setting a steady pace toward Renaissance.

During the Dark Ages of Europe, the Arabs contributed to the progress of humanity more than any other people of the time.

Truly, the distinct entity of the Arabs did not clearly manifest itself and assert its prominent position until the birth of Islam.

Around the year 570 A.D., the *Prophet Mohammed* was born in Mecca. He was a humble member of an Arabian tribe called Qoureish. To nearly a billion Moslems around the world today, the Prophet Mohammed is the last of all prophets of God, who included Abraham, Moses and Jesus.

The words that descended from God were gathered into various chapters called *Suras*. They constituted what is known as the *Holy Qoran*, (also known as the Koran) which in Arabic means recitation (from the verb qara'a meaning to read or recite). The Qoran is the cornerstone of the Moslem faith. It is the Moslem Holy Book, which in time became the greatest pillar of the Arabic language and Arabic literature. Beyond any doubt, the Qoran contains the finest and truly most imaginative prose of any literature in any time. Basic in the Moslem faith is the call to worship of one God, namely: "there is no God but God and Mohammed is His Prophet." The Arabic equivalent is: La Ileha Ila Lloh! Mohammed Rasoul Lloh.

The Arab Empire

A few years after Islam had been only an unknown doctrine, it spread into the northern countries: Palestine, Syria, Iran, Iraq, and also to the south into Egypt. The great political successes of this new religion, establishing itself next to the Byzantine and Persian empires, is very startling indeed, since the followers of the Prophet were poor, both in numbers and material resources.

The Moslem religion nourished its believers and Bedouin followers with a great zeal, especially at a time of feuds and wars between the neighboring empires in the North and East. The Roman Empire had succumbed long ago and its successor, the Christian Byzantine Empire at Constantinople, was continually engaged in warfare with the Sassanid of (Persia) Iran. These devastating wars, heavy taxation and disregard for the local population, along with sectarian differences in the never-ending theological debates in the Christian world, created a very ripe atmosphere to change the rules and to open the gates for the Moslem newcomers.

These differences among the Christians were very acute, to the point that on some occasions persecuted minorities opened the gates of Byzantine cities to the Moslems. The lightning speed with which Islam developed and spread like wildfire, with great impact on life and culture in the area extending from China to Spain, is indeed one of the most remarkable features of the history of mankind.

After the death of the Prophet Mohammed the leadership passed on to Abou Bakr, who was the first caliph or "Khalifa," meaning Successor. His most brilliant general was Khalid Ibn Al-Walid, who led the Arab drive to break the Byzantine and Sassanid Empires. As the Arab army moved forward, the number of Moujehidine swelled by large conversions to Islam.

The Byzantine army was defeated at the Yarmouk River in 636 A.D. Iraq and Persia fell between 637 and 650. The city of Jerusalem fell in 638 and Egypt was conquered in 640. Conquests continued for a century until the Arab Empire extended from China to France, giving a unique feature in history, the like of which, in vigor and lightning speed, has never been duplicated.

The Caliphate was first in the Oumayyad family "Al-Ouma-weeyyeen," from the Qouraish tribe, and their rule was centered in Damascus. Rivalries later developed and resulted in dividing the Moslem religion into Sunni and Shi'a (Shi'ite) sects. After the murder of the third Caliph Outhman, his cousin Ali, who was a son-in-law to the Prophet, became the fourth Caliph. But Mouaweeia, the governor of Syria, accused Ali of complicity in the murder of Outhman and finally gained the Caliphate after Ali was assassinated.

With this came the major division in the Moslem faith: The Sunni, who believed that the Caliphate was an elective office, and the Shi'a, who believed that the heirs of Prophet Mohammed, namely his daughter Fatima and her husband Ali, were entitled to the Caliphate.

One more attempt was made to wrest the Caliphate for Ali's son, Hussain. But he and his followers were murdered at Karbala, Iraq, in October, 680 A.D. The most important Shi'a Shrines are at Karbala and Al-Najaf.

As the divisions spread, Moslems were divided into several sects. Among them are these:

- Ismailees or Accessors, who developed into a political group about the Twelfth Century A.D. They have terrorized large parts

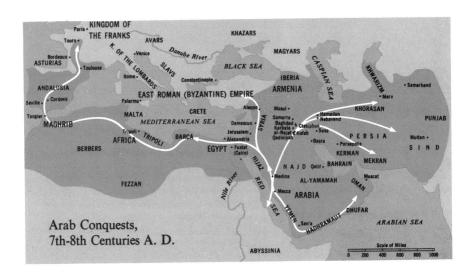

Arab Conquests,
7th-8th Centuries A. D.

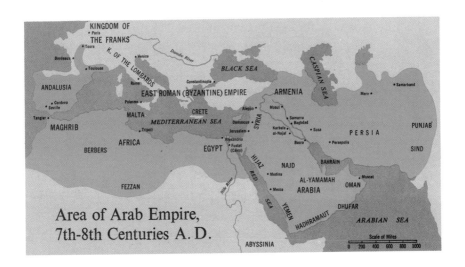

Area of Arab Empire,
7th-8th Centuries A. D.

of the Middle East. The Ismailees still live in northwest Syria and other communities in Iran and Oman. The Agha Khan is the head of this sect of Islam.

- *Alawis (Ansarieh or Nusayris).* These Moslems have adopted such practices as recognizing Christmas from Christianity and such other traditions as fertility ceremonies. The Alawis number nearly half a million. They live in Jabal Ansarieh in Syria.
- More recent *Shia offshoots*, which include the Zaidis, predominantly in Yemen; the Ali Ilahis, a sect recognizing Ali as the Deity, and the Bakhtahis, who live in Albania.
- *Qarmatians*, who lived in the area of Iran and Iraq during the Middle Ages. They have views of revolutionary and communistic nature. This sect has almost died away.
- *Druze*, who are people of the Ismailee heretical sect, numbering around half a million. They combined the Shari'a, a certain degree of animism, and the belief of the transmigration of souls. They are mainly in the Shouf mountains of Lebanon. Some of these Druze have migrated to the Houran area in Syria and a few settled in Northern Palestine and Iraq. Many of them believe that God will some day come back to earth.
- The *Bahais*, founded by Mirza Muhammed. This is a movement that has taken place during the Nineteenth Century in Iran as a reaction against materialism and corruption. Many of his followers were killed, but the movement still continues and its main creed is love for one another.
- *Sufism*, which is based on some mysticism in Islam. It has many groups and orders. The basic belief here is the mystical union between the human soul and Deity with the omnipresence of God's guidance. Spiritual possession, meditation, and prayer are basic to the Sufi way of living and these are in accordance with human behavior as determined by God's will.

The Oumayyad dynasty was finally overthrown in the year 750 by the descendents of Abbas, an uncle to the Prophet. The *Abbasid* dynasty ruled from Baghdad until its shattering by the Mongols in 1258. Prosperity reached its greatest peak during the Caliphate of Horoun Al-Rashid (786–809).

It was during the two decades of the rule of Horoun Al-Rashid that the Arab Empire distinguished itself with significant achievements in mathematics, medicine, astronomy, art, and philosophy. Translations in these fields flourished, and the works of Greeks, Romans and Persians were adapted, improved upon with innovations and later transmitted to the West when Europe was still in the Dark Ages.

In 1079, the *Crusaders* from Europe began their invasion of Syria.

This was done in the name of defending Christianity and the Holy Land. They held Jerusalem from 1099 until its recapture by *Saleh Eddine* in the year 1187. The Crusaders–with trading, commercial, and religious motives–felt the influence of Eastern civilization, which helped bring about the European Renaissance. They also left their impact on a segment of the people in the Middle East. By the year 1299, the last Christian stronghold had fallen.

The conquering of the two empires of the time, namely, the Sassanid and the Byzantine, was achieved with high speed. However, the first real setback for the Arabs and their conquests came from North Africa at the hands of none other than the Berbers who were much like the Arabs.

The Berbers were nomads who did not like either city dwelling or luxury living. Their features are of the Caucasian type. Some of them are slender and tall. They may be dark or blond and blue-eyed. For nearly one thousand years, beginning in 1200 B.C., the Berbers were ruled by the Phoenicians, who founded the Carthage state, based on Carthage near the City of Tunis in present-day Tunisia.

The Phoenicians were succeeded by the Romans after the destruction of Carthage in 146 B.C. The Roman rule remained for nearly 650 years and was followed by the vandals of the Byzantine Empire. Although there was disparity under the Byzantine rule, a small number of the people of North Africa became Latin-speaking Christians such as St. Augustine. The large majority of the people did not assimilate with the Roman conquest and culture. This was in contrast to the population of Western Europe. The Arabs took some time to subdue the Berbers and bring them under their empire. When this was done, it was done with great success. Where the Romans had failed, the Arabs succeeded in assimilating them as completely as could be. This was due mainly to the natural affinity in culture and way of life which existed between the Arabs and the Berbers, coupled with the vast power already mastered by the Islamic religion. Many of these facts have been reported by the Arab historian, Ibn Khaldoun, who was a native of Tunis.

Finally, Christianity was replaced by Islam, and Latin was replaced by Arabic in the entire North African area which had been under the Roman influence. The Latin and Greek populations of the cities left for Spain and Italy. The Berbers continued to use their own language after they had adopted Islam as their religion.

By the year 714 the entire countries of Spain and Portugal, were in the firm grip of Arab hands. Three years later their armies broke through the Pyrenées into the fertile land of France. At this point their advance was halted. Although they continued to carry on some raids and establish temporary colonies, the weather of Northern and Central Europe was never what the Arabs really desired.

During the Jaheeliyya time, great Arab poetry was written. It gives an insight into the Arab character, and brings forth one of the most impressive features in Arab tradition. Enthusiasm, hospitality and deep emotions are prevalent. However, some of the finest Arab poetry was authored during the Abbasid era where Baghdad reached the apogee of glory under the Caliph Horoun Al-Rashid, from the year 786 to 809, and his son, the Caliph Al-Mamoun (813–833).

A large number of mosques, government palaces with many beautiful gardens and pavillions were all about. Baghdad was a city of pleasure "the Paris of the Ninth Century."

The Golden Age of the Arabs brought to civilization skills in art, philosophy, science and a great culture, all of which enlightened many civilizations that followed. Several Arab cities prospered, and became centers of luxury and wealth, among them Baghdad, Basra, Cairo, Alexandria, Damascus, and Aleppo. One should never forget the fine contributions made by the Arabs in medicine, poetry, algebra and chemistry.

Arab ingenuity created new inventions and improved on previous civilizations through translations of many works of science, art, literature and technology. The Arabs not only brought to good use the knowledge that existed before them, but they have also kept the torch of wisdom and knowledge burning—a torch that enlightened Europe during its Dark Ages.

The great Abbasid Dynasty, which lasted nearly five hundred years, was declining toward the latter part of its rule. By the time *Mongol* General Hulagu Khan tore down Baghdad in 1258, the Caliph was kicked to death, and after 800,000 people died in the streets, the empire was finished. However, the decline of the Arab empire began slowly but surely much earlier, in fact after the death of Horoun Al-Rashid in 829.

Fall of the Arab Empire

On the 26th of November 1095, Pope Urban gave a speech at Claremont in Southeastern France. In that speech, he urged the faithful to "enter upon the road to the Holy Sepulchre, wrest it from the wicked race, and subject it." By the spring of the year 1097, nearly 150,000 men, mostly Franks and Normans, had answered the call and met at Constantinople. With the depressed economy and the poor social conditions in France, Lorraine, Italy and Sicily, the carrying of the cross was, essentially, a relief and not much of a sacrifice.

After the departure of the Crusaders, the Mongols or Tartars, coming from the highlands of Central Asia, attacked the Arabs mercilessly and caused destruction and devastation. Between the years 1220 and 1227, Genghis Khan and his men terrorized and destroyed many communities in Iran. By the year 1258, the Mongols' terror reached Mesopotamia. Baghdad was ruined and the Abbasid Caliphate was destroyed. One hundred years later, Timurlane and his armies reached Syria and burned its major cities.

The Mongols were finally stopped in Asia Minor, where they were challenged by the rising power of the *Ottoman Turks*, who invaded Asia Minor in the Thirteenth Century A.D. and received a grant of territory from a weakened Sultan. By the year 1453, they extended their rule to Constantinople, and around 1566, their Empire was expanded to include the entire Arab World and beyond. They ruled the Arabs in the name of Islam for many centuries.

The basis of the Sultan's Policy was: *divide and rule.* He turned Moslem against Christian, Sunni against Shi'a, Kurd against Armenian. This was a dark period in Arab history.

The Ottomans were repulsed outside Vienna in 1683 and this was the beginning of their slow decline. Their Empire ended in 1918 after the defeat of Turkey, which had entered World War I on the side of Germany.

During the barbaric attacks by Hulagu Khan, beautiful libraries and works of art were burned and thousands of inhabitants were massacred. The Mongols continued the destruction in various areas in Mesopotamia and also in Syria. The great system of irrigation which remained in this region to make it fertile and prosperous for many years also was ruined. The blow was devastating and beyond imagination.

The Ottoman empire was like the Romans' in the sense that it was essentially militaristic and dynastic in character. The major objective was not the welfare of the subjects, but the welfare of the governing state as represented by the Sultan or Caliph. These subjects were gathered in nationalities encompassing the Arabians, Iraqis, Syrians, Berbers, Armenians, Slavs, Kurds, Albanians, and Greeks, with many creeds, languages, and various ways of life. All of them were held by the power of the sword.

The Ottoman empire clearly distinguished between Moslems and Christians and encouraged differences even between Moslem Turks and Moslem Arabs. It played one Christian sect against another, very much along the lines of divide and rule. The seeds of decay were right in its structure from the early beginning. These conditions became aggravated, but the forces of nationalism prevailed after a long struggle.

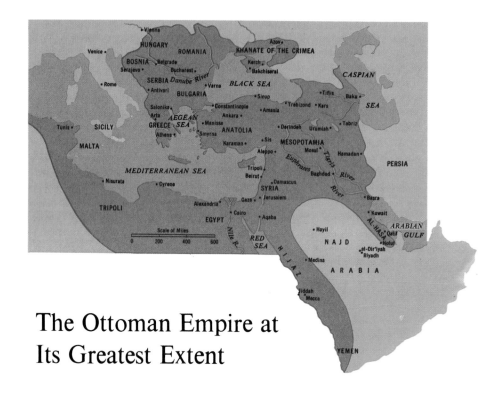

The Ottoman Empire at Its Greatest Extent

Their era of "Divide and Rule" was the darkest period in Arab History.

The Turks failed in their second attempt on Vienna, Austria, in the year 1683. That was the beginning of their major decline, a pathway that was long and very tortuous. The Turkish expansion into Europe made no more progress and after that the Turks had the problem of holding on to what already remained under their rule.

Six centuries of Ottoman rule are regarded by the Arabs today as the dark period in their history. It is indeed astonishing that such dynamic and creative people were held politically dormant and socially stagnant for such a long time. The end to this period of stagnation came with the rise of the Arab Nationalist movement in the latter part of the Nineteenth Century. This process which was culminated by Arabs joining forces with the Allies in World War I, and with the eventual end of Turkish rule in 1918.

Great Britain was the dominant force at the time. *King Abdulaziz Al-Saud, known in the west as Ibn Saud,* used his political genius to gain the necessary help in liberating those parts of Arabia under Turkish rule and foreign influence.

While Great Britain and France were determined to limit the Arabs to self-rule, the United States of America declared its support for self-determination. Good relations were established with the U.S. and careful diplomacy was used to avoid antagonism with the British.

King Abdulaziz Al-Saud was a legendary leader, truly known as the father of his country, which by 1932 was unified as the Kingdom of Saudi Arabia.

Oil discovery and production by 1938 added to the strategic and spiritual importance of this land, birthplace of the Prophet, and guardian to the Holy Moslem Shrines. It is the heartbeat of the Arab world, the spiritual leader for all Moslems of the globe, and the energy giant with undisputable worldwide moderating force and influence.

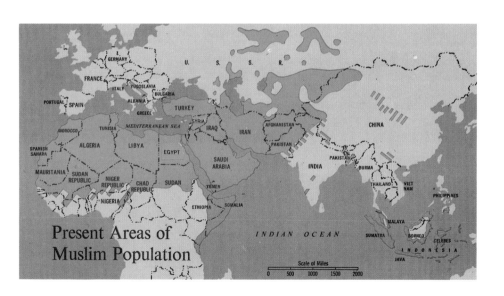

Present Areas of Muslim Population

The Kingdom of Saudi Arabia is the birthplace and guardian of Moslem Holy Shrines. (Every Moslem faces Mecca in his Prayers).

Arabs of Today

The tremendous impact of Arab oil on world energy needs has been coupled with greater awareness and importance for the Arab world as a whole, especially the oil-producing nations. Almost overnight, news about oil took prominence, and the migration of world technologies toward the Arabs has indeed reached a high point.

With the importance of Arab oil, especially the massive oil reserves of Saudi Arabia, came economic power and special attention to the Arab cause, that had been neglected for many centuries.

The Arabs need Western technology and the West is in equal need of their oil. Without it, many of the Western industries and economies would suffer severely or outright collapse. Thus, a very interesting equation has developed in the past few years, where Arab interests and Western interests must logically and ultimately lead to a common base of mutual benefit and understanding.

One of the thorniest points in Arab matters, as far as the international community is concerned, has been Western insensitivity to a major issue, namely the *Palestinian question, and the refugees' dilemma. World peace cries for a just and permanent solution to this problem which is at the core of Middle East conflicts.*

King Fahd with his wise leadership and political valor devised an ingenius peace plan. This inventive solution (described earlier) coupled with serious American peace initiatives, should clear the way toward an acceptable compromise for ending this devastating tragedy.

However, much destruction has taken place in the span of a few years. The Middle East has been wracked by bickering differences, wars, and the creation of nearly four million Palestinian refugees. This has resulted in a great burden that has settled upon and choked many nations of the region.

One nation that suffered the most in recent times from the aftermath of creating these refugees, is the once fascinating and beautiful country of *Lebanon,* best known as "the land of milk and honey" and the "Switzerland of the Middle East." It was a beauty crowned with majestic nature where the air smells of goodness and delight, an ancient land that was a shining example of tolerance among many religions and nationalities.

Unfortunately international intrigue, hatred and divisions in the Arab world brought an ugly civil war that tore the country apart. The result has been the transformation of Beirut, formerly known as the Paris of the Middle East, into the world capital for tragedy and terror.

It is imperative that the United States should exercise its unique position of leadership by helping this region in gaining peace and

Modern Architecture and "high rise" dot the desert landscape.

tranquillity. Such a policy will be beneficial to all the parties concerned. It will frustrate communist designs and shatter their dreams of dominating this strategic and vital part of the world.

Throughout the Arab world there is action on many fronts to modernize and build. Saudi Arabia, for example, is a nation with great wealth and deep religious traditions. Under the wise leadership of *King Fahd*, progress in every walk of life is mind-boggling. Because of its just and swift rules, this country is one of the safest on earth.

The Kingdom is carrying out an industrial and educational evolution of far-reaching consequences. To attract personnel with needed know-how, pay is lucrative and living quarters are similar to any suburban American community.

With the discovery of oil in the 1930's, the Arab world became gradually more important. With the impact and dangers of modern-day energy needs, the Arabs and their oil gained international stature and acquired great wealth and influence.

Billions of petrodollars have been pouring in and massive industrialization programs are under way. In this atmosphere of Arab renaissance, the West, especially the U.S.A., can make a great contribution in leadership and technology that will be beneficial to all.

The modern Arabs remain divided into many independent nations. They yearn for Arab unity and a single Arab nation from the Atlantic Ocean to the Arabian Gulf; but this remains largely a dream.

With the fires of nationalism have come faint communist "Eastern" winds that are basically alien to the Arab tradition and to the Moslem religion of the Arabs. These winds shall fade away, for the Arabs are God-fearing people, who have a deep respect for Western technology, and great pride in their heritage.

Appendix C

Simplified Diagram for the Government of Saudi Arabia

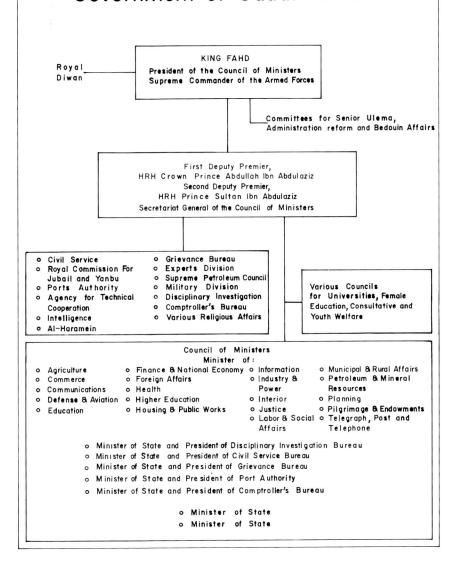

Royal Diwan

KING FAHD
President of the Council of Ministers
Supreme Commander of the Armed Forces

Committees for Senior Ulema,
Administration reform and Bedouin Affairs

First Deputy Premier,
HRH Crown Prince Abdullah Ibn Abdulaziz
Second Deputy Premier,
HRH Prince Sultan Ibn Abdulaziz
Secretariat General of the Council of Ministers

- Civil Service
- Royal Commission For Jubail and Yanbu
- Ports Authority
- Agency for Technical Cooperation
- Intelligence
- Al-Haramein

- Grievance Bureau
- Experts Division
- Supreme Petroleum Council
- Military Division
- Disciplinary Investigation
- Comptroller's Bureau
- Various Religious Affairs

Various Councils for Universities, Female Education, Consultative and Youth Welfare

Council of Ministers
Minister of :

- Agriculture
- Commerce
- Communications
- Defense & Aviation
- Education

- Finance & National Economy
- Foreign Affairs
- Health
- Higher Education
- Housing & Public Works

- Information
- Industry & Power
- Interior
- Justice
- Labor & Social Affairs

- Municipal & Rural Affairs
- Petroleum & Mineral Resources
- Planning
- Pilgrimage & Endowments
- Telegraph, Post and Telephone

- Minister of State and President of Disciplinary Investigation Bureau
- Minister of State and President of Civil Service Bureau
- Minister of State and President of Grievance Bureau
- Minister of State and President of Port Authority
- Minister of State and President of Comptroller's Bureau

- Minister of State
- Minister of State

Appendix D

Major Battles Fought by Abdulaziz In His Arduous Struggle to Unify Arabia*

Al-Sureif Battle on 26 zi Al-Ko'da 1318 A.H. (February 16, 1901)

Conquest of Riyadh, 5 Shawwal, 1319 (January 15, 1902)

Conquest of Ouneiza, 5 Muharram 1322 (March 23, 1904)

Al-Bukeireyya Battle, 1 Rabi'i Awwal 1322 (May 16, 1904)

Al-Shunana, 18 Rajab 1322 (September 29, 1904)

Rawdhat Muhanna (Death of Ibn Rashid), 18 Safar 1324 (April 14, 1906)

Al-Turefia, 5 Sha'aban 1325 (April 14, 1907)

Conquest of Bureidah and defeat of Abe-Al Kheil, 20 Rabi'i Thani 1326 (May 23, 1908)

Hudia, 1 Jumada Al-Thani 1328 (January 10, 1910)

Conquest of Al-Hasa, 5 Jumada Awwal 1331 (April 13, 1913)

Jurab, 7 Rabi'i Awwal 1333 (October 24, 1915)

Turba, 25 Sha'aban 1337 (May 25, 1919)

Conquest of Asir, Shawwal 1338 (July, 1920)

Al-Juhree 26 Muharram 1339 (October 11, 1920)

Conquest of Hail, 29 Safar 1340 (November 2, 1921)

Conquest of Taif, 7 Safar 1343 (April 7, 1924)

Conquest of Mecca, 18 Rabi'i Awwal 1343 (October 18, 1924)

Musaffahat, 18 Sha'aban 1343 (March 14, 1925)

Surrender of Madina, after a ten-month blockade, 19 Jumada Awwal 1344 (December 5, 1925)

Surrender of Jeddah after a blockade of one year, 6 Jumada Thani 1344 (December 22, 1925)

Source: for Appendix D and E, Amin Rihani and others.

Appendix E

Abdulaziz and His Companions in the Winter of 1901, on Their Way From Kuwait to Recapture Riyadh

These courageous men are:

Mohammed Bin Abdul Rahman Al-Faisal
Fahd Bin Jiluwi Al-Saud
Abdulaziz Bin Jiluwi
Abdullah Bin Jiluwi
Abdulaziz Bin Musa'ed Bin Jiluwi
Abdulaziz Bin Abdullah Bin Turki
Fahd Bin Ibrahim Al-Mushari
Abdullah Bin Huneitan
Nasser Bin Saud Al-Farhan
Saud Bin Nasser Al-Farhan
Fahd Bin Mu'amar
Muslim Bin Mujfal Al-Subei'ye
Hizam Al-Oujalein Al-Dosari
Falaj Bin Shanar Al-Dosari
Ibrahim Al-Nafisi
Mansour Bin Mohammed Bin Hamzah
Saleh Bin Saba'an
Mansour Bin Freij
Youssef Bin Mishkhess
Abdullah Bin Khuneizan
Sa'eed Bin Bishar
Massoud Al-Mabrouk
Abdul-latif Al-Ma'ashouk
Mohammed Al-Ma'ashouk
Fouheid Al-Ma'ashouk
Sa'ad Bin Bkheit
Farhan Al-Saud
Nasser Bin Oujiyyan
Motlak al-Maghrebi
Fahd Bin Al-Woubeir Al-Shaimri
Abdullah Bin A'askar
Mohammed Bin Huza'a
Majed Bin Mir'eed
Zeid Bin Zeid
Abdullah Al-Huzani
Mohammed Bin Shu'eil
Abdullah Bin Oubeid
Sattam Abal-Kheil
Abdullah Bin Jreiss
Fairuz Al-Abdulaziz
Mo'dhad Bin Khursan Al-Shaimri

Appendix F
Sons of King Abdulaziz
(Order Giving Chronological
Relation of Age[1])

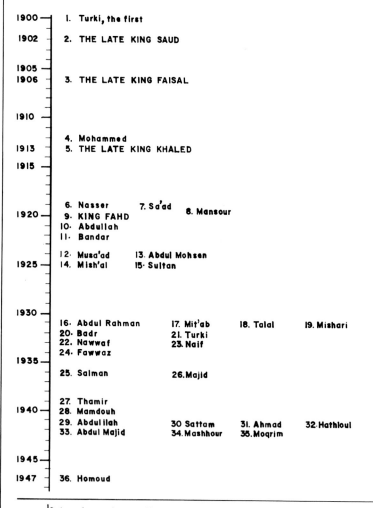

1900 —	1. Turki, the first
1902 —	2. THE LATE KING SAUD
1905 — 1906 —	3. THE LATE KING FAISAL
1910 —	
1913 — 1915 —	4. Mohammed 5. THE LATE KING KHALED
1920 —	6. Nasser 7. Sa'ad 8. Mansour 9. KING FAHD 10. Abdullah 11. Bandar
1925 —	12. Musa'ad 13. Abdul Mohsen 14. Mish'al 15. Sultan
1930 —	16. Abdul Rahman 17. Mit'ab 18. Talal 19. Mishari 20. Badr 21. Turki 22. Nawwaf 23. Naif 24. Fawwaz
1935 —	25. Salman 26. Majid
1940 —	27. Thamir 28. Mamdouh 29. Abdul Ilah 30 Sattam 31. Ahmad 32. Hathloul 33. Abdul Majid 34. Mashhour 35. Moqrim
1945 —	
1947 —	36. Homoud

[1]Order of age is according to number preceding name

THE SONS OF KING ABDULAZIZ[1]

1. Turki
2. SAUD

3. FAISAL

4. Mohammed
5. KHALED

6. Nasser

7. Sa'ad
12. Musa'ad
13. Abdul Mohsen

9. FAHD
15. Sultan
16. Abdul Rahman
21. Turki
23. Naif
25. Salman
31. Ahmad

8. Mansour
14. Mish'al
17. Mit'ab

10. Abdullah

11. Bandar
24. Fawwaz

19. Mishari

20. Badr
29. Abdulilah
33. Abdul Majid

18. Talal
22. Nawwaf

26. Majid
30. Sattam

27. Thamir
28. Mamdouh
34. Mashhour

32. Hathloul

35. Moqrin
36. Homoud

[1]Full Brothers Listed Together.
Order of age is according to number preceding name

Appendix G

Brothers and Children
of Ibn Saud

His **brothers** are:
1. *Faisal Ibn Abdul Rahman*–Oldest brother–Died in 1890 A.D.
2. *Mohammed*–Six months younger than Ibn Saud; grew with him and fought many battles–Died in 1943.
3. *Saud*–Helped his brother in many battles–Died in 1965.
4. *Sa'ad*–Died in the battle of Kanzan in 1915.
5. *Abdullah*–Was top advisor for his brother King Abdulaziz; he is a distinguished scholar and poet.
6. *Sa'ad* (the second)–Named after his brother Sa'ad (the first)– Died in 1955.
7. *Ahmad*–Resides in Jeddah.
8. *Musa'ad*–Born in 1914. He is a man of literature, knowledgeable in monetary matters and national commerce; he became Minister of Finance and National Economy.

King Ibn Saud married more than one woman, fathering a number of girls and thirty-six boys. Among them and their children are rulers, governors, military men, distinguished scholars, poets, businessmen, along with directors of social & welfare organizations.

His **children** are listed according to their date of birth (seven others died in childhood):
1. *Turki*, the first–Born in 1900, he is the oldest son of King Ibn Saud who was known according to Arab customs as father of Turki–Died in 1919.
2. *The late King Saud*–Born in Kuwait in 1902. He was Amir of Najd in 1924 when his father was in Hijaz. He participated in many battles; proclaimed Crown Prince in 1932. He became King upon his father's death on December 11, 1953, and was abdicated from the throne on January 11, 1964. He died in 1969.
3. *The late King Faisal*–Born in Riyadh on April 9, 1906. He was known for his patience and farsightedness. In 1926, he fought the battle of Asir for unifying the Kingdom, becoming government chief in Mecca and his father's representative in the Hijaz. In 1919, he traveled to England, France and Belgium. In 1926, he headed a delegation to a number of western coun-

tries. He became foreign minister in 1930, and in 1932 he made an extensive trip to some western countries and to Poland, Russia, Turkey, Iran, Iraq, and Kuwait. He attended the Conference on Palestine held in London in 1939, and visited President Roosevelt of the United States and the King of England in 1943. He represented his country at the founding conference of the United Nations in San Francisco, U.S.A., and at a number of other U.N. meetings. He became Crown Prince in 1953. In 1964, he chaired the second Arab Summit Conference, and became the King. He was assassinated in 1975.

4. *Mohammed*–Born in 1912, in Riyadh. He is the oldest living son. He headed the force which carried the blockade of Medina during the war of Hijaz. Upon entering the city, he was granted the title: "Amir of Medina," but excused himself from accepting any official post.

5. *The late King Khaled*–Born in Riyadh in 1913. He accompanied his brother Faisal to the United States of America. He was involved in agricultural work. When Faisal became King, Khaled was made a Crown Prince by Royal Decree, then became the King in 1975.

6. *Nasser*–Born in 1919, First Governor of Riyadh after the entry to Hijaz.

7. *Sa'ad*–Born in 1919.

8. *Mansour*–Born in Riyadh, 1920. He was the first Minister of Defense–Died in 1953.

9. *King Fahd*–Present Monarch of the Kingdom of Saudi Arabia (KSA). First son of Hussah bint Ahmad Al-Sudairi; born in 1920. He was appointed first Minister of Education, upon whom rested the responsibility to lay the strong foundations for the great academic and industrial evolution of the Kingdom. He headed the Saudi delegation to the Arab League Conferences in Morocco and Lebanon, then he became Minister of the Interior, and thus established the cornerstone for Saudi Security and Defense, on top of this was added the post of Deputy Prime Minister. In 1975, he was made Crown Prince, and in 1982, he became the KING.

10. *Abdullah*–Born in 1921. Head of the National Guard. He became crown prince in 1982. The right hand man to the King: a man of courage, and great contributions to national harmony and security.

11. *Bandar*–Born in 1922; known for his strict religious beliefs; he is interested in business.

12. *Musa'ad*–Born in 1924; private business.

13. *Abdul Mohsen*–Born in 1924; was Minister of the Interior 1961–1962; became Governor of Medina–Died in 1985.

14. *Mish'al*–Born in 1925, he was Minister of Defense in 1951–1955; at one time he was Governor of Mecca, then he moved on to private business.

15. *Sultan*–Born in 1925. He was Chief of the Royal Guard in Riyadh, then became Minister of Agriculture, Minister of Communication. He was appointed Minister of Defense and the Air Force in the early Sixties. His impressive contributions to National Defense cover the span of over twenty years.

16. *Abdul-Rahman*–Born in 1931; was active in business; became Vice Minister of Defense.

17. *Mit'ab*–Born in 1931; became Minister of Public Works & Housing.

18. *Talal*–Born in 1931; He was Ambassador to France, then became Minister of Finance during the reign of King Saud; now active in the United Arab Council for Children.

19. *Mishari*–Born in 1931; private business.

20. *Badr*–Born in 1932; was Minister of Communications 1961–1962; he is Vice Commander of the National Guard.

21. *Turki*–Born in 1932; named after his brother Turki the first; was Vice Minister of Defense and the Air Force; now in private business.

22. *Nawwaf*–Born in 1933; he became special Advisor to King Faisal, dealing with Gulf affairs; in private business.

23. *Naif*–Born in 1933; he became Governor of Riyadh, then Deputy Minister of the Interior; he is presently Minister of the Interior.

24. *Fawwaz*–Born in 1934; he became Governor of Mecca, until he resigned in December, 1979.

25. *Salman*–Born in 1936; he has been the Governor of Riyadh since 1962.

26. *Majid*–Born in 1936; was Minister of Municipalities 1975–1978; became Governor of Mecca in 1980.

27. *Thamer*–Born in 1939; Died in 1958.

28. *Mamdouh*–Born in 1940; Governor of Tabouk.

29. *Abdul Ilah*–Born in 1941; he became Governor of Kasim (Ouneiza & Buraidah) in 1980.

30. *Sattam*–Born in 1941; he became Vice Governor of Riyadh.

31. *Ahmad*–Born in 1941; he became Deputy Governor of Mecca, and presently Vice Minister of Interior.

32. *Hathloul*–Born in 1941; has business interests.

33. *Abdul Majid*–Born in 1942; formerly Governor of Tabouk; now Governor of Medina.

34. *Mashhour*–Born in 1942; has business interests.

35. *Moqrin*–Born in 1942; was an Air Force pilot; he became Governor of Hail.

36. *Homoud*–Born in 1947; has business interests.

Appendix H
The Moslem Calendar

It is based on the Hijra, or the year the Prophet Mohammed migrated from Mecca to Medina; this corresponds to July 16, 622 A.D. (Gregorian year) or the year 1 A.H (Anno Hegirae = Hijra year). It is a lunar year, where one lunar month covers the cycle between two new moons encompassing 29 days, 12 hours, 44 minutes and 2.8 seconds. The lunar year has 354 days and $\frac{11}{30}$ of a day; every 30 years, this amounts to 11 days. The twelve lunar months of the Hijra year are:

Mouharram
Safar
Rabi awwal
Rabi thani
Joumada awwal
Joumada thani
Rajab
Shaban
Ramadan
Shawwal
Zoul-Qa'dah
Zoul-Hijjah

The following are some corresponding years between the Moslem and Christian Calendars. The indicated months are the dates on which the Hijra years begin.

A.H. (Hijra Year)	A.D. (Gregorian Year)	A.H. (Hijra Year)	A.D. (Gregorian Year)
1	622 July 16	1321	1903 March 30
150	767 February 6	1322	1904 March 18
500	1106 September 2	1323	1905 March 8
600	1203 September 10	1324	1906 February 25
1000	1591 October 19	1325	1907 February 14
1305	1887 September 19	1326	1908 February 4
1319	1901 April 20	1327	1909 January 23
1320	1902 April 10	1328	1910 January 13

A.H. (Hijra Year)	A.D. (Gregorian Year)	A.H. (Hijra Year)	A.D. (Gregorian Year)
1329	1911 January 2	1382	1962 June 4
1330	1911 December 22	1384	1964 May 13
1331	1912 December 11	1395	1975 January 14
1332	1913 November 30	1396	1976 January 3
1333	1914 November 19	1399	1978 December 2
1334	1915 November 9	1400	1979 November 22
1335	1916 October 28	1401	1980 November 9
1336	1917 October 17	1402	1981 October 30
1337	1918 October 7	1403	1982 October 19
1338	1919 September 26	1404	1983 October 8
1339	1920 September 15	1405	1984 September 27
1340	1921 September 4	1406	1985 September 16
1341	1922 August 24	1407	1986 September 6
1342	1923 August 14	1408	1987 August 26
1343	1924 August 2	1409	1988 August 14
1344	1925 July 23	1410	1989 August 4
1345	1926 July 12	1411	1990 July 24
1346	1927 July 1	1412	1991 July 13
1347	1928 June 20	1413	1992 July 2
1348	1929 June 9	1414	1993 June 21
1349	1930 May 29	1415	1994 June 10
1350	1931 May 19	1416	1995 May 31
1351	1932 May 7	1417	1996 May 19
1356	1937 March 14	1418	1997 May 9
1357	1938 March 3	1419	1998 April 28
1362	1943 January 8	1420	1999 April 17
1373	1953 September 10	1421	2000 April 6

Appendix I

Glossary of Arabic Words

Abadan	Never
Abaya	Wide garment made from wool & worn by men over their clothes.
Abb	Father
Abou	Father of . . . men are traditionally called by the name of their eldest son. Thus, if the father's name is Ahmad and his son is Ibrahim, the father will be called Abou Ibrahim.
Aghal	Double headcord worn on the headdress
Ahlan wa sahlan	Welcome
Ajlis	Sit (sit down)
Akl	Food
Akthar	More
Al	In the upper case, it connotes or denotes belonging to a family, (for example, Al-Saud)
al	Lower case al is a definite article meaning "the" (e.g. al-Arab = the Arabs)
Al-Saud	The House of Saud, the Saud family
Alf	Thousand
Alhamdulillah	Praise be to God
Allah	Allah, God
Allahou akbar	God is Great
Ameen	Safe
Ameerkani, Amreekee	American
Amir	Prince, belonging to the royal family, someone who holds authority such as a commander, ruler or governor
Anta	You (for male), Anti for female
Arabi	Arab, arabic
Ardha	Traditional sword dance
Assalamou alaikom	Peace be upon you

AssaOudi	Saudi
Azeem (moumtez)	Great, wonderful
Azraq	Blue
Badawi (pl. Badu)	Bedouin
Badr	Full moon
Bahr	Sea
Bakhour	Frankincense giving good smell upon burning
Balad	Country
Bareed	Mail
Barmeel	Measure for crude oil production; one bpd (barrel per day) is equivalent to a volume measure of 42 U.S. Gallons per day. One ton is the weight of 17.3 barrels of average crude oil
Bass	Enough
Bay'ah	Oath of allegiance to the King
Bab	Door
Bedu	People of the desert, Bedouin
Beit	Home, house
Bin	Same as Ibn, son of . . . (Fahd bin Abdulaziz)
Bina'a	Construction
Bint	Girl
Bismillah	In the name of God
Bouldan	Countries
Boulis	Police
Caliph (Khalifah)	Successor, Title for the Moslem leaders that came to power after the Prophet's death. This title was later used by the Ottoman Empire to designate the Turkish Sultan
Daktour bil handasa	Doctor of engineering
Daqiqa	Minute
Darahim (foulous)	Money
Darb, Tareeq	Road
Dhahab (Thahab)	Gold
Diayfa	Hospitality
Dishdasha (Thobe)	White gown worn by men
Doukkan, dakekeen	Shop, shops
Doular	Dollar
Douwali	International

Eid al-Adha	Feast of Sacrifice celebrating the end of pilgrimage; it begins on the tenth day of the month Zul Hijjah
Eid al-Fitr	A festival of the breaking of the fast, occurs on the first of Shawwal, commencing with the sighting of the new moon at the end of Ramadan
Famm (Fami)	Mouth, my mouth
Fard	Individual
Farmasheeia	Pharmacy
Fatwa	Important pronouncement by moslem religious authorities.
Falleh (pl. Falleheen)	Peasant (peasants)
Fikra	Idea
Floos	Money
Fustan, fistan	Kaftan worn by women, dress
Garage	Garage
GDP	Gross Domestic Product
Ghazu	Bedouin raid
Ghutrah	Man's headscarf
Hadhar	Settled people deriving their livelyhoods from farming and trading (opposite nomad)
Hadith	Sayings of the Prophet Mohammed and his Companions
Hajj	Pilgrimage to Mecca
Hajja	Female moslem who made the Hajj
Hajji	The one who made the Pilgrimage
Hakeem	Doctor, wise
Haleeb	Milk
Hamd	Praise
Haram	Sacred sanctuary, such as the areas surrounding Mecca and Medina which are off limits to non-moslems.
Harām	Forbidden
Harara	Heat
Harb	War
Hareem	Women, female members of a family
Hareer (gazz)	Pure silk
Harr	Hot
Hazz	Luck
Hijra	Migration, for moslems it refers to the migration of the Prophet Mohammed and

	his followers from Mecca to Medina. It also refers to the moslem calendar (Hijra or Hijria)
Hina	Here
Hujar	The plural of hijra, agricultural settlements of the Ikhwan
Ibn	Son; used with the name of an ancestor, it denotes a family such as Ibn Saud
Id (eeid)	Holiday, holy day
Igal	Headband
Ingleezi	English
Ikhwan	Literally it means brotherhood (plural of akh, brother). Warriors organized by King Abdulaziz Ibn Saud. They were settled in the hujar. The first settlement was built in the fall of 1912, at the desert wells of Artawiya.
Imam	Moslem leader in Prayer, an acknowledged dignitary or anyone leading in a prayer. This title was given to Ibn Saud, and then, after he became a King, his father was called Imam.
Inshallah	God Willing
Intaj	Production
Islam	The Moslem religion, submission to the will of God
Ism	Name
Ismi	My name
Ismak	Your name
Istihlak	Consumption
Jabal	Mountain
Jame'e	Mosque
Jameel	Beautiful, handsome
Jawab	Answer
Jihad	Holy War
Jild	Leather (skin)
Jism	Body
Jouneina	Garden
Jawaher	Jewelry
Ka'aba	Cube-shaped stone building, fifty-foot high, containing the sacred black stone in Mecca to which a moslem directs himself during prayer. It is draped in black and gold

material which is traditionally renewed annually. It is the House of God built by Abraham. Its black cornerstone was cast down by God to Adam after he was removed from the Garden of Eden. This is a symbol of God's reconciliation with mankind.

Kabir	Large
Kafalah	Guarantee
Kaffiya	Arab head-dress
Kaftan	Long gown worn under abaya
Kahwa	Coffee
Keef al-hal	How are you?
Kalam	Talk
Kalima	God's Word, word
Khayma	Bedouin tent made from sheep's wool or goat's hair
Khanjar	Curved dagger
Kharab	Destruction
Khatar	Danger
Khateeb	Preacher, speaker
Khibrah	Experience
Khobz	Bread
Kilomitr	Kilometer
Kitab	Book
Kteer	Very much, a lot
La	No
Laban	Buttermilk, yogurt
Leil	Night
Leila saeeda	Goodnight
Libass	Dressing clothes
Ma'a assalama	Goodbye
Madrasa	School
Maghrib	Sunset
Mahr	Dowry
Majalla	Magazine
Majlis	Audience with the King, Prince, Governor or Sheikh. Such gathering is open to all citizens who may wish to offer a suggestion or grievance. Also reception or sitting room; from the Arabic ijlis meaning sit down
Maktab	Office
Maktaba	Library
Malioun	Million

Manzar	View
Mareedh	Ill
Marhaba	Hello
Marrah	Once
Masafah	Distance
Masroor (mabsoot)	Happy
Matar (shita'a)	Rain
Mat'haf	Museum
Mataar	Airport
Me'e (my'y) (ma'e)	Water
Meeyyah	Hundred
Mihnah	Profession
Minfadlak (m)	Please
Minfadlik (f)	Please
Misr	Egypt
Mistashfa	Hospital
Mnee'h, moumtaz	Good
Mootēr	Engine
Moujahid	Fighter in Holy War
Moujahideen	Plural for Moujahid
Moulawwath	Contaminated
Mou'minoun	Faithful, or followers of Islam
Moushkila	Crisis, trouble
Mouhandis	Engineer
Mu'akhkhar	Second part of dowry promised to wife in case of divorce.
Mu'azzin	Religious man calling for prayer time
Mufti	Highest religious authority of Islam, leading religious and legal official first appointed during the Ottoman Empire in 1539 A.D.
Muqaddam	First part of the dowry payment paid at time of engagement
Mutawa'a	Man of religion (who volunteer or obey); they remind the populace of prayer times and religious practices
Na'am	Yes
Nahawr	Day (during daylight)
Nay	Flute
Nedir (Qalil)	Rare (little)
Omm	Mother
Oud	Arabic musical instrument similar to the guitar
Otel	Hotel

Oureed	Would like
Passpor	Passport
Petrole (zeit)	Petroleum
Qadi	Judge
Qalb	Heart
Qamar	Moon
Qareeb	Relative (related to), near
Qif	Stop
Qoran	Holy book of Islam. It is God's revelation to the Prophet Mohammed through the Angel Gabriel. It contains 114 Chapters or Suras.
Qounsouliyya	Consulate
Rab'a al-khali	The famous barren desert in the southeast region of Saudi Arabia, known as the Empty Quarter
Radiater	Radiator
Ramadan	The Holy Month of fasting (Ramadan)
Ratib	Humid
Raudha (hadiqa)	Garden
Rajol	Man
Raml	Sand
Riyal	Saudi Riyal (SR); monetary unit with approximate value of 3.75 SR per one US dollar
Routouba	Humidity
Sabah	Morning
Sabah el-Kheir	Good morning
Sadeeq	Friend
Saffara	Embassy
Sa'hra	Desert
Salam	Peace, hello
Salamat	Regards, Hello
Salah	Prayer
Samn	Clarified Butter
Sana	Year
Sanawat	Years
Sawm	Fasting from sunrise to sunset during Ramadan
Sayyid	Sir
Samihni	Excuse me
Seyf	Sword
Shahadah	Profession of Moslem Faith: there is no God

	but God (Allah) and Mohammed is the Prophet of God
Shahr	Month
Shamal	North wind
Sharif	Noble, Honorable
Sharqi	Humid wind in Arabian Gulf, coming from the east
Sharikah	Company
Shari'a	Islamic Law
Sheikh	Honorific title denoting tribal chiefs, notables, and scholars (literally it means old man)
Shi'ite (shi'a)	A branch of Islam, (shi'at Ali-The party of Ali)
Shoubbak	Window
Shoukran	Thank you
Sifir	Zero
Sikkeen	Knife
Sondouq	Box
Souq	Bazaar, market place
Soura	Picture
Sourour	Pleasure
Sunnah	Traditions and practices set by the Prophet, and practiced by Moslems
Sufism	Referring to various Moslem mystics using different ways in order to achieve strong closeness to God
Sunnis	Major sect of the Moslem World. They are the followers of Sunna (guide to proper behavior from the Qoran and the sayings of the Prophet) of the Prophet)
Talab	Application
Taqa	Energy
Tayyara	Airplane
Tahéneena	Congratulations
Talifon	Telephone
Talleghrof	Telegram
Talvizion	Television
Taqteer (tasfia)	Distillation, refining
Tareeq	Road
Tareeqa	Method
Tasdir	Export

Tasfia (taqteer)	Refining
Tawb (Thawb)	Long dress worn by women, similar to the Thawb for men.
Taweel	Long, tall
Taxi	Taxi
Tayyib	OK; delicious
Thaman	Price
Thaqafa	Education
Thawb	Long sleeved, full-length garment, with high neck, worn by men; it is usually white and thin in the summer, heavier, dark or striped in the winter.
Ulama	Religious scholars, learned men who oversee the religious aspect of life. When terrorists seized the Grand Mosque of Mecca, the Ulama issued a Fatwa or religious ruling based on King Khaled's request, so that Saudi troops could enter the Mosque and fight the criminals
Umla	Money, coin
Umm	Mother
Wa alaikoumou'ssalam	Peace be with you
Wahid	Number one
Wadi	Dry river bed
Wahhabis	Adherents to wahhabism
Wahhabism	Puritanical concept of Islam, as it was preached by Mohammed bin Abdul-Wahhab, whose alliance with King Fahd's ancestors brought about a dynamic religious revival which culminated with the rise to power of King Fahd's father Abdulaziz Ibn Saud
Walad	Boy
Wallahi	By God!
Wasat	Medium
Ya	Used to call for someone (e.g. ya Ahmad; ya Allah = Oh God!)
Yadd	Hand
Yakol	Eat
Yasmine	Scent from Jasmine flower
Yasouq	Drive
Yaktob	Write
Yom	Day (for the whole day)

Zahab (Thahab)	Gold
Zakat	Religious tax
Zakee	Intelligent
Zawj	Husband
Zawjat	Wife
Zawjee	My husband
Zeit	Oil
Zeitoun	Olives

Appendix J

Worldwide Energy Demand by Sources

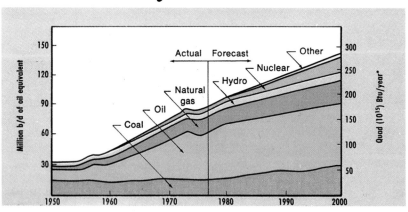

Source: Shaheen, E. I. and Vora, M. K., "Energy Yesterday, Today and Tomorrow," also International Petroleum Encyclopedia, PennWell Books, Tulsa, OK. U.S.A., 1980. (* 1 Quad = 10^{15}Btu/year = 471,233bbl crude oil/day)

Appendix K

Estimated Proven Recoverable Reserves of Crude Oil and Natural Gas of the World

Country	Crude Oil, 10^9 bbl	Natural gas, Tcf = 10^{12} cu ft
Abu Dhabi	31.0	20.5
Algeria	8.8	107.1
Australia	1.5	18.2
Canada	6.5	99.7
Indonesia	8.5	35.6
Iran	47.9	470.0
Iraq	44.1	29.0
Kuwait	89.8	32.5
Libya	21.3	21.4
Malaysia	3.1	52.7
Mexico	49.3	77.0
Netherlands	0.3	67.0
Nigeria	16.6	47.0
Norway	10.9	104.0
Saudi Arabia	169.0	121.0
U.K.	13.0	33.0
U.S.A.	28.0	197.0
USSR	61.0	1500.0
Venezuela	25.6	59.1
World total	700.1	3484.1

Source: Oil and Gas Journal, December 30, 1985 and Shaheen, E. I., "Catalytic Processing in Petroleum Refining," PennWell Books, Tulsa, OK. U.S.A., 1983.

Appendix L

Traveler's Advisory for Saudi Arabia

Visas: To obtain a visa, contact the visa section of the Royal Embassy of Saudi Arabia in Washington, D.C., or one of the Saudi Arabian consulates in New York, Los Angeles and Houston.

Business Hours: In Saudi Arabia, government offices are open from 7:30 a.m. until 2:30 p.m.; private businesses from 8 a.m. until noon, and from 3 p.m. to 6 p.m.; general banking from 8 a.m. until noon and from 5 p.m. to 8 p.m.; and markets and shops are open until 9 p.m. The beginning of the new fiscal year was March 11, 1986.

Holidays: The Saudi weekend is Thursday and Friday. Two special religious occasions are observed: *Ramadan,* May 9 to June 8, 1986, and *Hajj* season, August 6 to September 4, 1986. Official holidays include *Eid Al-Fitr* (Breaking of the Fast of Ramadan), June 5 to 14, 1986, and *Eid Al-Adha* (culmination of the Hajj), August 14 to 17, 1986. In general, businesses are closed during these times.

Saudi National Day: September 23.

Restrictions: Forbidden items include alcohol, narcotics, weapons, ammunition, pork and pornography. Prescription drugs must be fully documented. In addition, the cities of Makkah and Madinah hold special religious significance and only persons of Islamic faith are allowed entry.

Media: Some English radio/TV programming is transmitted daily throughout the Kingdom. Aramco provides English radio/TV in the Eastern Province. Three English-language daily newspapers (*Arab News, Saudi Gazette* and *Riyadh Daily*) are widely available.

Weights/Measures: Metric.

Telecommunications: Telex and direct dial to/from most countries are available. Telephone country code for Saudi Arabia is 966. City codes for major cities are: Riyadh—1, Adha—7, Abqaiq—3, Dammam—3, Dhahran—3, Hail—6, Hofuf—3, Jeddah—2, Jubail—3, Makkah—2, Madinah—4, Ras Tanurah—3, Tabuk—4, Taif—2, and Yanbu—4.

Time Zone: All of the Kingdom is under one time zone, which is Eastern Standard Time (Washington, D.C.) *plus* eight hours.

Climate: East/west coastal regions are humid; other regions are dry. Temperatures generally are hot, with midday summer temperatures around 100 degrees Fahrenheit and evening temperatures warm in coastal areas, cooler inland. Winter temperatures in central and northern

regions may drop below freezing. Average precipitation ranges from three inches annually to as much as 20 inches in the mountains of the Southwest. June temperatures for major cities are: Riyadh: 68°F—113°F, Dhahran: 73°F—112°F, and Jeddah: 70°F—114°F. July temperatures average: Riyadh: 80°F—108°F, Dhahran: 82°F—110°F, and Jeddah 80°F—107°F.

Health Care: Major cities are served by modern public and private hospitals with fully trained staffs. Most prescription drugs are available at local pharmacies.

Voltage: Most areas 110V/60Hz, some rural areas 220V/50Hz.

Dress: Western men usually wear slacks and a long-sleeved dress shirt for business. While in the Kingdom, however, some men prefer the comfort of Saudi dress, which includes a *thobe* (a long, generally white, robe) and a *ghutra* (headdress), held in place by an *ogal*.

Although Western women are not required to wear the traditional full-length *abaya*, or cloak, over their clothing, they are encouraged to wear a knee-length tunic/dress over slacks and a scarf on their heads.

Exchange Rates: As of July 21, 1986, the rate of exchange is approximately 3.74 Saudi riyals (SR) to the dollar.

Saudi Airlines: Flights leave frequently from New York to the Kingdom. Reservations may be made by calling: 1-800-472-8342. Schedule as follows: New York—Jeddah—Riyadh departs Tuesdays, Thursdays and Sundays.

Ground Transportation: Taxis, limousine service and car rentals are widely available. Jeddah and Riyadh both provide efficient bus transit systems. Major highways connect most cities.

Hotel Accommodations: Major international hotels in the Kingdom include the Sheraton, Hyatt, and Intercontinental.

Courtesy: Royal Embassy of Saudi Arabia–Washington, D.C.

References

Abal-Khail, Mohammad Ali Sheikh, H. E. "Economic Development in Saudi Arabia and Western Technology," American-Arab Affairs, #3 pp. 1–4, Winter, 1982–83.

Abbas, Hamed, *Fahd–The Nation and the Event*, Hodeil Agency for Information, Mecca, 1984 (in Arabic).

Abd Rabbou, Abdul Hafez, *Faisal in the Apogee of History*, Dar al-Kitab al-Misry, Cairo, Dar al-Kitab al-Loubnani, Beirut, 1977 (in Arabic).

Abraham, Nicholas A. (Hanna, Christine A., editor) "Doing Business in Saudi Arabia," Vol. 1, Tradeship Publishing Co., 1980.

Agency for Water and Sewage in the Riyadh Region, "Report," Directorate General of Projects, Riyadh, 1983 (in Arabic).

Al-Akkad, Abbas Mahmoud, *Woman in the Koran*, Nahdhat Misr for publishing, Cairo, 1976 (in Arabic).

Al-Ansari Abdul Koddous, *King Abdulaziz in the Mirror of Poetry*, Dar al-Umeir, Jeddah, 1983 (in Arabic).

Al-Banyan, Abdullah Saleh, *Saudi Students in the United States: A Study of Cross Cultural Education and Attitude Change*, Ithaca Press, London, 1980.

Al-Bilad, "Those Know Abdulaziz," al-Bilad, Special Issue, Sept., 23, 1984 (in Arabic).

Al-Farsy, Fouad, *Saudi Arabia A Case Study in Development*, Kegan Paul International, London, 1982.

Al-Hanbali Uthman Bin Bish al-Najdi, *Modern Library of Riyadh*, (in Arabic).

Al-Hoqeil, Hamad Bin Ibrahim, *Abdulaziz in History–History and Literature*, Modern Library of Riyadh, 1980 (in Arabic).

Al-Kabisy, Muhieyddine, *Fahd In Pictures*, Dar El-Ard, Riyadh, 1984 (in Arabic).

Al-Kabisy, Muhieyddine, *The Koran and the Sword*, (Collection of Speeches and sayings of King Abdulaziz), Dar al-Nasser, al-Ahlia Offset Printing, Riyadh (in Arabic).

Al-Keelany, Kamal, *Fahd Bin Abdulaziz and the Path of a Nation*, Saudi Arabian Publishing Co., Riyadh, 1984 (in Arabic).

Al-Khuli, Muhammad Ali, *The Light of Islam*, Al-Farazdak Press, Riyadh, 1983.

Al-Khuli, Muhammad Ali, *The Need For Islam*, Al Farazdak Press, Riyadh, 1981.

Al-Khuli, Muhammad Ali, *The Translations of The Meanings of Some Traditions of Prophet Muhammad*, Al-Farazdak Press, Riyadh, 1984.

Al-Mana, Mohammed, *Arabia Unified: A Portrait of Ibn Saud*, Hutchinson Benham, London, 1980.

Al-Mane'e Mohammed, *Unification of the Kingdom of Saudi Arabia*, translated from English by Uthaimeen al Abdullah al-Saleh, Mautaww'a Printing, Dammam, 1982 (in Arabic).

Al-Mukhtar Saleh Eddine, *History of the Kingdom of Saudi Arabia in its Past and Present*, Vols. 1 & 2, Dar Maktabat al-Hayat, Beirut (in Arabic).

Al-Rashid, Nasser I. and Shaheen, Esber I., "Oil Spill: Impact and Abatement," presented at the American Institute of Chemical Engineer's Symposium: Oil Pollution Abatement: Onshore, Offshore, On the High Seas, paper No. 73a, Philadelphia, PA., U.S.A., Aug. 20, 1985.

Al-Rihani, Amin, *History of Najd & Annexed Territory, and the Story of Abdulaziz*, fourth printing, Dar Rihani, Beirut, 1970 (in Arabic).

Al-Roueishid, Abdullah Bin Sa'ad, "Al-Imam Al-Sheikh Mohammed Ibn Abul Wahhab," al-Idara, Vol. 2, 9th year, Oct. 1983 (in Arabic).

Al-Salloum, Youssof Ibrahim, *Study in the Method of Planning*, Tihama Publications, Jeddah, 1982 (in Arabic).

Al-Saud, Moudha Bint Mansur Bin Abdulaziz, *King Abdulaziz and the Kuwait Conference, 1923–1924*, Tihama Publishing, Jeddah, 1982 (in Arabic).

Al-Sawwai, Mahmud (Shaikh Muhammad), *The Muslim Book of Prayer*, Dr. Miyahid Muhammad Al-Sawwaf, Mecca, 1977.

Al-Suweigh Abdulaziz Hussein, *Petroleum and Arab Politics*, Gulf States Information Documentation center, Riyadh, 1981 (in Arabic).

Al-Torki, S., "Family Organization and Women's Power in Urban Saudi Arabian Society," Journal of Anthropological Research, Vol. 33, Fall, 1977.

Al-Was'a, Abdul Wahhab Ahmad Abd, *Education in the Kingdom of Saudi Arabia*, The Arabic Saudi Book 79, Jeddah, 1983 (in Arabic).

Al-Yassini, A., *Religion & State in the Kingdom of Saudi Arabia*, WVSS on the Middle East Ser., Westview, 1984.

Ali, Sheikh Rustum, *Saudi Arabia and Oil Diplomacy*, Praeger, New York, 1976.

Ali, Abdullah Yusif, *The Holy Qur'an Text*, Translation and Commentary, American International Printing Co., 1946.

Allen, Robert C., "Regional Security in the Persian Gulf," Military Review, 63, pp. 2–11, December 12, 1983.

Amin, Mohamed, *Pilgrimage to Mecca*, The Islamic Center, Washington, 1980.

Anderson, I. H., *Aramco, the United States, and Saudi Arabia: A Study of the Dynamics of Foreign Oil Policy, 1933–1950*, Princeton University Press, Princeton, N.J. 1981.

Anderson, N., and Rentz, G., *The Kingdom of Saudi Arabia*, Salem House, Merrimack Pub. Cir. 1983.

Antonious, G., *The Arab Awakening*, Gordon Press Publishing, New York, 1976.

Anthony, John Duke, "The Gulf Coopertion Council," Journal of South Asian and Middle Eastern Studies, 5 No. 4, pp. 3–18, Summer, 1982.

Anthony, J. D., *Middle East; Oil Politics & Development*, American Enterprises, 1975.

Arab World Agribusiness, Vol. 1, #2–3, 1985.

Arabian Government and Public Services Directory, 1983, 3rd edition, Parrish-Rogers International, Northampton, 1982.

Aramco, *Exploration and Petroleum Engineering Center*, Aramco, Dhahran, Saudi Arabia, 1985.

Aramco, "Facts and Figures," Aramco, Dhahran, Saudi Arabia, 1983.

Aramco, *To Serve and Conserve*, Al-Mutawwa Press Co., Dammam, 1975.

Aramco, *The Master Gas System*, Public Relations Department, Aramco, Dhahran, Saudi Arabia.

Aramco World Magazine, "Science: The Islamic Legacy," A Special Aramco World's Fair Issue, 1982, along with several other issues through 1985, Houston.

Aramco, "The Caravan (Al-Qafila) Magazine," Al-Wafa Printing Press, Dammam, Saudi Arabia, Issues through March 1985 (in Arabic).

Asad, M., *The Road to Mecca*, Dar Al-Andalus ltd., Gibraltar, 1980.

A'ssah, Ahmad, *Miracle on the Sand*, Domestic Lebanese Press, Beirut, 1965 (in Arabic).

Assah, Ahmed, *Miracle Of The Desert Kingdom*, Johnson, London, 1969.

Ata, I. W., "Prospects and Retrospectives On The Role of Moslem Arab Women at Present: Trends and Tendencies," Islamic Culture, October, 1981.

Ba'albaky, Mounir, *al-Mawrid–a Modern English–Arabic Dictionary*, Dar el-Ilm-lil-Malayeen, Beirut, 1977.

Bahry, L., "The New Saudi Woman: Modernizing in an Islamic Framework," Middle East Journal Vol. 36, 4, pp. 502–515, 1982.

Bakalla, M. H., *Arabic Culture Through Its Language and Literature*, Kegan Paul International, London, 1984.

Barron, Louis, editor, *WorldMark Encyclopedia*, "Saudi Arabia," pp. 285–292, WorldMark Press, ltd., 3rd edition, N.Y., 1967.

Beling, W. A., ed., *King Faisal and the Modernization of Saudi Arabia*, Westview Press, London, 1980.

Bin-Khamis, Abullah Bin Mohammad, *al-Diriya–The First Capital*, al-Farazdaq Printing, Riyadh, 1982 (in Arabic).

Bindagji, Hussein H., *Atlas of Saudi Arabia*, 3rd edition, Oxford United Press, 1978.

Binzagr, Safeya, *Saudi Arabia: An Artist's View of The Past*, Three Continents, 1979.

Birks, J. S., and Sinclair, C. A., *Arab Manpower: The Crisis of Development*, St. Martin's Press, New York, 1980.

Birks, J. S., and Sinclair, C. A., *International Migration and Development in the Arab Region*, ILO, Geneva, 1980.

Bligh, Alexander, *From Prince to King: Royal Succession in the House of Saud in the Twentieth Century*, NYU Press, 1984.

Blunt, Lady Ann, *Pilgrimage to Nejd–The Cradle of the Arab Race*, second edition, London 1881, Translated by Ghaleb, Mohammed An'am, Second printing, Dar al-Yamama, Riyadh, 1978 (in Arabic).

Boardman, Francis, *Institutes of Higher Learning in the Middle East*, Middle East Institute, Washington, 1977.

Brockelmann, C., *History of the Islamic Peoples*, Putnam's G. P. & Sons., New York, 1960.

Bustani, Emile, *Doubts and Dynamite–The Middle East Today*, Allan Wingate, London, 1958.

Caroe, O., *Wells of Power, The Oilfields of South-Western Asia, A Regional and Global Study*, MacMillan, London, 1976.

Carter, J. R., *Investors in Saudi Arabia*, Scorpion Comm, England, 1982.

Catholic Press, *Student's English–Arabic & Arabic–English Dictionary*, Catholic Press, Beirut, 1953.

Central Intelligence Agency, "Issues In The Middle East," U.S. Government Printing Office, Washington, 1973.

Cheney, Michael S., *Big Oilman From Arabia*, William Heinemann ltd., London, 1958.

Chubin, Shahram, editor, *Security In The Persian Gulf, Pt. 1: Domestic Political Factors*, International Institute for Strategic Studies, 1981.

Clements, F. A., *Saudi Arabia*, Clio Press, Oxford, England; Santa Barbara, CA., 1979.

Cleron, J. P., *Saudi Arabia 2000: A Strategy for Growth*, St. Martin's Press, New York, 1978.

Collier's Encyclopedia, "Saudi Arabia," pp. 450–457, 1982.

Commercial Office, *Doing Business in Saudi Arabia*, Royal Embassy of Saudi Arabia, Washington, 1982.

Corcoran, K. R., editor, *Saudi Arabia: Keys to Business Success*, McGraw-Hill (UK) ltd., Maidenhead, England, 1981.

Cordesman, A., "Saudi Arabia AWACS, and America's Search for Strategic Stability in the Near East," International Security Studies Program Working Papers, #26A, Washington, 1981.

Cragg, K., and Speight, M., *Islam From Within: Anthology of a Religion*, Wadsworth Publishing Co., Belmont, CA., 1980.

Cranford, C. L., "Bedouin Life," Christian Science Monitor, pp 12–14, August 26, 1980.

Cressey, George B., *Asia's Lands and Peoples*, 2nd edition, McGraw-Hill, New York, 1951.

Daghistani, Abdal-Majeed Ismail, *Al-Taif, a City in Transition*, A Falcon Press Production, Jeddah, 1981.

Dar al-Watan, "Al-Sonbula," Dar al-Watan, Riyadh, March issue, 1985 (in Arabic).

Darwish, Madiha Ahmad, *History of the Saudi Nation Until the 1st Quarter of the 20th Century*, 3rd printing, Dar al-shourouq, Jeddah, 1985 (in Arabic).

Darwish, Salim Kamel, *Industrial Economy*, Tihama, Jeddah, 1985.

DeGaury, G., "An Arabian Bibliography," Royal Central Asian Society Journal, Vol. 31, pts. 3–4, pp. 315–320.

DeGaury, G., *Faisal: King of Saudi Arabia*, Atthur Barker, London, 1966.

Department of Studies & Organization, *The Bulletin of King Saud University*, King Saud University Press, Riyadh, June, 1983.

Dequin, H., *The Challenge of Saudi Arabia*, Eurasia Press Singapore, October, 1976.

Doermer, William R., "Opening Bids In The Middle East," Time, pp. 16–18, February 25, 1985.

Doing Business in Saudi Arabia & The Arab Gulf States: 1978–79, Inter Cresent, 1979.

Doing Business in Saudi Arabia & the Arab Gulf States, Inter Cresent, 1983.

Eckbo, P. L., *The Future of World Oil*, Ballinger Publishing Co., Cambridge, Massachusetts, 1976.

Eddy, William A., *FDR Meets Ibn Saud*, American Friends of the Middle East, Inc., New York, 1954, Translated by al-Uqba, Ahmad Hussain, under the title: *Secrets of the Meeting of King Abdul Aziz and President Roosevelt* (Expanded Study), King Abdulaziz University, Jeddah, 1984 (in Arabic).

El-Khatib, Abdel Basset, *Seven Green Spikes (1973–1979)*, Ministry of Agriculture and Water, Printed by Dar al-Asfahani, Jeddah, 1980 (in English and Arabic).

El Mallakh, Ragaei, *Saudi Arabia: Rush to Development*, Profile of an Energy Economy and Investment, Johns Hopkins University Press, Baltimore, MD., and Croom Helm, London, 1982.

El Mallakh, Ragaei and Dorothea, *Saudi Arabia: Energy, Developmental Planning and Industrialization*, Lexington Books, Lexington, MA., 1982.

Electric Corporation, "Eighth Annual Report, 1983–1984, Obeikan Company for printing & publishing, Riyadh, 1984 (Arabic and English).

Encyclopedia Americana, "Ibn Saud," Vol. 14, p. 618, American Corporation, New York, 1965.

Encyclopedia Americana, "Saudi Arabia," Vol. 24, pp. 316–316b, American Corporation U.S.A., 1965.

Falcon Publishing, "Arab World Agribusiness," Magazine, Falcon Publishing Europe Ltd., Vol. 1 No. 23, London, 1985 (English and Arabic).

Fisher, Eugene M., Bassiouni, M. Cherif, *Storm Over The Arab World: A People In Revolution*, Follett Publishing Co., Chicago, 1972.

Fisher, S. N., revised edition, *The Middle East, A History*, New York, Knopf Alfred A., 1968.

Fisher, W. B., *The Middle East*, 6th edition, Butler and Tanner, ltd, London, 1971.

Franco, Gaston L., editor, *World Communications*, Gaston Lional Franco publications, London, 1983.

Garaudy, R., *The Case of Israel: A Study Of Political Zionism*, Shorouk International, ltd, London, 1984.

Geddes, C. L., *Analytical Guide to The Bibliographics On The Arabian Peninsula*, American Institute of Islamic Studies, Denver, Colorado, 1974.

General Administration of Public & Industrial Relations of Saline Water Conversion, *The Fresh Water From Sea*, Middle East Press, Riyadh, 1983.

General Agency for Technical Education and Training, *Statistical Report, 1982–1983*, Riyadh (in Arabic).

Ghalib, Mohammed, Adib, *News of Hijaz and Najd In the History of al-Jabraty*, Dar al-Yamama, Riyadh, 1975.

Ghazal, Abdul Karim, *Saudi Arabia In Front Of Her Great Destiny*, second printing, Ta'ounia Printing, Damascus, 1984 (in Arabic).

Glubb, J., *Short History of the Arab Peoples*, Stein & Day, 1970.

Goldschmidt, A., Jr., *A Concise History Of The Middle East*, Westview Press, Colorado, 1979.

Grayson, B. E., *Saudi–American Relations*, University Press of America, Washington, 1982.

Griffith, William E., *The Middle East, 1982: Politics, Revolutionary Islam, and American Policy*, Cambridge: Center for International Studies, Massachusetts Institute of Technology, January 20, 1982.

Grolier Universal Encyclopedia, "Ibn Saud," Vol. 5, Grolier Universal Encyclopedia, p. 338, American Book, Stratford Press Inc., New York, 1966.

Grolier Universal Encyclopedia, "Saudi Arabia," Vol. 9, Grolier Universal Encyclopedia, pp. 119–123, American Book, Stratford Press Inc., New York, 1966.

Guillaume, A., 2nd edition, *Islam*, Harmondsworth, Penguin Books, England, 1956.

Gulf Bureau For Organization & Statistical Studies, *Saline Water Conversion*, Riyadh, 1983, (in English, French and Arabic).

Gulf States Information Documentation Center, *Guide to Arab Gulf Publishers*, Riyadh and Baghdad, 1984 (in Arabic).

Gulf States Information Documentation Center, *Mass Media and Journalism Annotated Bibliographies*, second edition, Baghdad, 1984 (in Arabic).

Habib, J. S., "Ibn Sa'ud's Warriors of Islam: The Ihwan of Najd and Their Role in the Creation of the Sa'udi Kingdom, 1910–1930," Social, Economic and Political Studies of the Middle East, Vol. 27, Leiden: Brill, 1978.

Haig, Alexander, "Saudi Security, Middle East Peace, & U.S. Interest," (Current Policy Series, No. 323), Department of State, Bureaus of Public Affairs, Washington, October, 1981.

Hathloul, Saud, Ibn, *History of the Kings of Al-Saud*, Medina Printing, Riyadh, 1982 (in Arabic).

Helms, C. M., *The Cohesion of Saudi Arabia*, Johns Hopkins University Press, Baltimore, MD and London, 1981.

Hersey, Regina, editor, *Directory of Saudi Arabian Companies, 1984: Saudi Products & Services*, Leland Publishing Co., 1983.

Hitti, Philip K., *History of the Arabs*, 10th edition, St. Martin's Press, New York, 1974.

Hobday, Peter, *Saudi Arabia Today*, St. Martin's Press, 1978.

Hopwood, D., editor, *The Arabian Peninsula: Society and Politics*, Allen & Unwin, London, Rowman & Littlefield, Lotowa, NJ, 1972.

Hopwood D., Jones, D. G., editors, *Middle East and Islam: A Bibliographical Introduction*, International Publication Service, New York, 1972.

Howarth, D. A., *The Desert King: A Life of Ibn Saud*, Collins, London, McGraw-Hill, New York, 1964.

Humphrey, R. S., "Islam and Political Values in Saudi Arabia, Egypt, and Syria," Middle East Journal, Vol. 33 p. 1–19, Winter, 1979.

Hurewitz, J. C., *Middle East & North Africa In World Policies: A Documentary Record*, Yale Univ. Press, 1975.

322   King Fahd and Saudi Arabia's Great Evolution

Ibrahim, A. Al-Moneef, *Transfer of Management Technology to Developing Nations: The Role of Multinational Oil Firms in Saudi Arabia*, Brouchey, Stuart, editors, Ayer Co., 1980.

Ibrahim, S. E. and Cole, D. P., *Saudi Arabian Bedouin: An Assessment of Their Needs*, American University in Cairo, Egypt, 1978.

Information Office of the Royal Embassy of Saudi Arabia, "Saudi Arabia," Vol. 1 #2, Washington, Summer, 1984.

International Monetary Fund, *Balance of Payments Statistics*, Washington, 1981–1985.

Ishaq, I., *The Life of Muhammad*, Translation by A. Guillaume, Oxford University Press, London, 1967.

Iskander, Marwan, "Gulf Cooperation: A Weighty Agenda," An Nahar Arab Report and Memo (Beirut), 6, No. 39, pp. 1–2, November 15, 1982.

Islami, A. Reza & Kavousi, Rostam, M., "The Political Economy of Saudi Arabia," Near Eastern Study Series, #1, University of Washington Press, Washington, 1984.

Issa, Seyyed, *Economic Development in the Kingdom of Saudi Arabia*, Saudi Presses, Riyadh, 1984 (in Arabic).

Jabbour, Abdel-Nour and Souheil Idriss, *al-Manhal, French–Arabic Dictionary*, Dar al-Edeb, Dar el-Ilm lil Malayeen, Beirut, 1973.

Jackh, E., *Background of the Middle East*, Cornell University Press, Ithaca, New York, 1952.

Jeddah Chamber of Commerce, *Jeddah Chamber of Commerce and Industry Annual Trade Directory, 1981–82*, Inter-Crescent Publishing Co., Dallas, Texas, Amsterdam: Arabesk, 1981.

Kal'aji, Kadri, *Faisal and the New Renaissance–The Islamic Conference*, Dar al-Kitab al-Arabi, vol. 8, along with other volumes, Nassrallah Publishing.

Katakura, Motoko, *Bedouin Village: A Study of A Saudi Arabian People in Transition*, University of Tokyo Press, 1977.

Kay, Shirley, *Saudi Arabia: Past & Present*, Quartet England, Charles Rivers Books.

Kelly, J. B., *Arabia The Gulf & The West*, Basic Books Inc., New York, 1980.

Kennedy, J. L., "Aramco Maintenance Operation Organized to Meet Unique Challenge," Oil & Gas Journal, 75 (29), 76, July 18, 1977.

Khan, Mir Bakadur Hussain, editor, *Genius Diplomat Crown Prince Fahd*, Bakur International Corp., Jeddah, September, 1979.

King Abdulaziz University, Various College "Bulletins," Jeddah, 1985.

King Faisal University, "Bulletins," Hassa, Dammam, 1985.

King Saud University, "Bulletins," Riyadh, Diriya, 1985.

Kirk, G. E., *Short History of the Middle East*, 4th edition, Methuen, London, 1957.

Klebanoff, S., *Middle East Oil & Foreign Policy: With Special Reference to the U.S. Energy, Crisis*, Praeger, 1974.

Knauerhase, Ramon, "Saudi Arabia: Fifty Years of Economic Change," Current History, 82 No. 480 pp. 19–23, January, 1983.

Koury, Enver M., *The Saudi Decision-Making Body: the House of Saud*, Institute of Middle East & North Africa, 1978.

Koury, Enver M., Nakhleh, Emile A., & Mullen, Thomas W., editors, *The Arabian Peninsula, Red Sea, & Gulf: Strategic Considerations*, Institute of Middle Eastern & North African Affairs, Maryland, 1979.

Lanier, Alison R., *Update: Saudi Arabia*, Intercult Press, 1982.

Lawrence, T. E., *Seven Pillars of Wisdom*, Penguin Books Inc., 1976.

Lawton, J., Clark, A., "Foundations: A Decade of Development," Aramco World Magazine, Vol. 33, #6, November–December, 1982.

Lebkicher, Roy, Rentz George, Steinke Max, *Aramco Handbook*, Arabian American Oil Co., Netherlands, 1960.

Lee, William F., "U.S.–Arab Economic Ties: An Interdependent Relationship," Journal of American–Arab Affairs, pp. 5–13, Winter, 1982–83.

Lees, Brian, *A Handbook of the Sa'ud Ruling Family of Saudi Arabia*, Royal Genealogics, London, 1980.

Lenczowski, G., *Oil and State In The Middle East*, Cornell Univ. Press, 1960.

Lengyel, E., *Oil Countries of the Middle East*, Watts, 1973.

Linden, F., Wyatt, F., Inst. S.M.M., *Arabian Transport Services*, 2nd edition, Anglo-Arabian Publishing, London, 1985.

Litwak, Robert, *Security In The Persian Gulf: Sources of Interstate Conflict*, International Institute For Strategic Studies, 2, London, 1981.

Long, D., *The Hajj Today: A Survey of the Contemporary Pilgrimage to Makkah*, State University of New York Press, Albany, New York, 1979.

Long, D. L. and Hills, B., *Saudi Arabia*, Sage Publications for the Center for Strategic and International Studies, Georgetown University 1976.

Looney, Robert E., *Saudi Arabia's Development Potential: Application of An Islamic Growth Model*, Lexington Books, 1981.

Makky, Ghazy Abdul Wahed, *Mecca: The Pilgrimage City; A Study of Pilgrim Accommodation*, Croom Helm for the Hajj Research Centre, London, 1978.

Mamoon, Adbul M., Ali, Zakir, Akhtanuzzaman, A. A., *Bulletin of College of Engineering*, King Abdulaziz University Press, October, 1983.

Mansfield, P., *Arab World*, T. Y. Crowell, 1976.

Mashreq Publishers, *El-Mounjid in Language and Information*, Published in Arabic, Dar el-Mashreq, Beirut, Lebanon, 1973.

McCaslin, J., editor, & Farrar, G. L., et Al Staff editors, International Petroleum Encyclopedia, Petroleum Publishing Co., Tulsa, Oklahoma, 1976–1986.

McHale, Thomas R., Whither, "Arabia In A Changing World Economy," (Middle East Problem Paper, No. 22) Middle East Institute, Washington, 1982.

Méchin-Benoist, *Ibn Saud Ou la Naissance d'un Royaume*, Editions Albin Michel 1955, translated from the French by Laund, Ramadan, Dar Aswad for Publishing, Beirut, 1976 (in Arabic).

Mian, Q. Javed & Lerrick, Alison, *Saudi Business & Labour Law: Its Interpretation & Applications*, Graham & Trotman, England, 1982.

Middle East Institute, *The Middle East Between War and Peace*, 37th Annual Conference, Washington, Sept. 30–Oct. 1, 1983.

Miller, A. D., *Search For Security: Saudi Oil and American Foreign Policy, 1939–1940*, University of North Carolina Press, 1980.

Ministry of Agriculture and Water, *A Guide to Agricultural Investment In Saudi Arabia*, Dept. of Agricultural Development, Riyadh, 1979.

Ministry of Agriculture and Water, *Agricultural Development In The Kingdom of Saudi Arabia*, Riyadh, 1975–1984.

Ministry of Communications, *Several Booklets on Land, Air and Marine Transportations*, National Offset Printing Press, Riyadh, 1982–1985 (in English and Arabic).

Ministry of Education, *Educational Statistics: in the Kingdom of Saudi Arabia*, 16th issue, Center For Statistical Data and Educational Documentation, Riyadh, 1982–1983.

Ministry of Education, Department of Antiquities and Museum, *An Introduction to Saudi Arabian Antiquities*, Kingdom of Saudi Arabia, Riyadh, 1975.

Ministry of Finance & National Economy, *Cost of Living Index: All Cities and Middle-Income Saudi Populations*, Department of Statistics, April, 1984.

Ministry of Finance & National Economy, *The Statistical Indicator*, Central Department of Statistics, Riyadh, Saudi Arabia, 1981, 1982.

Ministry of Finance and National Economy, *Statistical Yearbook*, Central Department of Statistics, Kingdom of Saudi Arabia.

Ministry of Finance and National Economy, "Saudi Arabian Manufactured Products," Saudi Industrial Development Fund, Safir Press, Riyadh, 1984.

Ministry of Finance and National Economy, *Foreign Trade Statistics*, Central Department of Statistics, Middle East Presses, Riyadh, Third Quarter 1983 (in Arabic and English).

Ministry of Higher Education, *King Abdulaziz University Directory*, Dar Al Asfahani, Jeddah, 1984.

Ministry of Higher Education, *Higher Education in the Kingdom of Saudi Arabia*, Riyadh, 1984 (in Arabic).

Ministry of Higher Education, *Statistics of Higher Education In The Kingdom of Saudi Arabia, 1981–1982*, issue 5, Directorate General For The Development of Higher Education, Riyadh, 1981–1982.

Ministry of Higher Education, *Progress of Higher Education In the Kingdom of Saudi Arabia During Ten Years 1970–1980*, Directorate General for the Development of Higher Education, Kingdom of Saudi Arabia.

Ministry of Information, *A Decade Of Progress*, Kingdom of Saudi Arabia, Obeikan Printing Co., 1985. (in English and Arabic).

Ministry of Information, "Message Of His Majesty King Fahd Ibn Abdulaziz," Pilgrimage, Mecca, 1983, (in English), and Message of 1982 (in French).

Ministry of Information, *HRH Prince Fahd Bin Abdul Aziz, Crown Prince of the Kingdom of Saudi Arabia*, General Directorate of Press, Riyadh.

Ministry of Information, *Saudi Arabia: The Second Five-Year Economic Development Plan*, along with a number of other booklets and literature, Riyadh, 1985.

Ministry of Information, *Saudi Arabia and Its Place In The World*, Kingdom of Saudi Arabia, 1979.

Ministry of Information, "Fahd At Islamic University–Medina, 1983," Farazdaq Presses, Riyadh (in Arabic).

Ministry of Information, "Meeting of King Fahd With Saudi Students Studying Abroad, Jeddah, Aug. 20, 1984," Yamama Press, Riyadh, 1984 (in Arabic).

Ministry of Information, "Frankness and Clarity," Dialogue Between King Fahd and the Faculty & Students at King Faisal University-Hasa, 1984, Mutawwa Press, Dammam, 1984 (in Arabic).

Ministry of Information, al-Kasim, Fertility and Growth, Obeikan Press, Riyadh (in Arabic).

Ministry of Information, Asir–The Land of Beauty and Resources, National Offset Printing Press, Riyadh.

Ministry of Information, Pictures From Hail, Riyadh.

Ministry of Information, "Agriculture and Water," National Offset Printing Press, Riyadh.

Ministry of Interior, Ninth Statistical Book, Riyadh, 1983 (in English and Arabic).

Ministry of Interior, Eighth Statistical Book, Riyadh, 1982 (in Arabic).

Ministry of Petroleum & Mineral Resources, Petroleum Facts In Saudi Arabia 1972–1981, Al-Mutawwa Press Co., Dammam, Saudi Arabia, 1981.

Ministry of Petroleum & Mineral Resources, Petroleum Statistical Bulletin, 1982, Saudi Arabian Printing Co., Riyadh, 1982.

Ministry of Petroleum & Mineral Resources, Petroleum Statistical Bulletins, 1980–1981, Al-Mutawwa Press, Co., Dammam, Saudi Arabia, 1981.

Ministry of Planning, Third Development Plan: 1400–1405 A.H.–1980–1985 A.D., Riyadh, Saudi Arabia.

Ministry of Planning, Achievements of the Development Plans (1970–1983), Ministry of Planning Press, Saudi Arabia.

Ministry of Planning, "Fourth Development Plan 1985–1990," Riyadh, 1985 (in Arabic).

Ministry of Planning, Summary of The Fourth Development Plan, Riyadh, April, 1985.

Ministry of Planning, Achievements of the Developments Plans, 1970–1983, Riyadh, 1983 (in Arabic and English).

Ministry of Planning, Achievements of the Developments Plans 1390–1402 A.H., Riyadh, 1982.

Modern Library, Abbas Mahmoud al-Akkad With The King of the Arab Island, Modern Library, Beirut, 1946.

Moliver, Donald M. & Abbondante, Paul J., The Economy of Saudi Arabia, Praeger, 1980.

Mortimer, Edward, Faith and Power: the Politics of Islam, Random House, New York, 1982.

Mostyn, T., editor, Saudi Arabia: A MEED Practical Guide, Middle East Economic Digest, 1981.

Mutawia, Hamid H., Faisal and the Fidelity of History, Mecca, Cultural Club, Mecca, 1979.

Naawab, Ismail I., Speers, Peter C., & Haye, Paul F., editors, Aramco and Its World: Arabia and the Middle East, Dhahran, 1981.

Nakhleh, E. A., Arab–American Relations in the Persian Gulf, American Enterprise Institute, Washington, 1975.

Nakhleh, E. A., The United States and Saudi Arabia: A Policy Analysis, American Enterprise Institute For Public Policy Research, 1975.

New York Times, "Kingdom Stops Wheat Imports," Vol. 18, issue 875, p. 5, July 25, 1984.

Niblock, T., editor, *State, Society and Economy In Saudi Arabia*, St. Martin's Press, New York, 1982.

Nicholson, Eleanor, *In The Footsteps Of The Camel*, Stacy International, London, 1984.

Nyrop, Richard F., editor, *Saudi Arabia–a Country Study*, Area Handbook Series, American University, Washington, Superintendent of Documents, U.S. Government Printing Office, Washington, 1985.

O'Leary, D. E., *Arabia Before Muhammad*, Reprint of 1927 edition, AMS Press.

Oran, Y., *Middle East Record*, 2 Vols., Halsted Press.

Oxford University Press, *Oil In The Middle East*, New York, 1954.

Park, Y. S., *Oil Money and the World Economy*, Westview Press, Boulder, Colorado, 1976.

Peet, R. C., "Doing Business in the Middle East: A Review of Current Publications," Middle East Journal, Vol. 35 #3, Summer, 1981.

Pendleton, Madge, Davies, D. L., Davies, Martina S., Snodgrass, Frances O., *The Green Book, Guide For Living In Saudi Arabia*, 3rd edition, Middle East Editorial Associates, Washington, 1980.

Pesce, Angelo, *Jiddah: Portrait of An Arabian City*, Falcon Press, London, 1977.

Peterson, J. E., editor, *The Politics of Middle East Oil*, Middle East Institute, Washington, 1983.

Petroleum Economist, "Aramco's Record Year in Saudi Arabia," Petroleum Economist, XLIV (7), 270, July, 1977.

Petroleum and Minerals Organization, *Petromin*, Public Relations Dept., Riyadh, 1977 (in French, English and Arabic).

Petromin Lubricating Oil Refining Co., *First In Saudi Arabia*, "Luberef," Jeddah, Saudi Arabia, 1978.

Petromin, "Jeddah Oil Refinery Co.," Tihama Publishing, Jeddah, 1982 & 1983 (in Arabic).

Philby, H. S., *Arabia of the Wahhabis*, Reprint of 1928 edition, Arno.

Philby, Harry, "Sa'udi Arabia," World Affairs series National & International Viewpoints, Ayers Co., 1955 (reprint 1972).

Philby, H., St. John B., *The Heart of Arabia*, Constable, London, 1922.

Philby, H., St. John B., *Arabian Oil Ventures*, Middle East Institute, Washington, 1964.

Philipp, Han-Jurgen, *Saudi Arabia: Bibliography On Politics, Society & Economics From 18th Century to The Present*, K. G., Saur, 1984.

Pickthall, M. M., *The Meaning of the Glorious Qur'an*, Orientalia, Inc., New York, 1970.

Plascov, Avi, *Security in the Persian Gulf: Modernization, Political Development and Stability*, International Institute for Strategic Studies, London, 1982.

Plastic World, "Saudi Arabia May Soon Replace the U.S. and Japan as One of the Biggest Exporters of Plastics to World Markets," pp. 56–57, March, 1985.

Powell, William, *Saudi Arabia & Its Royal Family*, Lyle Stuart, Inc., Syracuse, N.Y., 1982.

Price, D. L., *Oil & Middle East Security*, Sage, 1977.

Princeton University Press, *The Arabs; A Short History*, Princeton University Press, Princeton, New Jersey, 1949.

Projects Research Inc., *Projects In Saudi Arabia*, Falls Church, VA., 1983.

Quandt, William B., *Saudi Arabia's Oil Policy*, The Brookings Institution, Washington, 1981.

Quandt, William, *Saudi Arabia In The 1980's*, The Brookings Institution, Washington, 1982.

Rashid Engineering, Riyadh, 1986.

Rashid, Nasser I. and Shaheen, Esber I., "The Great Academic Evolution in the Kingdom of Saudi Arabia," to be presented at the Annual meeting of AIChE in New York, U.S.A., Nov. 1987.

Research and Publishing House, *Saudi Arabia: Record of Economic Development, 1983*, Sin el Fil, Lebanon, 1983.

Rihani, Ameen F., *Maker of Modern Arabia*, Greenwood, reprint of 1928 edition, Washington, 1983.

Riyadh Chamber of Commerce and Industry, *Businessmen Pocket Directory*, Riyadh, 1981.

Robertson, Nelson, editor, "Origins of The Saudi Arabian Oil Empire: Secret U.S. Documents, Documentary Publications, Washington, 1923–1944.

Robinson, Maxime, *The Arabs* (Translation by Arthur Goldhammer) University of Chicago Press, Chicago, 1981.

Ross, Heather C., *The Art of Bedouin Jewellery*, Arabesque Commercial, Switzerland, 1981.

Ross, R. C., *The Art of Arabian Costume: A Saudi Arabian Profile*, Arabesque Commercial SA, Switzerland, 1981.

Routledge & Kegan Paul, *Ibn Battuta Travels In Asia and Africa 1325–1354*, Routledge & Kegan Paul ltd., 1983.

Royal Commission For Jubail and Yanbu, *Annual Report*, Saudi Arabia.

Royal Commission for Jubail and Yanbu, "Industrial Yanbu," Directorate General of Yanbu Project (in Arabic and English).

Safran, Nadav, *Saudi Arabia: The Ceaseless Quest For Security*, Belknap Press of Harvard Univ. Press, Massachusetts, 1985.

Salem, Abdulaziz, *History of the Arab Nation*, Publishing Agency for University Youth, Alexandria, 1984 (in Arabic).

Saline Water Conversion Corporation, "Fresh Water From The Sea," Middle East Press, Riyadh, 1983 (in Arabic and English).

Sarhan, Samir, editor, *Who's Who In Saudi Arabia*; 3rd edition, Europa, Gale, England, 1984.

Sardar, Z., and Badawi, M. A., Zaki, editors, *Hajj Studies*, Croom Helm For The Hajj Research Centre, King Abdulaziz University, Jeddah, 1978.

Saudi Agency for Consulting Services, "Guide to Industrial Investment," sixth printing, Riyadh, 1984 (in Arabic).

Saudi Arabia–Central Planning Organization, *Development Plan 1395–1400*

(1975–80), (reproduced by National Technical Information Service, PB246,572), Springfield, Virginia: NTIS, 1976.

Saudi Arabia Construction Industry Directory, 2nd edition, Inter-Crescent Publishing Co., Dallas, Texas, 1980.

Saudi Arabia, "The 50th Anniversary of the Kingdom, A Two-Part Survey," International Herald Tribune (entire issue), Paris, July, 1982.

Saudi Arabian Airlines, *Successful Transition Into Saudi Arabia,* Kansas City, Missouri, 1980.

Saudi Arabian Monetary Agency, *Annual Report, 1984,* Research and Statistics Department, Riyadh, 1984 (in Arabic and English).

Saudi Arabian Standards Organization, *Proceedings Of The International Symposium For Standardization of Codes Character Sets and Keyboards For The Arabic Language Computers,* Albadia Printing Press, Riyadh, June 1–4, 1980.

Saudi Arabian Trade Directory, Inter-Crescent Publishing Co., Dallas, Texas, 1982.

Saudi Economic Survey, "Drive For Food Self-Sufficiency," Vol. 18, issue 876, p. 7, Aug. 1, 1984.

Saudi Economic Survey, "1.8 Million Students Go To Schools," Vol. 18 issue 882, p. 5, Sept. 18, 1984.

Saudi Press, "Numerous Articles From Newspapers, relating to the Kingdom and King Fahd," Riyadh, 1985–1986 (mostly in Arabic and some in English).

Saudi Press Agency, *Visit of His Majesty King Fahd Bin Abdulaziz to the United States of America,* King Saud University Press, Feb., 1985 (in Arabic).

Saudi-OGer ltd., Riyadh, June, 1980, 1982 and Personal Communication 1985–1986.

Sayigh, Yusif, A., *Arab Oil Policies In The 1970's,* Groom Helm ltd, Kent, Great Britain, 1983.

Schoellner, Joan, "Living In The Middle East . . . A Wife's View," Chemical Engineering issue June 20, 1977, pp. 125–130, McGraw-Hill, 1977.

Shah, Ali Sirdar Ikbal, *The Controlling Minds of Asia,* Herbert Jenkins ltd., London, 1937.

Shaheen, E. I., *Energy-Pollution Illustrated Glossary,* Engineering Technology, Inc., Mahomet, Illinois, 1977.

Shaheen, E. I., *Basic Practice of Chemical Engineering,* International Institute of Technology, Inc., Joplin, Missouri, 2nd edition, 1984.

Shaheen, E. I., *Environmental Pollution: Awareness and Control,* Engineering Technology, Inc., 1974.

Shaheen, E. I., "The Energy Crisis: Is It Fabrication or Miscalculation?," Vol. 8 #4, Environmental Science and Technology, April, 1974.

Shaheen, E. I., "Surviving Even Thriving Overseas," Chemical Engineering, issue December 6, 1976, McGraw-Hill, 1976.

Shaheen, Esber I. and Rashid, Nasser I., "The Energy Spectrum," presented at the AIChE Symposium: Energy: Yesterday, Today and Tomorrow, New Orleans, LA., U.S.A., April 6–10, 1986.

Shair Management Services, editors, *Business Laws & Practices of Saudi Arabia,* Graham Trotman, England, 1979.

Sharaf, Abel-Aziz M. and Sha'ban, Mohammad Ibrahim, *Abdel-Aziz Al-Sa'ud and the Genius of Islamic Personality*, Dar al-Ma'aref, Cario, 1983 (in Arabic).

Sherbiny, N. A., and Tessler, M. A., *Arab Oil–Impact On Arab Countries & Global Implications*, Praeger.

Shaw, John A., and Long, David E., "Saudi Arabian Modernization: The Impact of Change On Stability," 10, (Washington Papers #89.), Praeger, Center For Strategic and International Studies, Georgetown University, Washington, 1982.

Shilling, N. A., *A Practical Guide To Living And Traveling In the Arab World*, Inter-Crescent Publishing Co., Dallas, Texas, 1978.

Shwadran, B., 3rd edition, *The Middle East, Oil and the Great Powers*, Transaction Books, New Brunswick, New Jersey, 1973.

Stacey International, *The Kingdom of Saudi Arabia*, Stacey International, London, 1977, 2nd edition 1979 and 6th edition 1980–85.

Steward, Desmond and the Editors of Life, *The Arab World*, Life World Library, Time, Inc., New York, 1964.

Stork, J., "Middle East Oil and the Energy Crisis," Monthly Review, 1975.

Tabbarah, Riad, "Population, Human Resources, and Development in the Arab World," Population Bulletin of ECWA, No. 20, pp. 5–38, June, 1981.

Tahtinen, Dale R., "National Security Challenges To Saudi Arabia," American Enterprise, 1978.

Tarantino, Mardijah A., *Marvellous Stories From The Life of Muhammad*, The Islamic Foundation, 1982.

Tchekof Minosa, Massari, Patricia and Dagher Cherbel, *Najran–Desert Garden of Arabia*, Scorpio Editeur, Paris.

Thomas, Bertram, *The Arabs*, Butterworth, London, 1937.

Tibbits, G. R., *Arabia in Early Maps*, Oleander Press.

Topham, J., *Traditional Crafts of Saudi Arabia*, Stacey International, London, 1982.

Troeller, Gary, *The Birth of Saudi Arabia: Britain and the Rise of the House of Sa'ud*, Cass, London, 1976.

Tuncalp, Secil, and Ugur Yavas, "Agricultural Development in Saudi Arabia," Third World Planning Review 5, #4 pp. 333–347, Liverpool, November, 1983.

Twitchell, K. S., *Saudi Arabia*, 3rd edition, Princeton University Press, Princeton, 1958.

United Nations, Department of Economic and Social Affairs, *World Population Trends and Prospects by Country, 1950–2000: Summary Report of the 1978 Assessment*, New York, 1979.

United Nations, Statistical Office, *Demographic Yearbook*, New York, 1948–1985.

United Nations, *Yearbook of National Accounts Statistics*, United Nations Statistical Office, New York 1957–1985.

U.S. Department of Commerce, *An Introduction to Contract Procedures In The Near East & North Africa*, 3rd edition, International Trade Administration, Washington, November, 1984.

U.S. Department of Commerce, *Saudi Industry 83 Al-Dhiafa Exhibition Center*, International Trade Administration, Riyadh, November 20–25, 1983.

U.S. Department of State, General Publication Division, "Background Notes, On the Countries of the World," U.S. Printing Office, Washington, 1973– 1976.

U.S. General Accounting Office, Comptroller General, *Status of U.S.–Saudi Arabian Joint Commission on Economic Cooperation*, (GAD-ID83-32), Washington, May, 1983.

U.S. House of Representatives, Foreign Affairs, and National Defense Division, *Saudi Arabia and The United States: The New Context in An Evolving "Special Relationship,"* Congressional Research Service, Library of Congress, August, 1981.

U.S. Department of State, *Background Notes–Saudi Arabia*, Bureau of Public Affairs, Washington, February, 1983.

U.S. Department of State, Bureau of Consular Affairs, *Tips For Travelers To Saudi Arabia*, Department of State Publications, Department of Foreign Services, September, 1983.

United States–Saudi Arabian Joint Commission on Economic Cooperation, *Summary of Saudi Arabian Five Year Development Plan 1980–1985*, Riyadh, 1980.

University of Petroleum and Minerals, "Bulletins," Dhahran, 1985.

Vincett, Betty A. L., *Animal Life In Saudi Arabia*, Garzanti editore S.pa, Italy, 1982.

Vincett, Betty A. L., *Wild Flowers of Central Saudi Arabia*, Garzanti S.pa, Italy, 1977.

Viola, J. W., *The Development of Human Resources: A Case Study of United States–Saudi Arabian Corporation*, Center of International Higher Education Documentation, Boston, 1982.

Von, Pivka, Otto, *Armies Of The Middle East*, Mayflower Books, New York, 1979.

Walmsley, John, *Joint Ventures In Saudi Arabia*, Graham & Trotman, England, 1979.

Ward, Philip, "Ha'il Oasis City of Saudi Arabia," Vol. 11 p. 768, Oleander Press, 1983.

Wells, D. A., *Saudi Arabian Development Strategy*, American Enterprise Institute for Policy Research, Washington, 1976.

Wett, Ted, "Saudi Petrochem Complexes Make Debut," Oil and Gas Journal, March 25, 1985.

Weiss, Leopold, "Through Central Arabia: In The Kingdom of Nejd," Living Age, Translated from the Neue Zürcher, Zurich, German-Language Daily, Vol. 337, pp. 427–432, Boston, 1929–30.

Weiss, Leopold, "Trouble In Arabia," The Living Age, Translated from Neue Zürcher Zeitung, Vol. 334, pp. 806–813, Boston, 1928.

Weiss, Leopold, "New Travels In Arabia," from Neue Zurcher Zeitung (Swiss Daily), The Living Age, Vol. 334, pp. 1170–1180, Boston, 1928.

Wheatcroft, Andrew, *Arabia And The Gulf: In Original Photographs 1800– 1950*, Kegan Paul International, London, 1982.

Who's Who in Saudi Arabia, Europa, 1979.

Who's Who in Saudi Arabia, 2nd edition, International Publication Service, 1978–79.

Winstone, H. V. F., *Captain Shakespear*, Jonathan Cape ltd., the Chaucer Press ltd., London, 1976.

Wolfe, R. G., editor, *The United States, Arabia, and the Gulf*, Georgetown University Center For contemporary Arab Studies, Washington, 1980.

World Bank, *World Development Report*, International Bank For Reconstruction and Development/The World Bank, Washington, 1978–1985.

World Book, "Saudi Arabia," pp. 130–135, 1985.

Yale, William, *The Near East: A Modern History*, University of Michigan Press, Ann Arbor, Michigan, 1958, revised 1968.

Young, Arthur N., *Saudi Arabia: The Making of a Financial Giant*, New York University Press, New York, 1983.

Zirikli, Khir, al-Din, *Arabia Under King Abdul Aziz*, 4 Volumes (in Arabic), Beirut.

Additional References

Abdeen, Adnan M., Shook, Dale N., *The Saudi Financial System*, John Wiley & Sons, New York, 1984.

Al-Nashashibi, N., *The Talk of the Great (Hadith Al-Kibar)*, Novograph, Madrid, 1986 (in Arabic).

Al-Rashid, Z. M., *Su'ūdi Relations With Eastern Arabia and 'Umān (1800–1879)*.

Berlitz, *Berlitz Travel Guide*, Saudi Arabia, Switzerland, 1985.

Carter, Jimmy, *The Blood of Abraham*, Houghton Mifflin Co., Boston, 1985.

Doé, A. rahman I., *Shari'ah: The Islamic Law*, Ta Ha Publishers, London, 1984.

El-Mallakh, Ragaei, editor, *OPEC: Twenty Years and Beyond*, Westview Press, Boulder, Colorado, 1982.

Farid, Abdel Majid, editor, *Oil and Security in the Arabian Gulf*, St. Martin's Press, New York, 1981.

Findley, Paul, *They Dare to Speak Out*, Lawrence Hill & Co., Westport, Connecticut, 1985.

Hayes, John R., editor, *The Genius of Arab Civilization–Source of Renaissance*, 2nd edition, London, 1983.

Holt, P. M. *The Age of The Crusades*, Longman Group Ltd., London, 1986.

Johany, Ali D., Berne, Michel & Mixon, J. Wilson Jr., *The Saudi Arabian Economy*, Croom Helm, London, 1986.

Kiernan, Thomas, *The Arabs*, Little, Brown & Co., New York, 1975.

Lewis, Bernard, *The Arabian History*, Hutchinson & Co., London, 1950.

Mazboudi, W., *Date With Tomorrow*, gathering of newspaper articles, published mainly in the Beiraq newspaper, Beirut, Lebanon, 1986.

Ministry of Finance & National Economy, *The Saudi Fund For Development, Annual Report 1984–85*, Vol. XI Arabian Falcon Publishing/IBF, 1986.

Ministry of Finance & National Economy, *Real Estate Development Fund, Annual Report 1403/04*, Obeikan Co., Riyadh, 1985.

Ministry of Higher Education, *Statistical Index On Progress of Higher Education From 1969/70 to 1983/84*, issue no. 2, Directorate General for the Development of Higher Education, King Saud University Press, 1985.

PennWell Books, "Oil and Gas Journal," Vol. 83 no. 52, PennWell Publishing, Tulsa, December 30, 1985.

Polk, William R., *The Arab World*, Harvard University Press, Cambridge, Massachusetts, 1980.

Quandt, William B., *Decade of Decisions–American Policy Toward the Arab–Israeli Conflict 1967–1976*, University of California Press, Berkley, 1977.

Royal Embassy of Saudi Arabia, "Saudi Arabia," Vol. 3, no. 6, Washington, D.C., Several issues up to August, 1986.

Sheean, Vincent, *Faisal, The King and His Kingdom*, University Press of Arabia, England, 1975.

Smith, Pamela A., editor, *Middle East Yearbook 1980*, publisher Ahmed Afif Ben Yedder, (in USA distributed by Franklin Watts Inc., 1980).

Winistone, H. V. F., *Gertrude Bell*, Quartet Books, London, 1980.

Zahlan, A. B., *Science and Science Policy in the Arab World*, Croom Helm, London, 1980.

Biographical Sketch
About the Authors

Dr. Nasser Ibrahim Rashid

Dr. Esber Ibrahim Shaheen

Dr. Nasser I. Rashid is Chairman of *Rashid Engineering*, Box 4354, Riyadh 11491, Kingdom of Saudi Arabia (KSA). Dr. Rashid is a native of Saudi Arabia. He attended schools in the Kingdom, Syria and Lebanon prior to his university studies. In 1961, he joined the University of Texas in Austin. He graduated with a Bachelor of Science degree in Civil Engineering and then a Doctor of Philosophy degree from the same university. While acquiring his education, his performance was outstanding in high school and at the university level.

Dr. Rashid traveled extensively around the world and in the process he acquired basic practical education, know-how and insight into development in far corners of the globe. He is a man of justice with deep affectionate feelings for his native country. He was brought up under Shari'a and the tenets of Islam. He covered the practical spectrum of the Saudi Arabian way of life. His tremendous intellect, coupled with his deep rooted Saudi Arabian background and the positions of eminence that he occupied in the latter years, make him *uniquely qualified* to give a true picture and a vivid description of the gigantic progress that has been achieved in the Kingdom of Saudi Arabia in slightly over a decade. From his position of competence, leadership and common sense, his contributions are basic in complementing a major task for making this book "one of a kind." He published a number of articles pertaining to management, engineering and energy.

Dr. Rashid is listed in *Who's Who in Saudi Arabia, International Who's Who in the Arab World.* In 1980, he was selected as the *Distinguished Graduate of the College of Engineering at the University of Texas,* Austin, Texas, USA. He is a member of many honorary fraternities. A number of Islamic foundations granted him *honorary awards* for generous contributions and continuous support. He received from

St. Jude Children's Research Hospital, in Memphis, Tennessee, an award for humanitarian efforts and generous support. He received the *Ordre National de la Légion d'Honneur*, awarded by the president of the French Republic.

Upon graduating from the University of Texas, Dr. Rashid joined the University of Petroleum and Minerals in Dhahran, Saudi Arabia, as an Assistant Professor of Civil Engineering. He later became Dean of Business Affairs, then Dean of Engineering. During his years at this University, Dr. Rashid participated in establishing an accredited program for the College of Engineering and establishing ties with major U.S. universities, such as: MIT, Princeton, Rochester, University of Alabama, Colorado School of Mines, Wentworth Institute and others.

Under his management the university campus was completed on time and on budget. It turned out to be a *showplace for the Kingdom.* He was instrumental in equipping the laboratories with the most elaborate and sophisticated equipment for all branches of engineering and science. He also directed an active international recruiting program for the university, lasting for three years prior to leaving the university to go into private practice in engineering.

In 1975, he started his company: Rashid Engineering, a consulting firm, based in Riyadh, Saudi Arabia. It began with a small contract valued at the equivalent of twenty thousand dollars. In 1978–79, Rashid Engineering became the largest Saudi consulting firm in the Kingdom with a total volume of work exceeding two billion dollars. This was in excess of projects carried in association with U.S. firms.

He was a member of the Contractors Classification Committee. This was charged with prequalifying and classifying all contractors, local and international, prior to granting them permission to bid on government projects.

Dr. Rashid is very active in social work in the Kingdom. He is heavily involved in various charity works and organizations in the Kingdom and abroad. *He is a humanitarian, a man of justice and an international philanthropist.*

Dr. Rashid became actively involved in supporting various programs fighting childhood leukemia, giving generously to these programs. His donations exceeded four million dollars. He is currently building in Riyadh, at his own expense, the biggest research hospital. It is known as *King Fahd Children Medical Center* for fighting leukemia. The cost will be seventy million dollars.

Dr. Rashid is chairman of the board for a number of finance corporations in various parts of the world.

The King of Saudi Arabia, chose Dr. Rashid as his engineering consultant. Thus, Rashid Engineering was charged with the planning, design and construction management of all official as well as private residential and office complexes for the King and the Crown Prince. *Dr. Rashid did not only observe and admire what has been taking place in the Kingdom and its achievements, but he lived and partici- pated actively and most dynamically in the development process that has swept the Kingdom in its golden decade.*

Dr. Esber I. Shaheen is an international consultant and president of the *International Institute of Technology, Inc. (IITI)*, 830 Wall Street, Joplin, Missouri 64801 USA. Dr. Shaheen, as a young man with ambition and thirst for knowledge, *emigrated* to the United States of America and first attended the University of Texas in Austin for two years. He received his Bachelor of Science degree in Chemical Engineering from Oklahoma State University. He then completed his Masters of Science degree at the University of Arizona, and received his Doctor of Philoso- phy degree from the University of Tennessee.

He is actively involved in *training, writing, technology transfer, international consulting and management of international projects.* His wide travels and varied education covered a unique spectrum in formulating his forthright views and thoughts. His experience in the Arab world, and especially in the Kingdom of Saudi Arabia, along with the know-how and wide range of technology acquired in America, his sense for justice, *deep feelings of compassion and admiration for achievement,* all give him a *unique perspective* that was efficiently and dynamically used to portray the parade of progress that has taken place in the Kingdom of Saudi Arabia in the span of slightly over a decade.

Dr. Shaheen has served as Director of Education Services for the Institute of Gas Technology and as Director of International Education Programs for Gas Developments Corporation in Chicago, Illinois, USA. He was a *professor* and *distinguished lecturer* at more than six different universities throughout the United States of America and the World, including: University of Wisconsin, University of Petroleum and Miner- als in Saudi Arabia, Illinois Institute of Technology in Chicago and University of Tennessee. Many training and consulting projects both national and international have been designed and managed by Dr. Shaheen. He formerly was Senior Engineer and Manager of Education projects at the Algerian Petroleum Institute.

Dr. Shaheen is the *author* of six textbooks, along with more than fifty articles and presentations. He is the author, co-author or editor of nearly twenty training manuals in the fields of gas engineering, energy, environment and petrochemical processing. He has many years of experience in a wide variety of industrial and educational programs and takes pride in his practical approach. Dr. Shaheen is a *dynamic* and an *inspiring speaker*. He is listed in *American Men of Science, Men of Achievement* and *Personalities of the West*. He also is an *Honorary Texas citizen* and an *Outstanding Educator of America*.

After teaching at the University of Petroleum and Minerals in Dhahran, Saudi Arabia for two years, Dr. Shaheen returned to the United States of America and continued his education and training career. Several years had passed. He then returned to Saudi Arabia and was astonished to see the degree of miraculous progress that had been achieved in a short period of time. *Witnessing the amazing level of achievement that had taken place, Dr. Shaheen was deeply moved and bewildered. He embarked with his co-author on a campaign of far reaching research to document what has taken place in the Kingdom for the benefit of history, the benefit of men and women who treasure justice and admire achievement everywhere.*

INDEX

A

Abbasid Dynasty, 284, 286
Abdul Rahman, Ibn Faisal, 9, 11, 15
Abdulaziz Bin Fahd, see Fahd
Abdulaziz Ibn Abdul Rahman Al-Saud,
  see Ibn Saud
Abdullah Bin Abdulaziz, 74, 128, 142,
  245–252, 299
Abdulwahhab, Mohammed, 7–10
Academic Evolution, see Education
Ad-Dawish, Faisal, 30–31
Agricultural settlements, see Hijra
Agriculture, 202–207, 273–274
Aid, see Saudi Arabia
Air Force, see Royal Saudi Air Force
Airports, 196–198
Ajlan, 17–21
Al-Haramein, see Haram
Al-Hasa, see Hasa
Al-Hasan Zafer, 142
Al-Jaheeliyya, see Jaheeliyya
Al-Khalifa, Sheikh Isa Bin Salman,
  196
Al-Khalifa, Sheikh Hamad Bin Isa, 69
Al-Musmak, see Musmak
Al-Sabbah, see Mubarak
Al-Saud Family, 6
Al-Shaer, Ali, xi
Ali Bin Hussain, 29
Ali, Mohammed, 8–9
American-Saudi relations, see Saudi-
  American relations
Arab Empire, 6, 281–286,
  Fall of, 286–288
Arabia, see Saudi Arabia
Arabia Felix, 3
Arabian American Oil Company, see
  Aramco
Arabian Oil Company, 174
Arabian Peninsula, 275–277

Arabic language, see Glossary of Arabic
  Words
Arabs, a brief history of the, 275–292
Arabs of today, 290–292
Arabs, what are the, 275–280
Aramco, 35, 135, 169–174
Arms manufacturing, 258–260
Army, 257
Artawia, 25
Assyrians, 278
Awacs, 254

B

Babylonians, 275
Bandar Bin Sultan, 142, 159, 252, 264
Battles, see Ibn Saud
Beirut, see Lebanon
Bell, Gertrude, 12–13
Bin Bujad, Sultan, 31
Bin Jiluwi, Abdullah, 18, 21
Bin Sultan, Bandar, see Bandar Bin Sul-
  tan
British, see International relations
Brothers of Abdulaziz, see Ibn Saud
Bus transport, 199
Bush, George, 251, 256
Byzantine Empire, 281–282

C

Caliphate, 29, 282, 284, 286
Capture of Riyadh, see Riyadh
Carter, Jimmy, 153, 155
Chicago Tribune, 72–73
Children of Abdulaziz, see Ibn Saud
Chirac, Jacques, 151
Churchill, Winston, 42–43, 73
Climate, 314
Communications, 199–202

Companions of Abdulaziz on his way to conquer Riyadh, see Ibn Saud
Conquests, see Ibn Saud
Cox, Percy, 12
Credits by various fund organizations, 188–191
Crown Prince, see Abdullah Bin Abdulaziz
Crusaders, 284–285

D

Dams, 209
Debakey, Michael, 232
Defense, 241–260, 274
Desalination, see water desalination
Diriya, 6
Discovery Space Mission, 62, 74, 218–219, 264
Drilling for oil, see oil, Aramco

E

Eastern Province, see oil, Mohammed Bin Fahd
Eddy, William, 42–43
Education
  Kindergarten, 79
  General, 79–82
  Technical, 82–86
  Teacher training, 86–87
  Special programs, 87–92
  Higher education, 92–127
  Military colleges (see Defense) 241–260
  Profile: The Saudi Today, 268, 270–273
Education, first minister of, see Fahd
Electrical energy supply, 210–212
Empty Quarter, 12, 15
Energy, see oil, gas
Energy demand by sources, worldwide, 312
Energy sources, see oil, gas
Exhibits, 201–202
Exploration and Petroleum Engineering Center, 174

F

Fahd Bin Abdulaziz
  youth, 58–61
  family, 60–64
  the father, 62–64

Fahd Bin Abdulaziz (continued)
  Abdulaziz (son), 63–64, 131, 157
  unique qualities of leadership, 65–70, 299
  crown prince, 67, 72
  humanitarianism and compassion, 70–74
  first minister of education, 76–127
  special photos, 128–134
  national scene, 135–137
  regional arena, 137–142
  Fahd peace plan, 140–141, 154, 290
  moslem world (custodian of the two Holy Mosques) 142–145
  the international arena, 145–160
  redefining progress, 161–240, 292
  law and order, 241–245
  supreme commander, 241–260
  man of peace and achievement, 265–266
Fahd Peace Plan, 140–141, 154, 290
Fair, see exhibits
Faisal, King, 32, 54–55, 65–67, 73, 128, 146, 298–299
Faisal Bin Fahd, 62, 237–239
Fertile Crescent, 5, 275, 278
Fez Conference, see Fahd Peace Plan
First Deputy Prime Minister, see Abdullah Bin Abdulaziz
First five-year development plan, 180–181
First Minister of Education, see Fahd
Five-Year Plans, 178–188
Foreign aid, see Saudi Arabia
Foreign Relations Committee, see Richard Lugar
Fort Musmak, see Musmak
Fourth five-year development plan, 183–187, 264
Funds, 188–191
Future outlook, 261–266

G

GCC, see Gulf Cooperation Council
Gas, 172–173
Gas reserves, 173
General education, see education
General presidency of youth welfare, see Faisal Bin Fahd
Genghis Khan, see Mongol
Getty Oil Company, 174

Girl's colleges, the undersecretariat for, 93
Glossary of Arabic words, 303–312
Gold mining, see Mahd Al-Thahab
Government of Saudi Arabia, see Saudi Arabia
Gregorian calendar, see Moslem calendar
Gulf Cooperation Council, 137–139, 238, 260, 263

H
Hail, 27
Hajj, 222–224, 236
Haram, Haramein, 222–223, 305
Hasa, 27
Hassan II, King of Morocco, 72, 129
Health, 231–237
Henry, S. B., 33
Highways, see roads
Hijra (plan for settling the Bedouins), 25
Hijra year (A.H.), see Moslem calendar
Hoover, J. W. (Soak), 33
Hospitals, see health
Housing, Urban and Hajj development, 222–231
Hulagu Khan, see Mongol
Hussain, Sherif, 24, 27, 29
Hydrocarbons 212–215, see oil, gas

I
Ibn Rashid, Abdulaziz Ibn Mit'ab, 22
Ibn Rashid, Mit'ab Ibn Abdulaziz, 23
Ibn Rashid, Mohammed, 11, 13
Ibn Saud, 1–56, 161, 241, 289
    young man, 9–12
    capture of Riyadh, 10–22
    unifying the country, 22–32
    and the Ikhwan, 24–32
    the leader and the man, 36–38
    and president Roosevelt, 38–44
    and Churchill, 43
    interesting to know, 44–53
    U.N., 145
    major battles, 294
    companions on way to recapture Riyadh, 295
    children, 96–300
    brothers, 298
Ibn Saud, Mohammed, 6
Ibrahim Pasha, 8

Ikhwan, 24–32, 250
Imam Mohammed Islamic University, see universities
Industrial cities of Jubail and Yanbu, 215–217
Industrial development, 210–217
Industrial evolution, see industrial development
Industrial Fund, see funds
Industrialization, see industrial development
Information (television, radio and press), 201
Inspector General, see Sultan Bin Abdulaziz
Institute of Public Administration, see education
Instructor's Institute, see education
International relations,
    British 27, 29–32, 42, 45, 255–256, 289
    French, 255, 289
    Western, 254–258
    U.S.A. (see Saudi-American relations)
Islam, 10, 241–242, 244, 261, 266, 280–286, 306
Islamic sects, 282, 284
Islamic University at Medina, see universities

J
Jaheeliyya, 275, 280, 286
Jazeerat al-Arab, 12, 275, see Saudi Arabia
Jeddah, 29–30
Joint Commission on Economic Cooperation, 153
Joint ventures, 261–264
Jubail, 73, 170, 172, 215–217

K
KFCMC, see King Fahd Children's Medical Center and Research Hospital
Ka'aba, 306–307
Khafji, 174
Khaled, King, 54–56, 65–67, 71–74, 128, 146, 150, 299
King Abdulaziz Scientific City, 218
King Abdulaziz University, see universities

King Fahd Children's Medical Center and Research Hospital (KFCMC), 236–237, 263

King Fahd Medical City in Riyadh, 232, 272

King Fahd University of Petroleum and Minerals, see universities

King Faisal Specialist Hospital and Research Center, 232

King Faisal University, see universities

King Khaled Eye Specialist Hospital, 71, 231–232, 272

King Saud University, see universities

Kingdom of Saudi Arabia, see Saudi Arabia

Kohl, Chancellor, 149

L

Laskai, Harold, 154

Law and order, 241–245, 265, 274

Lebanon, 141–142, 290

Leukemia, 236–237

Lugar, Richard, 256–257

M

Madina, 59, 143–144, 306

Mahd al-Thahab, 177

Majlis, 74–76

Manufacturing plants, 212–215

Master Gas System MGS, 172

Mecca, 4, 27, 29, 59, 143–144, 261, 281, 306

Mesopotamia, 3, 5

Miller, Art P., 33

Minerals, 177

Minister of Defense and Aviation, see Sultan Bin Abdulaziz

Minister of Interior, see Naif Bin Abdulaziz

Minister of Petroleum and Mineral Resources, see Nazer, Hisham

Minister of Planning, former, see Nazer, Hisham

Minister of Information, see Al-Shaer, Ali

Modernization, 191–240, 292

Modernization Model for other countries, 239–240, 266

Mohammed Bin Abdulaziz, 73, 299

Mohammed Bin Fahd, 62

Mohammed, the Prophet, 4, 261, 281

Mongol, 286–287

Moslem, see Islam

Moslem Calendar, 301–302

Mubarak, 13, 15, 23

Musmak, 18–19, 21

Myrrh, 4

N

Naif Bin Abdulaziz, 60, 243–244, 300

Najd, see Saudi Arabia-History

NASA, 218

National Aeronautics and Space Administration, see NASA

National day, 32

National Guard, 245–252

National scene, see Fahd

National security chart, 248

Navy, see Royal Saudi Navy

Nazer, Hisham, xi, 154, 180

Newspapers, see press

North-South Summit, Cancun, Mexico, 153–154

O

Offset program, 262

Oil, 153, 278–280, 289–290,
  discovery, 32–36, 169, 240
  Dammam No. 7 (oil well), 34
  consumption, 163–164
  OPEC, 164
  production, 165, 170–171
  price, 166
  Aramco, 169–174
  reserves, 177–178, 313
  oil policy, 265–266

Omayyad, 282–284

OPEC, 164

Organization of Petroleum Exporting Countries, see OPEC

Ottoman (Turks), 15, 23, 27, 29, 286–289

P

Palestinian issue, 38–44, 138, 140–141, 154, 290

Petrochemicals, 212–215, see oil, gas, Sabic

Petroleum, see oil

Petromin, 174–178

Philby, St. John, 46

Phoenicians, 278, 285

Pilgrimage, see Hajj

Planning, former Minister of, see Nazer, Hisham
Plants, manufacturing, see industrialization
Ports, see seaports, airports
Post, see telephone, telegraph and post
Postal services, see telephone, telegraph and post
Postern Gate, see Musmak
Press, 201
Private sector, 261, 263–264, 273–274
Profile: the Saudi today, 268–274
Project expenditures during each five-year plan, 179

Q

Qoran, the Holy, 30, 38, 241, 281
Quandt, William, B., 148

R

Rab'a al-Khali (Empty Quarter), 12, 15
Radio stations, 201
Railroads, 198–199
Ramadan, 17, 309
Ras Tanura, 172, 177
Reader's Digest, 53
Reagan, Ronald, 141, 153–154, 156–158
Real Estate Fund, see funds
References, 316–332
Refineries, 176–177
Regional, see Fahd
Research, 217–219
Research Institute, 117, 218
Revenues and expenditures for each of the five-year plans, 185
Rise of the Arab Empire, see Arab empire
Riyadh,
    capture of, 10–22
    modern city of, 226, 229–231
Roads, 192–196
Roman Empire, 4, 281–282
Roosevelt, Franklin D., 3, 38–44, 73, 138, 145
Royal Commission for Jubail and Yanbu, 215–217
Royal Navy, see Royal Saudi Navy
Royal Saudi Air Force, 258
Royal Saudi Navy, 257–258

S

Sabic, see Saudi Basic Industries Corporation
Safco, 175
Safety, see law and order
Saleh Eddine, 285
Saline water conversion, 208–209
Salman Bin Abdulaziz, 60, 74–76, 300
Sancst, see Saudi Arabian National Center for Science and Technology
Sassanid Empire, see Sassanids
Sassanids, 281, 285
Saud Al-Fasial, 142, 146, 151
Saud Ibn Abdulaziz, King, 32, 54, 298
Saudi Airlines, see Saudia
Saudi-American relations, 3, 38–44, 73, 138, 145, 148–160, 254–257
Saudi Arabia
    history, 1–56
    tribal map, 16
    foreign aid, 147
    redefines progress, 161–240
    revenues and expenditures, 167, 183
    exports and imports, 168
    balance of payments, 169
    defense, 241–260
    profile: the Saudi today, 268–274
    government of, simplified diagram, 293
    traveler's advisory, 314–315
Saudi Arabian National Center for Science and Technology, 217–218
Saudi Basic Industries Corporation, 212–215
Saudi Industrial Development Fund, see funds
Saudia, 196–197, 252
Saudization, 264
Seaports, 198
Second Deputy Prime Minister, see Sultan Bin Abdulaziz
Second five-year development plan, 181
Security, see law and order
Semitic, 275
Shaer, Ali, see Al-Shaer, Ali
Shari'a, 8, 135, 241–242
Sherif, Hussain, 27, 29
Shi'a, see Shi'ite
Shihabi, Samir, 141
Shi'ite, 282, 310
Socal, 23
Social insurance, 219–220
Social justice and development, 219–222

Social security, 221–222
Social welfare, see social justice and development
Standard Oil Company of California, see Socal
Sultan Bin Abdulaziz, 60, 74, 252–260, 300
Sultan Bin Salman, 62, 76, 218–219, 264
Sunni, 282
Supreme Commander, see Fahd
Supreme Council for Youth Welfare, see Faisal Bin Fahd
Suras, 281

T
Taif, 29
Tailoring centers, see education
Teacher training, see education
Technical assistant institutes, see education
Technical education, see education
Telegraph, see telephone, telegraph and post
Telephone, see telephone, telegraph and post
Television stations, 201
Tewell, Bill, 135
Thatcher, Margaret, 149
Third five-year development plan, 181–183
Transport, 192–199
Travel, see Saudi Arabia
Tribal map of the Arabian Peninsula, see Arabia
Truman, president, 44
Turki, 60
Turks, see Ottoman
Twitchell, Karl S., 33

U
Ulama, 30–31, 135, 311
Umm Al-Qora University, Mecca, see universities
United Nations, 145–148

United States of America, see Saudi-American relations
Universities, 93–127, 268–272
King Saud University, 101–106
Islamic University at Medina, 107
King Fahd University of Petroleum and Minerals, 108–117, 170, 218
King Abdulaziz University, 117–121
Imam Mohammed Bin Saud Islamic University, Riyadh, 121–123
King Faisal University, 123–126
Umm Al-Qora University, Mecca, 126–127
University of Petroleum and Minerals (UPM), see universities
Uqair, 29
Urban development, 224–231
U.S.A., see Saudi-American relations
Uyaynah, 6

V
Visa, see Saudi Arabia
Vocational training, see education

W
Wahhabi movement, 7–10
Wahhabism, see Wahhabi movement
Water, 207–210
Welfare, social, see social justice and development
West, John C., 154
Wheat production, see agriculture

Y
Yanbu, 73, 170, 172, 176, 215–217
Yemen, Hodeida, 32
Youth welfare, 237–239

Z
Zakat, 25, 312
Zionism, 40–43, 254

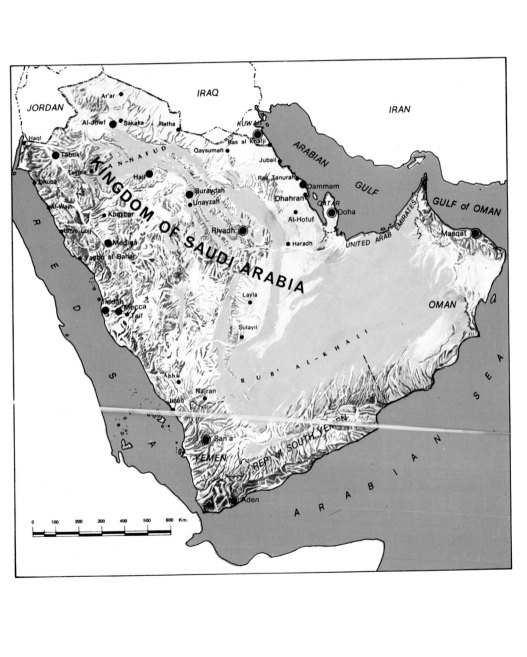

JORDAN

IRAQ

IRAN

Ar'ar

Al-Jowf ● ●Sakaka ● Rafha

KUWAIT

Haql● ●Ras al Khafji

Tabuk● ●Qaysumah

Tayma● Jubail●

ARABIAN

Dhuba● Hail● Ras Tanurah●

Al-Wajh● Buraydah● Dammam● GULF

Umm Lujj● Unayzah● Dhahran

Khaybar● QATAR● GULF of OMAN

Medina● Al-Hofuf● ●Doha

Yanbu al Bahr● Riyadh● Masqat●

UNITED ARAB EMIRATES

Haradh●

KINGDOM OF SAUDI ARABIA

Layla●

OMAN

R
E
D

S
E
A

Jiddah● Sulayil●

Mecca●

Taif●

RUB' AL-KHALI

Abha●

Najran●

Jizan●

ARABIAN

SEA

San'a●

YEMEN REP. of SOUTH YEMEN

Aden●

A
R
A
B
I
A
N

S
E
A

0   100   200   300   400   500   600 Km.